THE GREATEST GAME:

OUR LIFELONG ROMANCE WITH BASEBALL

by

Michael Anthony Ricci

Published by M.A. Ricci, Auburn, New York

Copyright 2018 by Michael Anthony Ricci

All Rights reserved, including the right to reproduce this book, or parts thereof, except for the inclusion of brief quotations in a review.

ISBN-13:
978-1724683984

ISBN-10:
1724683985

About the Author

Who is Michael Ricci? When Mike was a student in elementary school he had no inclination to write anything except to answer classroom questions. His parents, who both had a minimal elementary education, were unable to help him achieve the willingness to write creatively. He managed to get a rudimentary education in the secondary schools as well. It stymies all logic on how he might have begun to blossom as a writer.

The bigger question is, how did he develop his interest in baseball? He had no idea what baseball was all about before he was fourteen years old. Maybe some of his contemporaries were uninformed too. It is interesting how his interest, and later, his love for the game matured.

As he was growing up in Niagara Falls, New York, two of his friends were planning to play baseball at Ferry Avenue School's playground. They asked him if he would like to play too. He said, "sure," not realizing what was involved. It was nothing like "stick-in-the -mud" or "ringolevio," two common older-childhood games. (Ringolevio was a team form of "hide and seek.") Mike was game; he always enjoyed playing and learning something new. He and his friends were not aware that he needed a few new skills to play baseball. He was able to hit the ball well enough and ran like a deer, but he learned that he would need to learn something else, and that was being able to catch a ball. Because he was new to the game he was put in right field, which was the most unlikely place for a ball to be hit.

On that given day, the first ball that was hit to him in right field looked like it was going to be pretty easy to catch, but as the ball hit his glove, it bounced off and immediately dropped to the ground causing quite a furor among the batting team. Mike was so embarrassed because he didn't catch the ball, that he forgot to throw it so that a play could be made against the batting team. Time was called, and his teammates explained some quick rules of the game. No one thought to tell him that he had to relax his hand in order to catch the ball. He suffered the anguish of dropping the ball every time he tried to catch it.

Every day when everyone went home from school, they all rushed to go to the playground to play a baseball game. When it was time for supper, everyone would go home and within a half-hour they were back to play another game, playing until dark.

As soon as fall arrived, most of the players retreated to the front of the school where it was grassy, to play touch football—but not Mike. He was practicing, learning how to catch the ball. He did this, for hours at a time. He even got a friend, who was not interested in football, to hit him fly balls so that he would be able to become a better player the following spring.

When spring came, a few of the guys formed a team to play in the Kiwanis-Recreation baseball program. All of the guys were registered to play on the team, even Ricci, who was the last player on the team. Mike never thought to tell anyone that he had practiced to catch the ball during the prior fall while everyone else was playing football. Everyone else thought that he was just a bad player.

The name of the team was called the Casa Marinas and they were scheduled to play in the junior division of the city league. Mike went to every game to cheer his team on, but he never got to play. At the end of the season, the Casa Marinas team was good enough to participate in a one-game baseball playoff. They played a team from the LaSalle area of the city.

After the sixth inning (the games were seven innings long), the Casa Marinas were getting bombed. They didn't have chance of winning the game. In the seventh inning, after there were two out, the captain called time, walked over to Mike and told him to bat. Mike had finally got a chance to play in a game. When the other players heard that Mike would be batting, they all grumbled. The captain said, "He can't do any worse than you guys."

The pitcher on the other team was a southpaw and when he wound up, he kicked his right leg high like he was trying to reach the sky. He threw a blazing fast ball over the center of the plate. "Strike one," the umpire called. Mike was ready for the next pitch, he missed, fanning the air. It was strike two. Before Mike realized it, a third pitch came whizzing as it went by. "Strike three," the umpire yelled. Mike had struck out. The game was over and so was the season. The next baseball season, Mike and his two best friends, Jim and Joe, formed a baseball team of their own, calling it the Indians. The following year, Mike was 17 and too old for the Junior division. Jim and Joe stopped playing baseball, so Mike organized a team to play in the Intermediate Division of the Kiwanis Recreation Baseball League. The Intermediate Division was for 17- and 18-year-olds and their games were not played during the day like the younger divisions, but in the evening. Some of the guys were Mike's classmates from the high school. One day, during the season Mike was sitting on his porch, an interesting thing happened. A boy from the neighborhood walked up to Mike. He had a pained look on his face as if the whole world was on his shoulders. He told Mike that his Bantam Division team in the city league, the Tigers, needed a manager, badly. He said that his team manager had recently moved to California and he asked Mike if he would manage the team for the rest of the season. Now that he had immersed himself in baseball, Mike thought that it would be a good opportunity to manage a team as a non-player; he said he would. Mike scheduled a practice the next day so he could get to meet all the players. One of the players, asked Mike if he would let him pitch. For some reason, the players on the team called him "Tex," but he wasn't from Texas.

Every game, Tex kept pestering Mike to pick him to pitch. Finally

Mike had Tex pitch in one game. He struck out 11 batters in the game. On the down side, he also hit 11 batters. The batters he struck out, probably would rather strike out than being hit by one of his pitches.

One other game stood out in Mike's mind: One of the Tiger's opponents called the Pine Avenue Merchants had a pair of twins on their team, one of whom was their catcher. The game was played at 24th Street School playground. The playground supervisor also served as the umpire for all the games being played there. When the Merchants' catcher moved into his defensive position behind the batter, he wasn't wearing a mask. The umpire told him that he needed to wear a mask, but the boy said he didn't want to. After the two were bickering back-and-forth about the mask, the umpire finally allowed him to catch without one. About the second or third pitch, a batter fouled the ball directly back, hitting the catcher in the face. He was in agony. After applying first aid, the umpire had another player replace that catcher; it was his twin! He wouldn't wear a mask either. What were the odds of him getting hit too? The first pitch was fouled back to that twin too! After applying first aid, the umpire insisted that the next catcher had to wear a mask. We lent them our mask, and the game progressed without any further incident.

Finally, the season came to a close—except the playoffs. The Tigers were tied with the Pine Avenue Merchants and both managers were invited to the Recreation department offices where the assistant director flipped a coin and the Tigers were the winner of that toss. They played the first-place White Shoes team in a one-game playoff, ending in a dismal loss.

During the off-season, Mike didn't want to field another intermediate division team, but he had fun in managing the Tigers. He decided that he would organize another Tigers team for the next season. He had the help of a player who was too old to play the next season. Mike told him that they should have a left-handed pitcher. His response was that his newspaper boy was about the right age and he was left-handed. Mike asked that boy if he would like to play on the team. Mike contacted him in the spring, and he really pitched well for not having pitched before. The Tigers ended in first place, but lost in a playoff game.

On the days that Mike's team wasn't scheduled to play, he began umpiring Kiwanis-Recreation baseball games. It didn't pay much, only $2 per game, and only one umpire was used, calling pitches from behind the pitcher, and making calls for the bases from that position.

When the following season arrived, Mike decided to organize three teams in three different age groups--Midget (10-12 years old), Bantam (13-14) and Junior (14-15) age divisions. The Midget division team was sponsored by Mills Jewelers. He had a tryout at the Haeberle Field, which was used as an industrial league softball field in the evening. Surprisingly, the Mills Jewelers team was a good team and had beaten every team but the Pee Wees. The Bantam league team was called the Voelkers.

The Junior league team was sponsored by the Niagara Falls Boys Club and had a very good pitcher; he might have been the best pitcher in the City.

Before the next baseball season started in the Spring, Mike decided to have teams in all three divisions, but he added a new twist. He added another team in the Midget and bantam Division, as well as a team in th Intermediate division. The intermediate division was for boys who were 17 and 18 years old. They were called the Quakers. Why they were called that, no one knew.

The second team in the Midget division was called the Little Guys —that's because the kids were all little. It served as a "farm" team for the Mills team, but only one player from the Mills team was transferred before the deadline. A player who practiced with the Mills team had a habit of fooling around and not interested in improving himself. So Mike assigned him to play for the Little Guys. He played well because he was their best player, but he was not happy playing with them.

The second team in the Bantam division was called the Veterans. Mike had this team so some other kids could play on a baseball team.

At the end of the season, both the Boys Club and the Quakers both won city championships.

That same season, the recreation director Myron "Min" Hendrick asked Mike if he could organize a midget division All-Star team. In July a local men's All-Star game was scheduled to play a famous softball team, "The King and his Court," in a softball game. Min wanted the kid's All Star game to precede that one. On that day in July, Mike's All-Star team lost to that same Pee Wees team, 2-1.

While Mike was working at a department store as a stock clerk, he met Ed who had worked there since he was 15. Ed was a Cub Master for a cub pack from Bergholtz, a small community near Niagara Falls. The Holy Ghost Church sponsored the cub pack that had a softball team in a Cub Scout softball league. One day he talked Mike into coming to see that team play in Bergholtz. Mike was really impressed and attended a meeting of all the coaches. Before he knew it, Mike had volunteered to do the publicity for the league.

During that year, Mike organized an All-Star game and, later, a father and sons Cub Scout game too. The sons beat their dads. Everyone thought that the Dads threw the game so their sons would win. It was a fun day for both teams.

When Mike began organizing multiple teams, he also decided to become an umpire and he joined the local umpires group, which umpired softball games as well as baseball games.

In 1958, Mike began a new phase of his life as he and his future wife, Pat, met and were married the following year.

After his marriage, Mike moved to Buffalo, the home city of his wife. He joined the official umpires group to umpire Men's baseball games. He unfortunately found out that only one umpire was used, calling pitches while behind the pitcher. After a few games, which were much more faster than kids' games, they were difficult in making correct calls. Mike resigned after two weeks.

Mike graduated from Niagara University and soon after he found a high school English teaching job in Auburn, New York.

When one of his sons became eight years old, he wanted to join the Little League. But after a few practices, he was cut from the team. After Mike consulting with a friend, who was knowledgeable about Little League politics in Auburn, he was advised to start his own league. By June he organized an independent league, but he allowed girls as well as boys to play. All of his children who were not 13 yet, played in the league called "The Kids Sandlot Baseball League."

In 1979, he began working in Rochester and during the summer, umpiring youth league games. While there Mike organized a baseball school for eight-year old boys. That year, he also organized a new league in Auburn which eventually became a league for children five to eight years old, called "The Boys and Girls Baseball League."

After his first year teaching in Auburn, the three city high schools were consolidated to form a 3000-student central high school leading to his and other new teachers releases. Mike taught at Caledonia Mumford High School and later taught at African Road Elementary School in Vestal. Both were fill-in positions for teachers on maternity leaves.

He returned to Auburn, he continued umpiring for the Geneva, Syracuse and the Ithaca Umpires Associations. After retiring from the Ithaca' umpiring group in 2005, he spent most of his spare time in substituting. He embarked on a new avocation in writing a column about English called, "Watch Your Language" in his local Auburn Citizen newspaper. He began writing his column in March, 2010, and after 75 columns, resigned in December 2015. He then decided to write a book about Baseball's history, called The Greatest Game:Our Lifelong Romance with Baseball, published in 2018.

Preface For The Greatest Game

The Greatest Game: Our Lifelong Romance with Baseball is a history about the game of baseball, but it is different than any other book about baseball by narrating the history of baseball in the Mid-Nineteenth Century, from its sandlot beginnings, until the year this book was published in 2018.

It is not a drab compilation of numbers, but real stories of a total selection of players who ever played. The book conveys a min-biography of many players that many of you have heard about, but whose names do not mean anything to you. We all know that only the greatest players, managers, owners, umpires and executives get selected in the National Baseball Hall of Fame, the details surrounding their election, and which groups have been charged with selecting them.

All of the elected commissioners have been micro-sized in their little biographies, covering their tenures in those roles, in what years they performed those roles and what impact their decisions have in the formulation of the game. When the game of baseball rose from its amateur sandlot status, it eventually became professional during its evolution.

In the beginning, those organizations were known as the National Association, the National League, the American Association, the Union Association, the Players League, the American League, the Federal League and finally, the Continental League. The failure of those leagues left Major League Baseball with only the National and American League to play our National game. For many years both those leagues functioned with only eight teams. Since then, franchises have moved to other cities, while other cites were awarded expansion franchises to eventually accumulate to be a total of 30 franchises.

Each year since 1871, all pennant winner or winners were listed in this book, together with their number of wins and number of games their nearest rivals were behind. In addition, there were statistics concerning their best pitchers and best offensive players of each of those teams. In years where two teams compete in a series, a champion for that year was determined. When there were only two league champion winners, one of the two survived as World Series winner in that series competition.

Through the expansion of many teams, the competition in several playoff brackets determined which two teams would play in that year's series. In recent years, each league has three divisional brackets, named West, Central and East. This book will relate in detail which teams will compete in the playoffs, and which one would be the fourth competitor, called the wild card. Since 2012, an additional wild card competitor was added. The two wild card competitors play each other in a one-game playoff to determine which of them will continue in the divisional playoff.

There are many events that are mentioned in this book like Joe DiMaggio's 56 game hitting streak, Ted Williams travails to his .406 batting average, Lou Gehrig's final speech, Wille Mays' spectacular basket catch in the 1954 World Series, the Black Sox Scandal, when three runners ended up on third, and many more.

M.A.R.

Our American public considers baseball as being the greatest game because anytime you go to a game, even if you have seen and watched an innumerable number of them, you'll always see something that you've never seen before. George Carlin, who passed from our scene in 2008, thought so too, as he spoke about baseball in a stand-up routine and how it differs from other sports. This is his discussion about those differences.

"Baseball is different from any other sport, very different. For instance, in most sports you score points or goals; in baseball you score runs. In most sports, the ball, or object, is put in play by the offensive team. In baseball, the defensive team puts the ball in play, and only the defense is allowed to touch the ball. In fact, in baseball, if an offensive player touches the ball intentionally, he's out; sometimes unintentionally, he's
out.

"Also: in football, basketball, soccer, volleyball, and all sports played with a ball, you score with the ball, and in baseball, the ball prevents you from scoring. In most sports the team is run by a coach; in baseball the team is run by a manager. And only in baseball does the manager or coach wear the same clothing the players do. If you'd ever seen John Madden in his Oakland Raiders uniform, you'd know the reason for this
custom.

"Now, I've mentioned football. Baseball and football are the two most popular spectator sports in this country. And as such, it seems they ought to be able to tell us something about ourselves and our values. I enjoy comparing baseball and football. Baseball is a nineteenth-century pastoral game. Football is a twentieth-century technological struggle. Baseball is played on a diamond, in a park. The baseball park! Football is played on a gridiron, in a stadium, sometimes called Soldier Field or War Memorial Stadium.

"Baseball begins in the spring, the season of new life. Football begins in the fall, when every thing's dying. In football you wear a helmet. In baseball you wear a cap. Football is concerned with downs - what down is it? Baseball is concerned with ups - who's up? In football you receive a penalty. In baseball, you make an error. In football the specialist comes in to kick. In baseball the specialist comes in to relieve somebody.

"Football has hitting, clipping, spearing, piling on, personal fouls, late hitting and unnecessary roughness. Baseball has the sacrifice. Football is played in any kind of weather: rain, snow, sleet, hail, fog. In baseball, if it rains, we don't go out to play. Baseball has the seventh inning stretch. Football has the two minute warning. Baseball has no time limit: we don't know when it's gonna end - [we] might have extra innings. Football is rigidly timed and it will end even if we've got to go to sudden death.

"In baseball, during the game, in the stands, there's kind of a picnic feeling; emotions may run high or low, but there's not too much unpleasantness. In football, during the game, in the stands, you can be sure that at least twenty-seven times you're capable of taking the life of a fellow human being.

"And finally, the objectives of the two games are completely different: In football the object is for the quarterback, also known as the field general, to be on target with his aerial assault, riddling the defense by hitting his receivers with deadly accuracy in spite of the blitz, even if he has to use shotgun. With short bullet passes and long bombs, he marches his troops into enemy territory, balancing this aerial assault with a sustained ground attack that punches holes in the forward wall of the enemy's defensive line. In baseball the object is to go home! And to be safe! - I hope I'll be safe at home!"

The renowned poet, Walt Whitman, took pleasure in watching boys playing base ball. These are his thoughts about the game: "Let us go forth awhile, and get better air in our lungs and let us leave our close[d] rooms. The game of ball is glorious." That was spoken in the early days of baseball, probably in the 1880s.

A recent sportscaster on baseball, Bob Costas is convinced that there is no game like baseball and he says, ""First thing about it and this may seem so obvious that maybe we overlook it. Baseball is a beautiful thing. It's more beautiful in an old park thats asymmetrical and quirky. But even—I hate to say this because it might encourage them—but even in a dome with artificial turf it's beautiful the way the field fans out. The pace and rhythm of it that the place allows for conversation and opinion and comparison."

Some of the greatest baseball players think that there is no greater game like baseball too:
"Baseball was, is and always will be the best game in the world."---Babe Ruth

"I thank God for that wonderful game we call baseball"---Phil Rizzuto

"People ask me what I do in winter when there's no baseball. I'll tell them what I do. I stare out of the window and wait for spring." --Rogers Hornsby

"Baseball was one-hundred percent of my life." -Ty Cobb

In the annals of history, it was found that games were inventions of children's minds. Baseball, or some form of baseball, is part of those games that boys play. Many years ago, it started with two boys playing catch. So that other boys could play too, one boy would throw a ball to another boy who would hit it with a stick. The batter's ultimate goal was to hit the ball safely and begin his journey around the three bases, eventually scoring a run when he reached home safely. The pitcher and the other defensive player's goals were to create three outs before any runs were scored. Although originally baseball was a boys' game, soon men adapted baseball as a game of their own. Children played baseball as a game of enjoyment; men enjoyed baseball as work. They learned to play the game from which they received money.

Baseball is derived from earlier games. Some were called "base," "one old cat," "stool ball," "rounders," and many others.

Early Ball Games before 1845

Some form of baseball has been played since 1744 when the city of Boston forbade that no base ball playing would be allowed in its streets.

In 1845, Alexander Cartwright who was a member of the Knickerbocker Fire Company, the first baseball team, drew up a diagram of the first baseball field. Together with a Knickerbocker committee, Cartwright drew up the new rules for playing baseball. Unlike the pitcher of today who throws overhand from 60 feet 6 inches, the pitcher then threw underhand from 46 feet. The batter, as now, was out on three missed strikes, but there was no base-on-balls. All caught batted balls were outs, and until 1893, a ball caught after one bounce was also considered an out. Then, as now, nine players compose a team and nine innings was a complete game. The first documented baseball game under the Cartwright rules took place on June 19, 1846 at Elysian Fields in Hoboken, New Jersey. The Knickerbocker team, however, lost to the New York Nine by a 21-1 score. The umpire was Cartwright. Although the rules called for nine players, only seven players were recorded as playing for either team in that record book.

Alexander Cartwright was considered to be the father of baseball, due to the innovations he created that differentiated baseball from other ball-and-bat games. He designed the first diamond-shaped field and formed the rules for Knickerbocker baseball. The Knickerbocker club played the first game under the Cartwright's rules. Cartwright had played ball and bat games called town ball while serving as a volunteer at the Knickerbocker Fire Company. In 1842 Cartwright and a committee for the Knickerbocker club drew up rules converting that playground game to one which could be played by adults. The rules were similar, but not the same as the game of rounders. 1849, Cartwright headed to California to take part in the Gold Rush there, but he continued westward to the Hawaiian Islands when he served as a chief for Honolulu's fire department from 1850 to 1863. He set up a baseball field there and encouraged the development of baseball. That year the New York Knickerbocker baseball club was the first team to wear uniforms. There were quite a few developments in the early years. In 1853, the first box score of Knickerbockers style game was printed in the New York Clipper. Baseball had not as yet become a full-fledged sport.

Henry Chadwick became the first regular baseball reporter. That year, baseball rules standardizing the game were adopted in May, stating that (1) the bat was not to exceed 2.5 inches in diameter and the ball not to exceed 10.5 inches in circumference, (2) and the game was to last nine innings or until one team won 21 runs. Previously each team played under its own set of rules. These led to three delegates from each team to attend a baseball meeting in 1856. The clubs represented were: Atlantic, Baltic, Bedford, Continental, Eagle, Empire, Excelsior, Eckford, Gotham, Harmony, Knickerbocker, Nassau, Olympic, Putnam and Union. Baseball teams then were not yet representing towns or cities, instead represented social clubs.

The following year, in 1857, it was decided that the game was won when one side scored 21 aces. Then it was a nine-inning contest and the highest scoring team wins. Although the first organized baseball group was known as the National Association of Baseball Clubs, each team designed its own schedule.

On July 20, 1858 was the first time that spectators were charged admission to a game at the Fashion Race Course in Long Island, N.Y. Two amateur teams participated and the admission fee was charged to pay for the rental of the field. It was the opening game of the first series ever played and the 50-cent admission was charged to 1,500 spectators. That year, a series of three games was played between the Brooklyn Brooklynites and the New York All-Stars on July 20, August 17 and September 10. New York won the first game 22-18, then took two-out-of-three games.

The first year that called strikes were introduced was in 1858. It was the first time that a batter was out on a batted ball, fair or foul, if caught on the fly or after one bounce. (It is hard to conceive that catching a ball on one bounce as being the same as catching it on the fly.) This rule continued to be in force until the National League baseball season in 1893.

Another rule introduced in 1858, stipulated that a base runner was no longer required to touch each base in order. (Imagine the confusion that that rule created.

In 1859, many colleges introduced baseball in their sports programs. That year, there was a record that an Intercollegiate baseball game was played between Amherst College and Williams College on July 1 in Pittsfield MA. Amherst won, 72-32. The game was played on a 60-foot square with the pitcher throwing 35 feet from the batter. It began at 11 AM and continued for four hours without interruption. Each team had 13 players and the game lasted 26 innings. One would imagine that the basis of the game was whoever scored 100 runs would be the winner. The game was concluded before that score was achieved because everyone must have been exhausted after four hours in that sweltering summer heat.

The first enclosed baseball park that was constructed was the William Cammeyer's Union Grounds in Brooklyn which opened on May 15, 1862.

A few rule changes occurred in 1863 as it was the first time that balls and strikes were called. The pitcher's box was designated to be 12 by four feet and the pitcher was no longer to take a step during his delivery and he had to pitch with both feet on the ground at the same time. Bat size was also regulated. Additionally, home base and the pitcher's box had to be marked. The most important rule that was made was that no base could be made on a foul ball.

Two additional rule changes were made in 1864 : (1) the "fly catch" of fair balls was adopted, (2) It was stipulated that each base runner must touch each base in proper order. Henry Chadwick's scoring system was also introduced.

A baseball game in which one team scored more than 100 runs was played on Sunday, October 1, 1865 in a nine-inning game in Philadelphia PA. The Philadelphia Athletics defeated the Jersey City Nationals By a whopping 114-2 score. There were two developments that year: Ed Cuthbert of the Keystones was the first person to steal a base and the batting averages began to be included in the records of each game.

Until 1866, all pitchers threw a straight ball, but during that year, William Arthur "Candy" Cummings was the first player to throw a curve ball. He played for the Excelsior Junior Nine and the Stars of Brooklyn. Also that year Bob Addy of the Rockford employees was the first one to slide while stealing a base. Tom Barrow of the Brooklyn Atlantics added a little excitement to the game by laying down the first bunt.

Baseball teams for women were first organized in the 1860s. In 1866, college women formed two baseball clubs. The Laurel Baseball Club and the Abenakes at Vassar female college. Women baseball teams played on a non-collegiate level as a Poughkeepsie, New York team was organized in Peterboro in 1868.

Baseball rule changes in 1867 continued to interest the players and teams as the pitcher's box was made into a 6 foot square and the pitcher is now permitted to move around inside this box. Then the batter was given the privilege of calling for a low or high pitch.

The first baseball team whose players receive a salary began in 1869 with the Cincinnati Red Stockings led by Harry and George Wright. That team was established on June 23, 1866. After playing four games that summer, Cincinnati Red Stockings joined the National Association of Baseball Players in 1867. In that league, many of the teams' players had been playing in Cricket leagues and soon converted by playing baseball. Harry Wright, the team's playing manager, organized that first team to play during the 1869 baseball season. They traveled to many cities engaging competition with local teams, and from 1869 to 1870 they played without losing a game. The 1869 Cincinnati Red Stockings baseball team posted a 69-0 record and has not been matched since then.

The other players on that team were pitcher Asa Brainard, catcher Doug Allison, first-baseman Charlie Gould, and Harry's brother George, who played short-stop. The outfielders besides Harry in center, were Andy Leonard in left and Cal McVey in right. Dick Hurley was a utility player who played in any position where he was needed.

The Cincinnati Red Stockings were the first fully professional baseball team; they were the first team to wear knickers. The first listing of at-bats in box scores occurred in the New York Clipper in 1870.

The Cincinnati club was disbanded after the 1870 season because the owners said that it was too expensive to pay all of the players. With the breakup of the Cincinnati team, all players signed up with the new Boston Red Stockings or Washington Olympics teams in the newly formed National Association of Baseball Clubs.

Harry Wright took the Red Stockings logo with him as he organized and managed the Boston team. Other players who followed him there were his brother George McVey and Charlie Gould, who all signed with the team for the 1871 season. Harry also signed Al Spalding and Ross Barnes who had played with the Rockford Forest Citys in 1870.

The remaining Cincy players who signed with the Olympics were pitcher Asa Brainard, catcher Doug Allison, Charlie Sweasy, third-baseman Fred Waterman and left-fielder Andy Leonard. Dick Hurley, a substitute player, signed with the Washington Club later in 1872. McVey was the first catcher (regular one in today's terms) for the 1871-72 seasons, and was the playing manager for the Baltimore Orioles in 1873, but returned to the Red Stockings the following year. With the breakup of the National Association at the end of 1875, some of the Boston team signed with the Chicago White Stockings in 1876. McVey, Spalding, Deacon White and Ross Barnes all played in the newly formed National League.

Baseball was played professionally since 1851, but no organized Major league was in existence. During the 1868 to 1870 seasons, the Cincinnati Red Stockings was a barnstorming baseball team that played all other teams. In 1869, the Red Stockings team was undefeated until they played a game against the Unions of Lansingburgh, New York (now part of Troy) known as the Haymakers. They played on August 26, 1869. After five innings, the score was tied at 17-17. In those days, gambling infringed upon the game being played on "a level field." Congressman John Morrisey, the most prominent backer of the "Haymakers," had placed a bet of $17,000 on his team. In the top of the sixth, the home team Red Stocking's Cal McVey hit a ball back to the catcher (the catcher then played five feet or more behind the batter—no masks nor protective equipment were worn by the catcher.) If the catcher caught the ball on the fly, or even on the one bounce, the batter was out. John Brockway was the umpire and he determined that the ball was caught on the second bounce and was only a foul ball. It appeared at that point that the home team had taken control of the game. Their late-inning hits presented a challenge for the Haymakers. The visitors president, a man named McKeon, protested the call and to protect the gambling interests of his club, removed his team from the field. In those days there was no forfeit rule in effect when one team refused to take the field. After giving the offending team a few minutes to return to the field, and when they did not return, the umpire awarded the win to the Red Stockings. The person in charge of the gate receipts refused to give any part of the money to the Haymakers. The Red Stockings continued to win a total of 57 games that season, but the contested game was ultimately called a tie. They did not play the Haymakers again in 1869.

Many of the Red Stockings players continued to play with new teams when the National Association was begun in 1871. The members of the Red Stockings team were: Asa Brainard, pitcher; Doug Allison, catcher; Charlie Gould, first base; Charlie Sweasy, second base; Fred Waterman, third base; George Wright, shortstop; Andy Leonard, left field; Harry Wright, center field/manager; Cal McVey, right field, and Dick Hurley, substitute.

Harry Wright entered his Red Stockings, no longer as the Cincinnati Red Stockings, which then had become the new Boston Red Stockings. His brother George, Cal McVey and Charlie Gould became part of that new team too. Pitcher Asa Brainard and Andy Leonard instead chose to be part of the Washington Olympics.

Albert Spalding

Albert Spalding, who was a dominant pitcher early as his youth, pitched for the Rockford Pioneers at the age of 15. After pitching his team to a 26-2 win, he was contracted by the Forest Citys, with whom he played for two years. With the formation of the first professional league, the American Association, he played for the Boston Red Stockings (an ancestor of today's Atlanta Braves) for the duration of the league, from 1871-1875, pitching 206 wins, losing only 53, and a batting average of .323. In 1876 with the formation of the new National

League, he finished his career playing for the Chicago White Stockings (a precursor of today's Chicago Cubs).

Cap Anson

One of the most outstanding players during the early baseball years was "Cap" Anson. Adrian Constantine "Cap" Anson played baseball for 27 seasons. When he was 14 and in high school, he boarded at the University of Notre Dame. He was always a mischievous child and his father thought that by his going to that school, they might curb some of his son's antics. However, his son's behavior was beyond curbing. When he came home, his father sent him to the nearby University of Iowa. His continued bad behavior resulted in his expulsion after only one semester. Anson played baseball for a number of competitive teams in his youth, and began playing professionally in the new National Association of Professional Baseball Players in 1871. He played third base for the Rockford Forest Citys. In 1872 he was traded to the Athletics of Philadelphia. He was one of the five best batters in the National Association with a .415 batting average and .455 on-base percentage. He led all batters league in 1872, but his numbers were reduced slightly in 1874 and 1875. His stats were good enough for him to be selected to play for the Chicago White Stockings in the National League in 1876. He was reluctant to leave Philadelphia because he was recently engaged to a girl there. But despite his reluctance to leave Philadelphia, the Chicago owner, William Hulbert, paid him more money to play in the "Windy City." City."

Hulbert selected Anson to improve his club at the opening of the new National League season, Hulbert had broken the rules by negotiating with Anson, and some other players, during the 1875 NA season, but because Hulber was the prime mover in the establishment of the new league, disciplinary action was overlooked. Morgan Buckeley was the first National League president, but only served for one year in 1876.

The National Association

Initially, the pitchers threw underhand from a distance of 46 feet from the batter. Baseball was played professionally since 1851, but no organized Major league was in existence . The first major league was the National Association which started play in 1871 and completed its last season in 1875.

Harry Wright organized some of the players to form a new team in that league called the Boston Red Stockings. The players who followed him there were brother George and Gould, McVey joined the team the following season, and continued playing with them until 1878. Asa Brainard and Doug Allison were the remaining players from the original team, who opted to play with the Washington Olympics in 1871.

Even though the Boston Red Stockings were the best team in the league's 28--game schedule during the 1871 season, the Philadelphia Athletics (21-7) beat them out by two games. Boston, which had a 20-10 record was also tied for second with the Chicago White Stockings (19-9). There were only nine teams in that first season: Boston Red Stockings, Philadelphia Athletics, Chicago White Stockings, Cleveland Forest Citys, Fort Wayne Kekiongas, New York Mutuals, Rockford Forest Citys, Troy Haymakers, and the Washington Olympics. Two teams dropped out before the end of the first season. They were the Kekiongas (7-12) and the Rockford Forest Citys (4-21).

In demonstrating the Red Stocking's dominance, Ross Barnes' batting led their offense with 66 runs scored, 63 hits (including five triples), 91 total bases and a .401 batting average. However, the Athletics' Levi Meyerle was a perpetual batting dynamo with 81 hits and a .492 batting average. No other player since has ever attained such a high batting average. It has never been considered to be a record because the 1871 season was so short. Harry Wright, the Boston

Red Stockings playing manager, was disappointed that his team had fallen two games short in 1871, but he was sure that it would not happen again.

Many baseball-related events occurred in 1871 as baseball had experienced many drastic changes since the Knickerbockers first game in 1846. There were a great number of baseball clubs that had not yet represented cities, but only represented various fraternal social clubs.

Baseball was only one of many activities which were scheduled between clubs. Most of these clubs were located in the New York City area like the Brooklyn, Atlantics and Eckford clubs.

The first teams in 1871 were the Boston Red Stockings, Chicago White Stockings, Cleveland Forest Citys, Fort Wayne Kekiongas, New York Mutuals, Philadelphia Athletics. Rockford Forest Citys, the Troy Haymakers, and the Washington Olympics. Fort Wayne dropped out after the first year and Troy withdrew after the 1872 season.

The cost of operating a baseball club became too expensive for most clubs. The Association only lasted for five seasons.. Some of the reasons for some teams to continue were (1) The instability of most franchises, which were unable to continue because they were placed in cities which were too small to financially support professional baseball, (2) the Boston club dominated the league from 1872 to 1875—Other teams were unable to compete, (3) there was a lack of a central league authority, and (4) there were suspicions that the game may have been influenced by gamblers.

We would be surprised to know that none of their players had team contracts and easily left their teams to join others, sometimes during the same season. Baseball, although organized into a league, did not pay players to play. The league frowned on paying players although secretly paid some of their top players. Most teams had as few as twelve or thirteen players and had only two players to be their pitchers.

1872

In 1872, despite racial discrimination, the first double-header was played between the Resolutes (a black team) and Boston played on July 4, 1873. The Red Stockings won 38 games in 1872 in a 50-game schedule. The Baltimore Canaries were 7-1/2 games behind. Albert Spalding won 38 games and had a 1.85 ERA. The best hitter on the Red Stockings was Ross Barnes who batted .430, had 99 hits, including 18 doubles, a 452 OBP, .583 SA and 134 TB. Spalding who was a good hitter for a pitcher batted .354, hitting 12 doubles and he had the most team RBIs at 47, beating out Barnes who had 44. Shortstop George Wright scored 87 runs.

1873

In 1873, the Boston Red Stockings won 43 games in a 60 game schedule. The Philadelphia White Stockings finished 4 games behind. The Red Stockings were such a good team that they rolled over much of their competition not only in 1873, but also in 1874 and 1875. Al Spalding had a 41-14 record a .745 WP, 2.99 ERA and 50 strikeouts. In those early days each team had only one pitcher, but because there were several days in between games, that pitcher was not over worked. He was a good hitting pitcher batting .328 and hitting 15 doubles and 71 RBI.

Ross Barnes numbers were continuing to be great as he scored 125 runs, peppered 138 hits, hit 29 doubles. 8 triples, a .431 BA, 197 TB, 43 stolen bases, 465 on-base 29 doubles. 8 triples, a .431 BA, 197 TB, 43 stolen bases, 465 on-base percentage (OBP) and a .616 SA. Catcher Deacon White hit 77 RBIs and George Wright had 20 bases-on-balls. Any fans of Barnes think Initially, the pitchers threw underhand from a distance of 46 feet from the batter. Baseball was played professionally since 1851, but no organized Major league was in existence. The first major league was the National Association which started play in 1871 and completed its last season in 1875.

Harry Wright organized some of the players to form a new team in that league called the Boston Red Stockings. The players who followed him there were brother George and Gould, McVey joined the team the following season, and continued playing with them until 1878. Asa Brainard and Doug Allison were the remaining players from the original team, who opted to play with the Washington Olympics in 1871.

Even though the Boston Red Stockings were the best team in the league's 28--game schedule during the 1871 season, the Philadelphia Athletics (21-7) beat them out by two games. Boston, which had a 20-10 record was also tied for second with the Chicago White Stockings (19-9).

There were only nine teams in that first season: Boston Red Stockings, Philadelphia Athletics, Chicago White Stockings, Cleveland Forest Citys, Fort Wayne Kekiongas, New York Mutuals, Rockford Forest Citys, Troy Haymakers, and the Washington Olympics. Two teams dropped out before the end of the first season. They were the Kekiongas (7-12) and the Rockford Forest Citys (4-21).

In demonstrating the Red Stocking's dominance, Ross Barnes' batting led their offense with 66 runs scored, 63 hits (including five triples), 91 total bases and a .401 batting average. However, the Athletics' Levi Meyerle was a perpetual batting dynamo with 81 hits and a .492 batting average. No other player since has ever attained such a high batting average. It has never been considered to be a record because the 1871 season was so short. Harry Wright, the Boston Red Stockings playing manager, was disappointed that his team had fallen two games short in 1871, but he was sure that it would not happen again.

Many baseball-related events occurred in 1871 as baseball had experienced many drastic changes since the Knickerbockers first game in 1846. There were a great number of baseball clubs that had not yet represented cities, but only represented various fraternal social clubs. Baseball was only one of many activities which were scheduled between clubs. Most of these clubs were located in the New York City area like the Brooklyn, Atlantics and Eckford clubs.

The first teams in 1871 were the Boston Red Stockings, Chicago White Stockings, Cleveland Forest Citys, Fort Wayne Kekiongas, New York Mutuals, Philadelphia Athletics. Rockford Forest Citys, the Troy Haymakers, and the Washington Olympics. Fort Wayne dropped out after the first year and Troy withdrew after the 1872 season.

The cost of operating a baseball club became too expensive for most clubs. The Association only lasted for five seasons.. Some of the reasons for some teams to continue were (1) The instability of most franchises, which were unable to continue because they were placed in cities which were too small to financially support professional baseball, (2) the Boston club dominated the league from 1872 to 1875 —Other teams were unable to compete, (3) there was a lack of a central league authority, and (4) there were suspicions that the game may have been influenced by gamblers.

We would be surprised to know that none of their players had team contracts and easily left their teams to join others, sometimes during the same season. Baseball, although organized into a league, did not pay players to play. The league frowned on saying that he was good enough to be in the Hall of Fame, but so few of them don't realize that one of the rules to be considered is that all prospective Hall of Fame members needed to have played as least 10 years in the majors. Barnes only played for nine seasons.

1874

Alfred James Reach, an outfielder for the Philadelphia Athletics in the National Association played from 1871-1875 and became the first professional baseball player. In 1874 he was paid $1000 for playing in

14 games. While playing for the Philadelphia Athletics in 1874, Reach formed a sports product manufacturing company called "A.L. Reach and Co.."

The Boston Red Stockings and Philadelphia Athletics conducted the first foreign tour in 1874.

In 1874, the Red Stockings continued to dominate with a 52-18 record, playing with only 11 players and finished 7.5 games ahead of the New York Mutuals. Outfielder Cal McVey led the team in runs (91), hits (123) and doubles (21) George Wright hit 15 triples and Jim O'Rourke hit a then record-smashing five home runs, had 165 TB, .359 BA and a .481 SA. Al Spalding continued to pour on wins every year that he pitched with a 52-16 record, including four shutouts, a 1.82 earned-run average (ERA), 31 strikeouts (SO) and issued 19 walks. Spalding didn't disappoint in hitting either as he garnered 119 hits including 13 doubles, a .329 BA and 54 RBI.

1875

The first baseball glove was worn by Charles Waite in 1875. He was the first baseman of the Boston Bostons team. The glove was flesh-colored so that it would not be noticed by the fans who thought that catching barehanded would be more manly. The glove had a large round opening in the back for ventilation. Fred Thayer invented the first catcher's mask.

The first baseball game, during which no runs were scored in nine innings was played at Red Stocking Park, St. Louis between the Chicago White Stockings and the St. Louis Reds of the National Association on May 11, 1875. In the tenth, Chicago won over St. Louis 1-0.

In 1875, the Red Stockings, rolled over most of the league overcoming their nearest runner-up Athletics with a 15 game chasm. Ross Barnes led the Red Stocking' attack scoring 115 runs and collecting 143 hits and even stole 29 bases. Jim O'Rourke established a new home run hitting record by hitting six while Cal McVey hit 21 doubles, nine triples and knocked in 87 runs. Catcher Deacon White wasn't very quiet that year, as he broke out with a .367 BA. Al Spalding ratcheted his win record to 54 wins and only five losses, a 1.59 ERA, 72 SO and 12 walks.

Joseph Emely Borden pitched a no-hitter for the National Association Philadelphia Athletics that beat the Chicago White Stockings 4-0 on July 28, 1875. The following year he also pitched a no-hitter for the Boston Red Stockings, and in 1877 he was the grounds keeper.

William Hulbert

William Hulbert was the National League organizer while he was the Chicago White Stockings owner. When that league was formed in 1876, Morgan Buckeley, the owner of the Hartford Blue Stockings, was elected in 1876, but he was only a figurehead president. The real power belonged to Hulbert, who was officially elected in 1877 when he served until 1922.

There was a lot of chicanery going on in the early days of baseball. Hulbert was a booster of the Chicago White Stockings and in 1874 became the president of the club. Baseball as a professional sport was in the doldrums. The Chicago team was not involved in competition since 1874 because all of the team's equipment and playing field complex were destroyed by the the Great Chicago Fire. There didn't appear to be a central authority, it was permeated by gamblers, and the Boston Red Stockings seemed to have a grip on the league's pennants from 1872 to 1875. Hulbert had a plan for a new league, the National League, when it appeared that the National Association program was in disarray. As president of the Chicago White Stockings, he planned to stock his team with the best players from the Association. Al Spalding, a stalwart pitcher for the Red Stockings was convinced to play for Chicago's team. A few others were awarded an increase in their 1875 contracts like Cal McVey, Deacon White, Ross Barnes, Cap Anson and Ezra Sutton. Sutton later withdrew.

There seemed to be a problem with Hulbert approaching those players while they were playing during the 1875 season. It was in violation with the NA rules. Hulbert wasn't too concerned with it because once he formed the NL, he no longer was in violation of their rules.

Two changes were instituted in 1883. A "foul-bound catch" was abolished and the pitcher could deliver the ball from above his waist. Previously it was below the waist because the pitcher pitched underhand.

In 1884, pitching was further developed as all restrictions on the pitcher's delivery were removed, and six "called balls" became a base-on-balls. One big decision on championships, they were on a percentage basis only. John Ward pitched the second perfect professional game on June 17, 1885 as Providence Grays defeated Buffalo Bisons, 5-0.

1876

The National League

The National League began competition in 1876 and is still is competing. The American Association was the National Leagues' competition in the early years from 1882 to 1891. During that time, another league was being formed called the Union Association played games in 1884.

The Player's League only played games during 1890. By 1900, the National League was the only one in existence. That year the National League had eight teams, New York Giants, St. Louis Cardinals, Philadelphia Phillies, Boston Beaneaters, Brooklyn Superbas, Cincinnati Reds, Pittsburgh Pirates, and Chicago Orphans.

John Ward pitched the second perfect professional game on June 17, 1885 as Providence Grays defeated Buffalo Bisons, 5-0.

In the first year of the National League, the Chicago White Stockings were the best team with a 52-14 record, only playing 66 games. The St. Louis Brown Stockings played tough against them, but ultimately fell six games behind.

Al Spalding, who previously pitched for the Boston Red Stockings to win four consecutive National Association pennants from 1872-1875, continued with his pitching magic winning 47 games in 1876, while appearing in 61 of 66 games for the Chicago White Stockings. He also pitched eight shutouts and had a 1.75 ERA.

The American Association was the National Leagues competitor in the early years from 1882 to 1891. During that period, another league formed called the Union Association which played games for three seasons from 1883-1885. Later a new Player's League joined the fray, only played games during 1890.

In 1877, canvas bases 15 inches square were introduced; home plate was placed in an angle formed by the intersection of the first and third base lines; and the batter was exempted from a time at bat if he walked.

The Player Reserve Clause was instituted in 1879 because many players left the team that they were playing for, leaving the next season or during the same season to play for another team. Then, the number of "called balls" became nine and all pitched balls were either called strikes or balls. Then it was necessary for the pitcher to face the batter before he pitched to him. That season a staff of umpires was first introduced.

The next year in 1880, a further change in the number of balls to make a base-on-balls was reduced to eight. More developments were made when a base runner was declared out, when being hit by a fair batted ball, and a catcher had to catch a batted pitch (foul tip) to register an out on a third strike.

The National League's first game was played between Boston Red Caps at Philadelphia Athletics on April 22, 1876. Final score: Boston 6, Athletics 5. Dave Force, Jim O'Rourke and Tim McGinley hit well that day. Force for the Athletics, recorded the first assist; O'Rourke, for Boston, had the first hit while his teammate McGinley scored the first run.

William McLean, from Philadelphia, became the first professional umpire, when he umpired the first game in National League history.

A few days later, on April 25, Albert Goodwill Spalding pitched the first shutout for the Chicago White Stockings, defeating Louisville Grays 4-0. The first baseball players to hit home runs were the Chicago White Stockings' Ross Barnes and the Cincinnati Reds' Charles Wesley "Baby" Jones, on May 2, 1876 at Cincinnati as Chicago won 15-9.

Levi Meyerle, third baseman for the Philadelphia Athletics, was credited with the first double and triple on April 24, 1876.

Ross Barnes, Chicago White Stockings second baseman, hit the first home run on May 2, 1876. Bill Harbridge, playing for the Hartford Dark Blues, was the first left-handed catcher, playing on May 6, 1876. George Bradley threw the first no-hitter in National League history on July 15, 1876. Candy Cummings was the first to pitcher and win two games on the same day, on September 19, 1876 .

All performances that year were the league's highest as Ross Barnes led the parade of hitters when he scored 126 runs, peppered 138 hits, including 14 triples, 140 TB, .404 BA, .590 SA and a .462 OBP and Paul Hines hit 21 doubles, Deacon White had 60 RBIs.

On February 12, 1876, Al Spalding announced that he planned to open a retail sporting goods store. More developments occurred in 1878, as (1) a staff of umpires was first introduced and (2) the Providence Grays were the first team to build the first safety net behind the catcher to protect the fans.

1877

In 1877, there were several developments or changes in major league baseball in 1877: (1) The International league became the first minor league, (2) Tecumseh and Maple Leafs are the first foreign professional teams, (3) The first professional gambling scandal—four

Louisville players were expelled from the game, (4) Will White is the first player to wear eyeglasses, (5) Albert Spalding made the first baseball glove, (6) the first schedule appeared so the fans will know when their team is playing, (7) the first rule appears stating that the ball must stay in fair territory to be a hit.

    The Boston Red Caps won 42 games in a 60 game schedule to capture the National League pennant, while runner-up Louisville Grays remained seven games behind. Tommy Bond was the best pitcher in the league as he had 40 wins, a 2.11 ERA and striking out 170 batters. He also had a team best in pitching six shutouts. Deacon White had a few league-high marks as he had a .387 BA and 49 RBIs. White also led his team with 103 hits including 11 triples, a .545 SA and collecting 145 TB. Jim O'Rourke scored 68 runs, walked 20 times and earned a .407 OBP as shortstop George Wright sliced 15 doubles.

1878

    More changes or developments occurred in 1878 such as (1) turnstiles in the major leagues were first introduced at Providence, (2) the baseball catcher's chest protector was invented by William Green of the Hartford C.P. Team and used in 1878. (He sold his rights in the 1880s to A.B. Spalding company for $5,000) and (3) the National League instructed home teams to pay umpires $5 per game.

    Frederick Winthrop Thayer of Waverly, MA invented the baseball catcher's mask. Thayer was captain of the Harvard University Baseball club who obtained a patent (face guard or safety mask) on Feb, 2, 1878. It was made by a tinsmith in Cambridge MA, and tried out in a gymnasium in the winter of 1876-1877 and used by James Alexander Tyng with the Live Oaks team of Lynn MA on April 12, 1877. Louis Trauschke, catcher for the Forest Baseball Club, Lawrence MA, who had been hurt by a pitched ball, adopted the mask. Eventually, it was manufactured by Peck and Snyder, New York City.

Paul Hines, center fielder for the Providence Grays, completed an unassisted triple play on May 8, 1878 by catching a short line drive over the infield. His impetus continued his movement toward third. Since both front runners had passed third, Hines tagging third made two more outs.

The Spalding company published the first "Official Rule Guide" for baseball on May 8, 1878. Two more developments occurred in 1878, as (1) a staff of umpires was first introduced and (2) the Providence Grays were the first team to build the first safety net behind the catcher to protect the fans.

The Boston Red Caps, in 1878, captured their second pennant in a row, winning 41 games while Cincinnati Reds trailed by four games. Tommy Bond pitched 40 wins again, had a .678 WP, nine shutouts, a 2.08 ERA while striking out 182 batters. Pitching was dominant that year, while Jim O'Rourke had 71 hits, seven doubles, and seven triples.

1879

In 1879, National League president William A. Hulbert appointed a group of 20 men from which teams could choose an umpire, therefore becoming baseball's first umpiring staff, and umpires were given the authority to impose fines for illegal acts.

In 1879, the Providence Grays had a little more punch, winning 59 games, forcing the Boston Red Caps to take a back seat, five games behind. John Montgomery Ward powered the Grays defense by winning 47 games. He also had a .712 WP and struck out 239 batters. Paul Hines and Jim O'Rourke provided the offensive punch. Hines had 146 hits, 147 TB and sported a .357 BA. O'Rourke had 62 RBIs and claimed a .371 OBP.

1880

The 1880 baseball season experienced newer rules such as (1) base-on-balls was reduced to 8 "called balls," (2) the base runner was out if hit by a batted ball and (3) the catcher had to catch the pitch on the fly in order to register an out on a third strike.

Other developments were observed that year as Lee Richmond pitched the first perfect game in professional history as Worcester defeated Cleveland 1-0 on June 12, 1880. Five days later John Ward was the second member of the Worcester club to pitch a second perfect game during the same season.

On June 17, 1880 the first night game was played between two department store teams at Nantasket Beach in Boston. The Chicago White Stockings, out of the running for a few years, came to life in winning 67 games in a 85-game schedule, outdistancing the Providence Grays by 15 games. Larry Corcoran won 43 games, striking out 268 batters while teammate Fred Goldsmith pitched 21 wins, had a .875 WP and a 1.75 ERA. Abner Dalrymple and George Gore spear-headed the offense. Dalrymple scored 91 runs, sprinkled 126 hits, including 25 doubles and 12 triples. Gore claimed a .360 BA, .399 OBP including 21 walks.

Old Hoss Radbourn

Charles "Old Hoss" Radbourn played 12 years in the major leagues. He was born in Rochester , NY on Dec. 11, 1854, but was raised in Bloomington IL. Radbourn was a pitcher who played for 12 years for five teams, Buffalo Bisons (1880), Providence Grays (1881-85), Boston Beaneaters (1886-1889), Boston Reds (1890) and the Cincinnati Reds (1891). He played for the Bisons as a utility fielder and only played in six games. During his career, there were no substitutions allowed. If he had a replacement as a pitcher, he played right field, so that if he was needed to close the game, he could finish the game.

In 1881, Radbourn won 25 games and a winning percent .694, both were league highs. He led the league in 1882 with 206 strike outs. In 1883, he won 48 games and finished all 73 games that he started. After that season, many of his teammates jumped to join Union Association teams. At that 32-win-point in the season. Radbourn promised to stay with the Providence Grays until the end of the season, if he were allowed to pitch the rest of the 27 games, all of which he won. He holds the all-time record for season wins with 59.

1881

Roger Connor of Troy hit the first grand slam in National League history off Worcester's Lee Richmond on September 10, 1881.

The Chicago White Stockings claimed another pennant in 1881, winning 56 games, while the Providence Grays were closer this time, by nine games. Fred Goldman won 28 games while Larry Corcoran won 27. Corcoran also had a .692 WP and whiffed 170 batters. Cap Anson led the offense with 137 hits, 82 RBIs, .399 BA, 175 TB, .442 OBP and a .510 SA. George Gore scored 86 runs, hit nine triples and earned 27 base-on-balls. King Kelly hit 27 doubles.

1882

The American Association

In 1882, there was some dissatisfaction how the National League was run and another league, the American Association was established. The league continued until 1891. The Brooklyn Bridegrooms left the AA in 1890 and joined the NL as did the Cincinnati Reds in 1890, the Pittsburgh Pirates in 1887, and the St. Louis Browns in 1892. The American Association was a more liberal league on comparison to the puritanical National League. The AA established itself in what was known as "river cities," which led to the limitation of lower morality and social standard in these cities which included Pittsburgh, Cincinnati, Louisville and St. Louis. The AA added teams from Philadelphia and Baltimore.

With the new league, it was decided on November 8, 1881, that individual teams would operate their own affairs, and set their own admission prices known as the "guarantee system." In comparison to the NL that prohibited the sale of alcohol on its grounds, the AA had no restrictions and had lower admission prices than the NL.

The original AA franchises were the Baltimore Orioles and the Cincinnati Red Stockings who were expelled from the NL for selling alcohol and playing Sunday games, which were prohibited by the NL.

Beginning in 1884 and continuing every year until 1890, the AA champion met with the NL pennant winner every year for the first "World Series." The number of games involved in this event was anything from three games to fifteen, with the 1885 and 1890 contests ending with disputed ties. One of the problems that weakened the AA was the tendency of many teams to jump to the NL or the Players League, which entered the league competition in 1890. The AA survived, and earlier entry into the fray by the Union Association in 1884-1885. Many of the baseball owners in the AA also had a team in the NL which contributed to the AA woes.

Major League baseball claimed a few developments in 1882 with (1) Paul Hines being the first player to wear sunglasses on the field, (2) Paul Browning was the first player to have his bats custom made, (3) the American Association introduced the first salaried umpire staff, (4) the first professional double-header was played with Providence opposing Worcester on September 25, 1882. In 1882, National League umpire Richard Higham became the only major league umpire ever expelled from the game after the League judged him guilty of collusion with gamblers.

The American Association started playing in 1882 as th Cincinnati Red Stockings won 55 games. Louisville Eclipse were unable to catch up as they remained 13 games out of first place. Will White won 40 games, including eight shutouts while striking out 122 batters. Hick Carpenter spearheaded the attack with 120 hits, 15 doubles, 67 RBIs, .342 BA, 148 TB, .360 OBP and .422 SA. Joe Sommer scored 82 runs while waiting out 29 bases-on-balls.

The National League champion was the Chicago White Sox who won 55 games, The Providence Grays were three games behind. Larry Corcoran won 27 games with a .692 WP, striking out 122 opponents. Cap Anson led the attack in a big way as he produced 126 hits, 83 RBIs, .362 BA, 174 TB, .397 OBP and a .500 SA. George Gore scored 99 runs, walking 29 times. King Kelly contributed 27 doubles to the cause.

The American Association's Cincinnati Red Stockings copped the pennant, winning 55 games. The Louisville Eclipse could not keep up, as they fell 13 games behind.

1883

A few new developments occurred in 1883 as (1) the "foul bound catch" was abolished, (2) the pitcher could deliver a ball from above his waist, (3) the Philadelphia Phillies started their first major league season.

The first night baseball game was played on June 2, 1883 at League Park, Fort Wayne IN between a club of boys known as M.E. College and the Quincy professional team from Adams County IL.; Seven innings were played, witnessed by 2,000 spectators. The field was illuminated by 17 lights of 4,000 candlepower each.

The Boston Beaneaters took the National League title winning 63 games. The Chicago White Stockings took a back seat this time, four games behind Boston. Jim Whitney won 37 games striking out 345 batters while Charlie Buffington won 25 and pitched four shutouts.

John Morrill hit 33 doubles, collected 212 TB and had a .525 SA. John Hornung. Ezra Sutton and Jack Burdick helped the powerful offense. Hornung scored 107 runs, Sutton peppered 134 hits and a .350 OBP. Burdock had 88 RBI and a .330 BA.

The Philadelphia Athletics won the 1883 American Association crown capturing 66 games. The St. Louis Browns were real close, until the last day of the season, missing by one game. Bobby Mathew won 30 games, had a 2.46 ERA and whiffed 203 batters.

1884

Interesting changes were made in 1884 : (1) All restrictions on the delivery of a pitcher were removed, (2) six "called balls" became a base on balls, (3) championships were to be decided only on a win-loss percentage basis (4) Joe Quinn is the first Australian-born player to enter Major League Baseball on April 26, 1884, (5) Moses and Weldy Walker of Toledo (AA) are the first African-American players to appear in a major league game on May 1, 1884 (6) the first post season games occurred—the National League versus the American Association, (7) the first third major league, the Union Association began playing in the 1884 season, and (9) it was ruled that a batter who is hit by a pitch allowed the batter to take first base.

The Union Association

In 1884 the Union Association was formed by Henry Lucas. His league did not institute the "reserve clause" which was used by the NL since 1879. The reserve clause stated that a certain number of players could be retained by their team for the following season and were not to be persuaded to play for another club. The original UA teams were: Altoona Mountain Cities, Baltimore Unions, Boston Reds, Chicago Browns/Pittsburgh Stogies, Cincinnati Outlaw Reds, Philadelphia Keystones, St, Louis Maroons and Washington Nationals. Four other teams played part of a season: the Kansas City Unions, Wilmington (DEL), Milwaukee Grays and the St. Paul White Caps.

The St. Louis Maroons won the pennant, winning 94 games and only 19 losses. When Lucas formed the third league, he hired the best players available. Unfortunately, his team was so powerful it ran away with the league. They won the pennant by 35.5 games over a replacement team, the Milwaukee Grays.

The 1884 season turned out to be a great season for seven strong strikeout pitchers They were: Hugh Daily, Dupree Shaw, Old Hoss Radbourn, Charlie Buffinton. Gary Heckler and Bill Sweeney.

One-arm Daily had 483 whiffs (469) for Chicago Browns/Pittsburgh Stogies and 14 for the Washington Nationals, both teams in the UA); Shaw had 451 strikeouts (142 for Detroit Wolverines in the NL and 309 for the Boston Reds in the UA); Radbourn had 441 whiffs for the Providence Grays in the NL; Buffinton struck out 417 for the Boston Beaneaters of the NL; Heckler had 385 Strikeouts for Louisville Colonels,in the AA; Bill Sweeney (not to be confused with Charlie Sweeney, who jumped from the Grays, to pitch for the UA champions St. Louis Browns) whiffed 374 batters for the Baltimore Orioles of the UA. Association; the the Chicago Browns/Pitttsburgh Stogies, Union Association, (469 SO) and the Washington Nationals, UA, for a 483 total.

The Providence Grays were victorious in claiming the National League 1884 crown winning 84 games. The Boston Beaneaters couldn't quite keep up, as they fell 10.5 off the pace.

Charles "Old Hoss" Radbourn set an all-time record for 59 wins. Midway through the season, another Grays pitcher, Charlie Sweeney, jumped into the newly formed Union Association with the St. Louis Maroons. Radbourn convinced the Grays ownership that if they would have him pitch the rest of the games that season, he would not follow Sweeney in jumping to another team.

During the Grays 1884 season, Radbourn, because of his sole position of competing in every game, besides his all-time record of winning 59 games, he also topped the National League in many categories. As he only lost 12 games, his .831 WP led all of his performances, as he sported a 1.38 ERA, pitched in 75 games, but he also pitched 678.2 innings.

Paul Hines was a whirlwind for the Grays as he scored 94 runs, had 148 hits including 36 doubles, 10 triples, with 213 TB, .360 OBP, .495 SA and collected 44 walks. Second baseman Jerry Denny had 59 RBIs.

Meanwhile, the New York Metropolitans captured the American Association title winning 75 games. The Columbus Buckeyes finished 6.5 games behind. The Metropolitans two-man pitching staff were always trying to outdo each other, as Jack Lynch won 37 games and was also matched by Tim Keefe with another 37. Lynch also had five shutouts, while Keefe struck out 334 batters and sported a 2.25 ERA. David Orr led the offense, hitting 32 doubles, 112 RBIs, 247 Rba .354 BA coupled with a .539 SA. Dude Estabrook and Candy Nelson supplemented other hitting categories on their own. Estabrook led the team with 150 hits, as Nelson scored 114 runs, had a .375 OBP and 74 base-on-balls.

In the third league, for only one year, the St. Louis Maroons demolished the rest of the Union Association teams as they won 94 games, while losing only 19. Their closest competitor, the Cincinnati Outlaw Reds, could do no better than 21 games trailing behind. Billy Taylor had 25 wins and a 1.68 ERA, while turncoat Charles Sweeney racked up 24 wins, striking out 192 batters. Leading the offensive barrage of the Maroons, Orator Shafer hit 40 doubles, had a .360 BA, .398 OBP, 234 TB, .501 SA and 33 walks. To supplement his performance, Fred Dunlap, who also served as manager for last part of the season, scored 160 runs, sprayed 185 hits, including 13 home runs, while Dave Rowe sliced 11 triples. The Union Association's champion Maroons did not get involved in any World Series.

In the first World Series, the Providence Grays (NL) defeated the New York Metropolitans (AA), 3-0. The first World Series championship was played at the New York City Polo Grounds on October 23-25, 1884. The Providence Grays defeated the New York Metropolitans 3-0.

Moses Fleetwood "Fleet" Walker was the first African-American to played in the major leagues in 1884 when Toledo joind the American Association. He was a catcher when he played in 41 games (in the early days, some teams played only 50 or 60 games) and batted .251 He also was the first African-American college baseball player playing for Oberlin College in 1888, and later for the University of Michigan where he was a law student.

1885

In 1885, the following baseball changes were made, such as (1) umpires and catchers first use of chest protectors, (2) one portion of the bat could be flat (one side), (3) home base could be made of marble or whitened rubber and (4) Joe Harrington is the first player to hit a home run in his first at-bat on September 10, 1885.

The Chicago White Stockings won the National League title by winning 87 games. Their closest competitor, the New York Giants challenged the Chicago Club until the last day, but their 85 wins left them two games behind. Abner Dalrymple's 11 home runs, Cap Anson's 108 RBIs, and John Clarkson's 53 wins and 308 strikeouts, best in the NL paced the White Stockings to the crown.

The Giant's ace was the best in the NL with 1.57 ERA.

The St. Louis Browns copped the American Association crown winning 79 games, but their runner-up Cincinnati Red Stockings could do no better than 16 games behind.

Dave Foultz, the Browns sparkling right-hander won 33 of 46 games. Teammate Bob Caruthers had a great season winning 40 games, a 2.07 ERA and a .755 WP. Bill Gleason's 119 hits, Curt Welch's .271 BA and 8 RBIs and Tip O'Neills' .350 BA led the Browns attack.

Chicago and St. Louis met in the 1885 series, but the series ended in a draw. In a seven game series, both teams had a 3-3 record and one tie. Game one finished in a tied called for darkness. Game two was awarded to Chicago by forfeit after six innings, because St. Louis refused to continue after disputing an umpire's decision. Both teams claimed that each of them was the champion.

1886

Only two changes occurred in 1886, with (1) players organizing their first union, "The Brotherhood of Ball Players" and, the first spring training camp was established by Chicago White Stockings at Hot Springs AR.

The Chicago White Sox captured the National League pennant by winning 90 games. while the closest team, the Detroit Wolverines were just behind them at 2.5 games.

John Clarkson won 36 games and struck out 313 batters. Jim McCormick won 31 games while Jocko Flynn won 23 games and had a 2.24 ERA.

The St. Louis Browns won 93 games in a 140 game schedule to top the American Association. Philadelphia Quakers playing them tough all the way, eventually beating them byl 3.5 games. Dave Foutz won 41 games, struck out 283 batters, had 11 shutouts and earned a 2.11 ERA. Bob Caruthers won 30 games and pitched 166 strikeouts.

Browns left-fielder, Tip O'Neill led the Browns offensively with 190 hits, including 14 triples, 107 RBIs, .385 OBP and a .440 SA. Arlier Latham scored 152 runs, stole 60 bases while Curt Welch knocked out 31 doubles.
The St. Louis Browns (AA) defeated the Chicago White Stockings (NL) in the 1886 World Series, 4-2.

1887

Jim Toy was the first Native-American to play in the Majors, playing first base for the Cleveland Blues of the American Association in 1887 and later was a catcher for the Brooklyn Gladiators in 1890.

The 1887 season had several changes: (1) The pitcher's box was reduced to 4 feet by 5 1/2 feet, (2) calling for high and low pitches was abolished (3) five balls became a base-on-balls (4) four "called strikes" were adopted for that season only, (5) bases on balls were recorded as hits for this season only, (6) home plate was to be made of rubber only - dropping the marble type, and was to be 12 inches square, (7) coaches were recognized by the rules for the first time ever, (8) the first rule defining the strike zone appears.

Charles Zimmer was first catcher to play consistently behind the batter. Mike Griffon of Baltimore and Cincinnati's George "Whit Wings" Tabeau were the first to homer in their first at bat on the same day, April 16, 1887.

The Dauvray Cup was a trophy given to the first three-time winners of the World Series, after 1887. The cup was donated by actress Helen Dauvray.

The New York Giants were the first team to win two titles in 1888 and 1889. But a turmoil between the National League and American Association, in 1890 and 1891, resulted in the end of post season play. When the American Association folded in 1891, the cup was given to the National League pennant winner in 1892 and 1893.

The Detroit Wolverines (NL) won the 1887 World Series, defeating the St. Louis Browns (AA), 10-5. In playing the World Series, MLB played the games in ten different cities. They were St. Louis, Detroit, Pittsburgh, Brooklyn, Boston, Philadelphia, Washington, Chicago, New York and Baltimore.

1888

Bud Fowler was the first African-American baseball player who played in the 1870s. Later Fleetwood Walker and Welday Walker were the first blacks to play in the major leagues, when they were members of the Toledo Blue Stockings in the American Association. Another black, Frank Grant joined the Buffalo Bisons in the minor International League, hitting .340 in 1888.

In 1885, a first national black team was founded. Through the first part of the twentieth century, many black teams and leagues were formed, but many were unable to finish their first season.

When baseball became popular, it was enjoyable to everyone. Ever since the African-Americans were released from captivity, the white man has excluded them from playing in the majors. By the end of the 1860s, the city of Philadelphia had a population of 22,000 blacks and that was where the many Negro teams and leagues were formed. It would be almost another century, when a white man would take up their cause so the African-American men could play in the majors.

The Player reserve clause was written into the contracts of minor leaguers for the first time in 1888. Then, the base-on-balls exemption from a time at bat was restored and a rule that a batsman was credited with a base hit when a runner was hit by his batted ball.

The New York Giants gained first place in the National League in 1888, winning 84 games. The Chicago White Stockings, their closest competitor, finished eight games back, Tim Keefe won 35 games, including pitching eight shut outs, struck out 335 batters and earned a 1.74 ERA. Mickey Welch, who had 26 wins, adding another 167 strikeouts of his own.

The Giants' Roger Connor put on an overwhelming hitting show while scoring 98 runs, scattered 140 hits, including 17 triples and 14 fence busters. He also had 71 RBIs, 231 TB, .389 OBP, .480 SA, and 73 bases-on-balls. Buck Ewing hit 18 doubles, while sporting a .306 BA.

In the American Association, the St. Louis Browns snatched first place, with 92 wins in a 135-game schedule. The Brooklyn Bridegrooms finally came into their own, finished second place at 6.5 games behind.

The Browns' Silver King was an outstanding pitcher, winning 45 games, including six shutouts, a 1.63 ERA and striking out 258 batters. Teammate Nat Hudson won 25 games, five shutouts and whiffed an additional 138 batters.

The epic poem "Casey at the Bat," made its first debut in print and on stage. Ernest Lawrence Thayer on June 3, 1888 wrote a poem, "Casey at the Bat" which made him famous. It was so popular that De Wolf Hopper, a stage actor, recited it during one of his stage shows on August 14, 1888, on Thayer's 25th birthday. Soon, many school boys would recite the poem in school, and anywhere else they had an audience.

Casey at the Bat
   By Earnest Lawrence Thayer

"The outlook wasn't brilliant for the Mudville nine that day;
The score stood four to two with but one inning more to play.
And then when Cooney died at first, and Barrows did the same,
A sickly silence fell upon the patrons of the game.

A straggling few got up to go in deep despair. The rest
Clung to that hope which springs eternal in the human breast;
They thought if only Casey could but get a whack at that—
We'd put up even money now with Casey at the bat.

But Flynn preceded Casey, as did also Jimmy Blake,
And the former was a lulu and the latter was a cake;
So upon that stricken multitude grim melancholy sat,
For there seemed but little chance of Casey's getting to the bat.

But Flynn let drive a single, to the wonderment of all,
And Blake, the much despised, tore the cover off the ball;
And when the dust had lifted, and men saw what had occurred,
There was Jimmy safe at second and Flynn a-hugging third.

Then from 5,000 throats, and more, there rose a lusty yell;
It rumbled through the valley, it rattled in the dell;
It knocked upon the mountain and recoiled upon the flat,
For Casey, mighty Casey, was advancing to the bat.

There was ease in Casey's manner as he stepped into his place;
There was pride in Casey's bearing and a smile on Casey's face.
And when, responding to the cheers, he lightly doffed his hat,
No stranger in the crowd could doubt 'twas Casey at the bat.

Ten thousand eyes were on him as he rubbed his hands with dirt;
Five thousand tongues applauded when he wiped them on his shirt.
Then while the writhing pitcher ground the ball into his hip,
Defiance gleamed in Casey's eye, a sneer curled Casey's lip.

And now the leather-covered sphere came hurtling through the air,
And Casey stood a-watching it in haughty grandeur there.
Close by the sturdy batsman the ball unheeded sped—
"That ain't my style," said Casey. "Strike one," the umpire said.

From the benches, black with people, there went up a muffled roar,
Like the beating of the storm-waves on a stern and distant shore.
"Kill him! Kill the umpire!" shouted some one on the stand;
And it's likely they'd have killed him had not Casey raised his hand.

With a smile of Christian charity great Casey's visage shone;
He stilled the rising tumult; he bade the game go on;
He signaled to the pitcher, and once more the spheroid flew;

But Casey still ignored it, and the umpire said, "Strike two."

"Fraud!" cried the maddened thousands, and echo answered fraud;
But one scornful look from Casey and the audience was awed.
They saw his face grow stern and cold, they saw his muscles strain,
And they knew that Casey wouldn't let that ball go by again.

The sneer is gone from Casey's lip, his teeth are clinched in hate;
He pounds with cruel violence his bat upon the plate.
And now the pitcher holds the ball, and now he lets it go,
And now the air is shattered by the force of Casey's blow.

Oh, somewhere in this favored land the sun is shining bright;
The band is playing somewhere, and somewhere hearts are light,
And somewhere men are laughing, and somewhere children shout;
But there is no joy in Mudville—mighty Casey has struck out."

Also in 1888, the Nationals is the first major league club to train in Florida, and the first rule giving three strikes for an out, appeared. The New York Giants (NL) defeated the St. Louis Browns (AA) in the 1888 World Series, 6-4.

1889

Three more new developments appeared in 1889 including that (1) the first rule giving four balls for a walk, (2) a sacrifice bunt was statistically recognized, (3) the first batter to be used in major league history on August 10, 1889, Mickey Welch, playing for New York becomes the first pinch-hitter, and he struck out.

The New York Giants copped the 1889 National League crown collecting 83 wins, edging out the Boston Beaneaters by one game. Mickey Welch won 27 games, including three shutouts, a 3.02 ERA and

125 strikeouts. Hall-of-Famer Tim Keefe won 28 games while striking out 225 batters. Right-fielder Mike Tieran carried the brunt of the offense, scoring 147 runs, spreading 147 hits and had a .335 BA, .447 OBP, .497 SA and had 96 walks. Jim O'Rourke, Roger Connor and John Montgomery Ward contributed some hitting of their own. O'Rourke hit 36 doubles, Connor 17 triples, 13 homers and 262 TB. Ward, showed off his speed stealing 62 bases.

The American Association's Brooklyn Bridegrooms took the 1889 crown winning 92 games, while perennial league winner, St. Louis Browns, slowed down a little, only two games back. Bob Caruthers won 40 games, including seven shutouts and whiffing 118 batters while Adonis Terre won 22, while adding 186 strikeouts.

Darby O'Brien led the hitting attack while scoring 146 runs, peppering the field with 170 hits including 30 doubles, .391 OBP, 237 TB, while burning the base paths with 91 steals. Oyster Burns and Darby O'Brien took off some of the pressure with their performances. Burns hit 13 triples, , had a .304 BA, a 391 OBP and a .423 SA. O'Brien scored 146 runs, had 170 hits including 30 doubles, 237 TB and 91 SB, while Foutz drove in 113 runs and Hub Collins displayed his great eye in being walked 80 times. The New York Giants (NL) defeated the Brooklyn Bridegrooms (AA) in the 1889 World Series, 6-3.

1890

The Players League

The American Association and the National league decided to abide by the same rules for the 1887 season, but on November 4, 1889 John Montgomery Ward helped formulate the Player's League which began playing in 1890. In October 1885, he formed the Brotherhood of Professional Base Ball Players in an effort to unionize the players to promote their best interests. Two key provisions of the Player's League was they would not have a reserve clause. A player could not be traded without his permission and could not be released outright without the consent of each team's board of directors. The teams that started playing during the 1890 season were: the Boston Reds, Brooklyn Ward's Wonders, Buffalo Bisons, Chicago Pirates, Cleveland Infants. New York Giants, Philadelphia Quakers and Pittsburgh Burghers.

Cy Young

Denton True 'Cy" Young was born on May 29, 1867 in Gilmore OH. He was a major league pitcher who played for five different teams: Cleveland Spiders, 1890-98; St. Louis Cardinals, 1899-1900; Boston Puritans/Red Sox, 1901-1908; Cleveland Naps, 1909-1911 and the Boston Braves, 1911. During his 22 year career he won 511 games and lost 316 a .618 WP and a 2.63 ERA. Due to his proficient winning career, an award for the best pitcher in the American and National League each year is called a Cy Young award as the best pitcher. Initially, the Cy Young Award covered both leagues in establishing the winner from 1956 to 1966. Since 1967 a winning pitcher in each league was selected. Young was elected to the Baseball Hall of Fame in 1937.

Some 1890 new developments were that (1) twelve games on July 30, 1890 were played making it the only time in major league history in which at least ten games were played with every game being won by the visiting team, (2) Ed Cartwright, of the St. Louis Browns, on September 23, 1890, became the first player to hit a grand slam and three run homer in one inning against the same pitcher (Ed Green ofross the Philadelphia Athletics.)

1891

The National League continued as an eight -team league and enjoyed another season without change.

There were many changes in the AA as the league wound down to its final season and while it expanded to nine teams. The Toledo Solons that only started playing in 1890, dropped out in 1891. Brooklyn, Rochester and Syracuse teams followed to create gaping holes in the league. On the plus side, Cincinnati returned after leaving the previous season. The Washington Statesmen, Milwaukee Brewer and the Boston Reds were accepted as replacements. The Reds had transferred from the 1890 Players League.

The Boston Beaneaters won the 1891 National League crown winning 87 games, leaving the Chicago Colts 3.5 games behind. John Clarkson led the defense, winning 33 games, backed up by Kid Nichols' 30 and Harry Staley's 24 winners. Clarkson also fanned 240 batters, Harry Stovey, like many other baseball players, did not want his family to know that he was playing baseball, because his family was against it. Stovey's real name was Harry Stowe. He earned three league best marks as he led Boston in hitting with 38 doubles, 20 triples, 16 home runs, 271 TB, 95 RBI and a .498 SA. Herman Long scored 129 runs and led the team in walks with 80.

The Boston Reds reach the end of the American Association 1891 season in first with 93 wins, 8.5 games ahead of the St. Louis Browns. The Reds ace, George Haddock had 34 wins while pitcher Charlie Buffinton had the leagues highest winning percentage at .763.

Both Reds Duke Farrell and Hugh Duffy had 110 RBI. While Farrell hit 12 homers. The offense was spread around with Tom Brown, Dan Brouthers, and Paul Radford. Brown scored 177 runs, 189 hits, 30 doubles, and 21 triples. Brouthers had a league high .350 BA, .471 OBP and SA. Radford walked 96 times.

Inter-league squabbles prevented series games that year. As the American Association folded, four of its teams were accepted in the National League as the Louisville Cyclones, Washington Senators, St. Louis Browns and Baltimore Orioles made the move.

In 1891, substitutions, for the first time, were permitted at any point in a game, and large padded mitts were allowed for catchers.

No World Series was played in the American Association last season because they and the National League owners were involved in many opposing issues and the World Series was not played in 1891.

1892

On March 4th, following the collapse of the American Association, it was decided that the schedule would be split in two halves. The first Sunday game is played on April 17, 1892 with Cincinnati Red Stockings beating St. Louis 5-1.

On June 6, Benjamin Harrison was the first United States President to watch a MLB game. The Cincinnati Reds defeated the Washington Senators 7-4 in a ll inning game.

On July 13, the last games in the first round are played. In the second half, the Cleveland Spiders were the second half winner. The Boston Beaneaters, the first half winner played the Spiders for the league play-off.

On September 21, John Clarkson of the Spiders recorded his 300th win.

In the 1892 championship, the Boston Beaneaters defeated the Cleveland Spiders 5-0, with one tie.

The players who hit the Boston Beaneaters to win the first half were Hugh Duffy scoring 125 runs, peppering 184 hits, 12 triples, 60 walks, a .301 BA, 418 SA and 251 TB. Herman Long, Billy Nash and Tommy Tucker finessed some hits too. Long Hit 33 doubles while stealiing 57 bases; Billy Nash had 95 RBIs and Tommy Tucker claimed a .365 OBP.

The Cleveland Spiders, while winning the second half powered their team as Ed McNear scored 135 runs, Cupid Shields spread 177 hits, had 177 walks and a .443 OBP. Chief Zimmer hit 29 doubles and claimed a 404 SA while Jake McAleer stole 540 bases. Jake Virtue slammed 20 triples, collected 228 TB.. Boston Beaneaters defeated the Cleveland Spiders for the league championship, winning 5-0 and one tie.

Brooklyn's Tom Daly hit the first pinch-hit homer on May 24, 1892.

Wee Willie Keeler

William "Wee Willie Keeler was a right-fielder who played for the National League teams Baltimore Orioles, the Brooklyn Superbas and the American League New York Highlanders from 1892 to 1910. He was born in Brooklyn on March 3, 1872. During his career he had 810 RBI, 485 stolen bases and has a lifetime batting average of .341. He was five feet, four inches tall, weighing 140 pounds, which accounts for his being called "Wee Willie." He batted with his hands apart which allowed him to get on base with bunt singles. He often would hit the ball straight down and was fast enough to reach first before a fielder could field the ball and throw to first. Legend has it that because he played for Baltimore, the type of his hits were called the "Baltimore Chop." He had advice for all hitters: "Keep your eye clear" and "Hit 'em where they ain't" (meaning the outfielders). Keeler was elected to the Baseball Hall of Fame in 1939.

1893

In 1893 there were new rules like (1) Pitching distance increased from 50 feet to 60 feet 6 inches (2) the pitching box was eliminated and a rubber slab, 12 inches by 4 inches was substituted, (3) the pitcher was required to place his rear foot against the slab, (4) the rule exempting a batter from a time at bat on a sacrifice was instituted, (5) the rule allowing a flat side to a bat was rescinded and (6)- the requirement that the bat be round and wholly of hard wood was substituted.

There was no championship series, but the Boston Beaneters won 86 games to cop the 1893 championship. The up- and-coming Pittsburgh Pirates lagged behind by five games.

1894

Boston Beaneater's Bobby Lowe became the first player to hit four home runs in in one game on May 30, 1894. In 1894, a new rule was added: foul bunts were classified as strikes.

In 1894. William Teller offered a cup for the World Series from 1894-1897. Teller was the President of the Pittsburgh Pirates and when his team finished second in 1893, he though that his team might win it. In those four years that the cup was offered, the Pirates never finished higher than sixth.

The Baltimore Orioles were in first place in 1894 with an 89-39 record. Sadie McMahon won 25 games, had a .758 WP, struck out 60, but gave up 11 walks. Bill Hake won 16, struck out 68 batters and he had trouble finding the plate too, walking 78 swingers.

Joe Kelley hit 48 doubles, had a .393 BA, .502 OBP, a .622 SA and 107 SB. Willie "Hit 'em where they ain't" Keeler scored 165 runs sliced 219 hits, but he duplicated Kelley's 305 TB. Heinie Reitz hit 31 tripl;es while Dan Brouthers collected 128 RBI.s

The New York Giants finished second with 88 wins, but won the World Series Temple Cup, 4-0.

The Giants Amos Rusie won 36 games for the Giants and struck out 195 batters. Jouett Meekin won 33 games, a .788 WP and whiffing 125 swingers. Jack Doyle led the Gaints with 30 doubles, a .368 BA, 496 SA and stole 44 bases. George Davis scored 125 runs, hit 19 triples, collected 263 TB and had 67 walks. Eddie Burke spread 176 hits and had a .434 OBP while George Van Haltren knocked in 105 runs.

The New York Giants finished second with 88 wins, but won the World Series Temple Cup defeating the Baltimore Orioles, 4-0.

1895

There were more rule changes in 1895: (1) the pitching slab was enlarged to 24 inches by 6 inches, (2) bats were permitted to be 2 3/4 inches in diameter and not to exceed 42 inches in length, (3) the infield-fly rule was adopted and (4) a held foul tip was classified as a strike.

The infield fly rule was codified in 1895. It went into effect when some infielders instead of catching a infield fly, chose to drop, or not catch an infield fly so they could complete a possible double play and jeopardize the runner or runners, who tagged their base. In the rule, there must be less than two outs and runners on first and second or first, second and third, and the ball was hit in the air, and must be caught in the infield with ordinary effort. In usual circumstances an umpire or umpires can call the infield fly rule, if the ball was deemed to be in fair territory. Occasionally, a ball could be viewed as being foul, but circumstances such as wind could bring the ball in fair territory, and the officials could then call the infield fly. In 1895, only one previous out was necessary. Further adjustment to this rule occurred in 1901, and in 1904.

The Baltimore Orioles had a 87-43 record in winning the 1896 National League pennant. The Cleveland Spiders played the Orioles tight, but at season's end, they were three games behind. Bill Hoffer won 31 games. The Spiders, however beat the Orioles in the World Series, 4-1.

1896

Nap Lajoie

Nap Lajoie played MLB for the Philadelphia Phillies, the Philadelphia Athletics (twice) and the Cleveland Naps from 1896 and 1916. He managed the Naps from 1905 to 1909. He led the AL in batting average five times and had a lifetime .338 BA. He also had the most hits in the AL four times. Lajoie was enshrined in the National Hall of Fame ion 1937.

Lajoie started his MLB career playing for the Philadelphia Phillies. At his signing he was assured that his salary would be the same as Ed Delahanty. In his fourth year with the Phillies, he saw the checks and he found out that his $2,600 salary was $400 less than Delahanty's. In the off-season, Lajoie thought that he would get his revenge from Phillies owner, John Rogers. He jumped to the Philadelphia Athletics of the new American League. Rogers went to court to block Lajoie's ability to play for the Athletics. The court issued an order that Lajoie could not play in the State of Pennsylvania for no one else, but the Phillies. Lajoie was granted Free Agency on April 21, 1902 and on May 31, 1902 signed with the Cleveland Broncos. When Cleveland played the Athletics, and because of the earlier court order, Lajoie never played against he Athletics while the Broncos played in Philadelphia.

Professor Charles Hinton demonstrated the first pitching machine in 1896.

Cap Anson was the first person to get 3,000 hits. When he began playing, walks were considered hits and some previously recorded hits were removed, but they were restored more than a century later.

In 1896 Ed Abbaticchio was the first Italian-American player in the major leagues. The Baltimore Orioles, bouncing back after their 1895 Series loss to the Spiders, won the 1896 pennant with a 90-39 record while those pesky Spiders lagged behind by 9.5 games. The Orioles Bill Hoffer with a 25-7 record, had a league high .781 WP. Right-fielder Joe Kelley also had a league high swiping 87 bases, but also had a team-high with 31 doubles, 19 triples, eight homers, 383 TB, .543 SA and 91 bases-on-balls. Wee Willie Keeler helped out by scoring 153 runs and rifled 210 hits. The Orioles had finished in first for therecord straight year, but this time they took the Temple Cup in winning the 1896 World Series, defeating second place Cleveland Spiders, 4-0.

1897

In 1897, the Boston Beaneaters compiled a 93-39 record to win the National League pennant. The second-place Baltimore Orioles finished two games behind. Both the position players and pitchers were credited with top league categories. Kid Nichols won 31 games and Fred Klobedanz had a .768 WP. Nichols also had to share his high three saves with Washington Senators pitcher Win Mercer, who also had three saves. The three offensive league highs were shared by Hugh Duffy (11 home runs), Jimmy Collins (132 RBIs) and Billy Hamilton (105 walks). Duffy also led his team in other categories in scoring 130 runs, scattering 187 hits and 41 base thefts.

The Baltimore Orioles won the Temple Cup for the second time, even though they had finished second in the standings. They defeated pennant winner Boston Beaneaters, 4-1. However, there was a downside to the fourth year of the Temple Cup Series. When the Orioles were winning the last game, only 700 fans were there. The Orioles management were so embarrassed that they refused to release the figures. The league gave back the cup to Mr. Temple rather than sponsor another future unprofitable series.

1898

There were a few rules changes and new developments occurring in 1898: (1) the first modern rules defining a balk and the stolen base appear, (2) the first time base stealing statistics are officially recorded.

The Boston Beaneaters won 102 games for the 1898 National League pennant, as they beat the Baltimore Orioles by six games. Kid Nichols' 31 wins and four saves were the league's best. He also had team highs with a .721 WP, five shutouts and a 2.13 ERA. Vic Wills, with 25 wins, struck out 160 batters. Billy Hamilton and Jimmy Collins had league-high marks: Hamilton with a .480 OBP while Collins hit 15 home runs and 287 TB. Hamilton also had several team highs, scoring 110 runs, 54 stolen bases, 87 walks, and a .369 BA. Collins scattered 106 hits, 35 doubles, 111 RBIs and a .479 SA. There were no playoffs at the end of the 1898 season.

1899

John Frank "Bucky" Freeman was the first "Home Run King" when was an outfielder for the Washington Senators of the National League in 1899. He hit 25 home runs and 25 triples.

Arm Signals in Baseball

It's hard to imagine a baseball game not using arms signals to indicate strikes, outs, foul or fair balls, or signals to indicate why a runner was safe. How about pitching signals. A catcher, who is the "general" of the defense, displaying finger signals for the kind of pitch that he wants the pitcher to throw. Usually using one finger to signal a fast ball, two for a curve and three for any number of different pitches. That number can change when the offensive team has a runner on second. The reason, the offensive team has signals for their own is to let the batter know what kind of the pitch the next pitch will be. Under those circumstances, the catcher will go to the mound to change what the different fingers required for a new assortment of pitches. How about when the manager or base coaches use an assortment of signals to send to the batter or runner(s). These signals led the fans to wonder if these persons have a skin or neurological problem. All the players on each team knows exactly what they mean, and act accordingly.

Sometimes missing a signal or disregarding it can present a problem in the outcome of a game. A famous manager, John McGraw, signaled to a batter to bunt the ball, but the batter disregarded the signal, and hit a home run. His failure to execute a signal cost him a tongue-lashing and a stiff fine. Let's see where the use of hand signals originated and how we can't imagine a game without their use.

It's not often that we can credit someone for having completely changed a sport, but Dummy Hoy might be an exception. Hoy's real first time using s hand signal was because he had the disability of being unable to hear or speak. The term for this problem was called "dumb," but through the years the "dumb" connotation has been that a person was "stupid." Hoy was not stupid—he was very intelligent. That talented center fielder played for several teams during his career. He is remembered not only for having been very talented, but he is regarded as the best deaf player in history. Not only that, but it is strongly argued, that as a direct result of Dummy Hoy, we see hand signals that are in vogue today. Dummy Hoy was baseball's third deaf player, but also the first member of this group that did not pitch as well. While many credit Hoy with having pioneered hand signals, there were others too!

Ed Dundon was the first deaf player recorded in baseball history. It is thought that while Dundon was umpiring a game in 1886, he used hand signals.

Charles "Cy" Rigler was also an umpire in the National League from 1906 through 1935. He is credited for having invented hand signals for balls, strikes and outs at the plate as a way for outfielders to see the calls more clearly. Later, when Rigler was umpiring in the minor leagues, MLB umpire Bill Klem began using them in the National League. Rigler, in should be noted, as one of the umpires, he was the first one responsible for using the chest protector.

During the course of a game, a the catcher or the pitching coach (sometimes a manager) would call "time" so they can talk with the pitcher. At one game, it was was discovered that someone in the stands who could read lips was transmitting that information to the batting team. Sometimes, that information which was received would affect the outcome of the game. Then it became necessary for the pitcher to cover his mouth with his glove, sometimes that catcher too, if his mask is off. A coach sometimes will cover his mouth with his hands.

The Brooklyn Superbas took the 1899 National League pennant, winning 101 games, while their runner-up the Boston Beaneaters finished 7.5 games behind. Jay Hughes's .824 WP and his 28 wins were league-highs. His record was shared with Joe McGinty, of ther Baltimore Orioles, who also had 28 wins. Team-highs were recorded by Wee Willie Keeler who scored 140 runs, peppered 216 hits, stole four bases, had a .425 OBP, .325 BA and 257 TB. Tom Daly hit 24 doubles while Joe Kelley had 93 RBIs and walked 70 times. There were no playoffs in 1899. There was also a downside in 1899, the Cleveland Spiders recorded the worse losing record in baseball history when they posted a 20-134 record.

1900

Some interesting facts from the 1900 baseball season were: (1) First pitcher to hit a grand slam was St. Louis pitcher Mike O'Neill on September 4, 1900 and, (2) the first pentagon shaped home plate appeared on the diamond.

During the NL off season of 1900, a few teams tried to revive the AA, after three of the four teams taken in by the NL from the AA, were dropped. This problem was resolved as the Baltimore Orioles, Washington Senators, the Louisville Colonels, and with the addition of the Cleveland Spiders formed the new American League.

The National League reduced its team rosters from 12 to 8 teams. The lineup of teams in the National League in 1900 was the Pittsburg Pirates, Philadelphia Phillies, Brooklyn Superbas, St. Louis Cardinals, Chicago Orphans, Boston Beaneaters, New York Giants and Cincinnati Reds.

In 1900, the New York Giants wanted to sign a rookie pitcher called Christy Mathewson, but they would have to trade Amos Rusie, who had been their best pitcher, having won 245 games. When he was traded to the Cincinnati Reds, he failed to win another game again. Mathewson appeared to have been a godsend as he won 373 during his 16 years with the Giants. As a rookie, he developed an assortment of pitches and had great control that was unusual for a first-year pitcher. To offset McGraw's rowdiness, Mathewson maintained a record of clean play so that he was dubbed the "Christian Gentleman." He would not pitch on Sunday, and an examination of his World Series record showed that he did not appear in any Sunday game there either! His fair-mindedness spilled over in his interviews. He would not give any interview to any sportswriter who he thought had been unfaithful to his wife.

Ban Johnson and the American League

Ban Johnson was the founder and first president of the American League (AL). He developed the AL which was then a descendant of the Western League, then considered to be minor league. Johnson viewed the National League to be notoriously rowdy. He wanted the new league to encourage a more orderly environment by supporting the new league's umpires. He thought that many of the NL umpires were constantly verbally abused. He would tolerate none of that in the new league.
With the help of the Western League owners and managers, like Charles Comiskey, Johnson convinced top talent from the National League to join the new league, which soon out-rivaled the older National League. Johnson maintained control over the AL until he was ousted in the mid 1920s, when he resigned, after a confrontation with the first baseball commissioner, Judge Kenesaw Mountain Landis. Johnson was born in Norwalk, Ohio and later studied law at Marietta College but did not pursue his degree. He became the sports editor of a Cincinnati newspaper. He befriended the then-manager of the Cincinnati Reds, Charles Comiskey.

At the urging of Comiskey and Red's owner John Bush, Johnson was convinced to assume the presidency of the beleaguered minor league, the Western League, at an organizational meeting in 1893. he later criticized the National League for its rowdy playing atmosphere which he said was driving away families and women from the games. He embarked on a crusade in making baseball friendly to them.

Contrary to the baseball atmosphere at time, he gave his umpires unqualified support and had little tolerance for players and managers who disrespected the umpires. Johnson fined and suspended players who used foul language on the field. Soon the Western League was recognized as the strongest and most efficient league in all of baseball.

Johnson had a bigger plan—to organize a new major league. After he had resigned as manager of the Reds, Comiskey purchased the Sioux City franchise and moved it to St. Paul. Then Johnson initiated a plan of expansion. His chance came after the 1899 baseball season, when teams from Baltimore, Cleveland, Louisville and Washington D.C. Were dropped from the National League. Johnson moved the Grand Rapids franchise to Cleveland, where they would later become the Indians. Johnson convinced Comiskey to move his St. Paul's franchise to Chicago to become the White Sox.

For the 1900 season, the Western League was renamed the American League, but it was still a minor league. The 1900 season was an unqualified success as Johnson received a ten-year extension to his contract. In October he withdrew the American League from the National Agreement (A formal agreement between the National League and the minor leagues). On January 28, 2001, he decalared that the American League would operate as a major league, and he placed teams in Boston, Washington, Philadelphia, and Baltimore.

Buffalo had been assured as a franchise in the new league as late as January 29, 1901, but Johnson proceeded to dump Buffalo and placed their franchise in Boston. Unknown to others, Johnson had been negotiating with the Boston people for months. He had invested money in the Boston franchise and also had a large stake in the Washington franchise, only withdrawing that stake later in 1903.

Johnson found that the National League had made a monstrous mistake in putting a cap on salaries at $2,400, which was extremely low at that economic period. We could imagine Johnson clapping his hands in glee, because it gave him an opening for American League teams to offer contracts which were much higher than the "senior league."

The eight team lineup for the new American League included the Boston Americans, Chicago White Sox, Baltimore Orioles, Philadelphia Athletics, Cleveland Blues, Detroit Tigers, Milwaukee Brewers and Washington Senators. Milwaukee's team experienced difficulty in its first season, and its franchise was transferred to become the St. Louis Browns in 1902. The Baltimore Orioles had difficulty as a team, and their franchise was transferred to New York to become the Highlanders in 1903. The league's lineup became stable until 1954.

By the end of the 1902 season, all the American League franchises were drawing more fans than the National League. The National League sued for peace and under a new national agreement, the National League recognize the American League as a new major league.

A three-man commission was set up composed of the two leagues presidents and Garry Herrmann. Cincinnati Red's owner. Although Herrmann was the nominal president for the commission, Johnson soon dominated the body.

1901

In 1901, catchers were compelled to remain continuously under the bat. Thomas Connolly umpired the first game in the National League between Cleveland Blue Birds and Chicago White Stockings.

The New York Giants took a great risk in trading Amos Rusie, their best pitcher who had won 245 games and was traded to the Cincinnati Reds for a rookie. Rusie only pitched three games for the Reds in 1901, and never won a game again. Christy Mathewson had never previously pitched in the majors.

The infield fly rule was amended to eliminate any line drive to be considered in the rule. The requirement as to the number of outs, to less than two went in effect.

At the turn of the new 20th century, there was a formation of new league —the American League. Since 1892, the National League was the only major league.

At season's end in 1901 the Pittsburg Pirates won the National League title with a 90-49 record during their 150-game season. The Philadelphia Phillies tried to come close, but they lagged behind by 7.5 games.

The Pirates pitching and hitting came together to claim a winning season. In the pitching department, Deacon Phillippe 22-12, Jack Chesboro's 21-10 and Jesse's Tannehill's 18-10 ruled the hill. Each of them also excelled in other pitching categories. Chesboro led the league with six shutouts. Tannehill struck out 118 batters and Phillippe claimed the lowest era of 1.02.

Honus Wagner, a sophomore player with 194 hits, 37 doubles, and 271 TB dominated the Buc's offense with 194 hits, 37 doubles, 271 TB, 126 RBI, .353 BA and a .417 OBP and stole 49 bases. He had a little help from Ginger Beaumont who scored 120 runs, and Lefty Davis' 56 bases-on-balls. With the advent of the new league, several cities now had two teams, one in each league, like Chicago, Boston, St. Louis, New York and Philadelphia.

In the American League, Chicago White Stockings won the pennant in 1901, winning 83 games while the Boston Americans trailed by four games.

The White Sox, like the Pirates, had three top-of-the-line pitchers. Clark Griffith led this trio with 24 wins and only 7 losses. The other two, Nixey Callahan's 15-8 record and Roy Patterson's 15-11 tally helped the Sox's tie down the pennant while Griffith notched the best league's winning average at .774.

A menagerie of offensive players nailed down the pennant for the Sox with contributions by Sam Mertz hitting 17 triples and 98 RBI. Fielder Jones scored 120 runs and a OBP of .412. Frank Isabell stole 52 bases while Dummy Hoy walked 86 times.

The two pennant winners never met in a playoff series because neither league was ready for the challenge, but later got together for the 1903 World Series.

Mordecai "Three Finger" Brown

Mordecai Peter Centennial "Three Finger" Brown was born on October 19, 1876 in Nyesville, Indiana. (His name "Centennial" was given to him because he was born on the 100th year of the United States Independence.)

He derived the "three Finger" moniker because he had a farm-machine accident on April 17, 1888 in his youth when he lost one and parts of two other fingers in his right hand. He turned his handicap into developing an exceptional curve ball which broke very sharply and sometimes broke downward before reaching the plate. He also developed a deceptive fastball, a screwball and change up. These special techniques spiraled him into being one of the best pitchers of his era.

Brown had an extensive career playing for the St. Louis Cardinals (1903), Chicago Cubs (1904-12), St. Louis Terriers (1914), Brooklyn Tip-Tops (1914), and the Chicago Cubs (1916) Chicago Whales (1915) and the Chicago Cubs (1916). The Terriers, Whales and Tip-Tops were in the Federal League. Brown served as playing-manager for the Terriers. His most productive playing years were from 1904-12, while playing for the Cubs, he took part in two World Series. He finished his career with 239 wins 130 losses, 1,375 Strikeouts and the best 2.09 ERA in 1906. He died on February 14, 1948. He was enshrined in the Baseball Hall of Fame in 1949.

The First Baseball Concessionaire

Harry M. Stevens began printing and selling baseball scorecards in the 1880s. By 1901 he was selling food items at the baseball games from stadiums from New York to Ohio. He had diversified and was selling hard-boiled eggs, ham sandwiches, slices of pie and ice cream.

On one cold afternoon when ice-cream sales at the Polo Grounds were almost non-existent he sent out for dachshund sausages which he put on long buns. A sports reporter in writing about the new delicacy did not know how to spell dachshund so he called them hot dogs. Stevens had made a great contribution in baseball with his hot dogs. No game is complete without hot dogs.

Connie Mack

Connie Mack is considered the manager with the most wins in baseball history. He began playing in the National League for ten years and one year with the Buffalo Bisons in the Players League in 1890. During his playing days in the 19th Century, he was well-known as being very intelligent and also as a light-hitting catcher as he batted .244. From 1894 to 1896, he was the playing manager. In 1896. he was fired, and he then agreed to be the playing-manager for the minor league Milwaukee Brewers from 1897-1900. While at Milwaukee, he first signed left-handed pitcher Rube Waddell whom he brought with him when began managing and becoming part-owner for the Philadelphia Athletics of the new American League in 1901. He continued managing the Athletics until 1950, when he retired at age 87. One facet that separated him from all other managers was that he managed the team in street clothes and directed his players from the bench.

Besides holding the record for managing the same team for 50 years during which he managed for 7,755 games and holds the records for the most games won, 3,731 (1,000 more than anyone else) and most 3,948 losses.

Mack was born on December 22, 1882 as Cornelius Alexander McGillicuddy in Brookfield (new East Brookfield), Massachusetts. He was one of the first catchers to station himself behind home plate. He was elected to the Baseball Hall-of-Fame in 1937 and he died on February 8, 1956.

1902

The Milwaukee Brewers franchise was transferred to St. Louis playing as the Browns. The Cleveland Blues of the American league changed their name to the Cleveland Bronchos.

The Pittsburg Pirates won the National League pennant for the second consecutive year with an amazing 103 wins as the Brooklyn Superbas finished a distant 27.5 games behind.

Pitcher Jack Chesboro, the Pirates' ace was the best pitcher in the National League with 28 wins and a .824 WP. Deacon Phillippe and Sam Leever also had wins with 20 and 15, respectively. Honus Wagner continued his excellence as a future Hall-of-Famer while he established National League marks for 1902 scoring 105 runs, hitting 30 doubles, 91 RBI, .407 SA. And 42 stolen bases. He also had team highs for 247 Total Bases. Tommy Leach and Ginger Beaumont also had league marks with six homers and .357 BA respectively.

Christy Mathewson of the New York Giants led the NL, pitching eight shutouts.

Meanwhile in the American League, Connie Mack's Philadelphia Athletics took the league crown with 83 wins in a 140-game schedule while the St. Louis Browns remained five games back. Rube Waddell led the A's pitching with 24 wins and a 2.05 ERA, both league marks. The offense had league highs also with Sock Seybold's six home runs. He also had team highs with 264 TB, .506 SA. Teammates Topsy Hartwell won league marks with 87 walks and 47 steals, and team highs in scoring 109 runs. Lave Cross had 191 hits and 108 RBIs..

1903

In 1903, the following events occurred: (1) the foul-strike rule was adopted by the American League, (2) the Baltimore Orioles American League franchise was sold to become the New York Highlanders, (3) the National League Chicago Orphans changed their name to the Chicago Cubs, (4) the Cleveland Bronchos of the American League changed their name to the Cleveland Naps in honor of their manager Napoleon Lajoie.

Christy Mathewson led the NL in striking out 267 batters.

The Pittsburg Pirates won the National League pennant winning 91 games from a schedule of 140. The New York Giants did not fare so well, lagging 6.5 games behind.

Two of the Pirates' pitchers both won 25 games: Deacon Phillippe and Sam Leever, but Leever also captured the league high with a .781 winning percentage and a 2.06 ERA.

Ginger Beaumont led their offense with 137 runs, 209 hits and 272 TB. He had help from Fred Clarke who had 32 doubles and a .592 SA. Tommy, Leach had 17 triples and speedy Honus Wagner stole 46 bases.

Coincidentally, the American League's Boston Pilgrims also had 91 wins, but the Philadelphia Athletics were no match as they were 14.5 games behind. Cy Young, who joined the Pilgrims from the St. Louis Cardinals, won an amazing 28 games, a .757 WP and seven shutouts, all of which were league highs. Young had the lowest 2.08 ERA . He had some pitching help from Tom Hughes and Bill Dinneen who won 20 and 21 wins, respectively.

Buck Freeman led the Pilgrims attack with 39 doubles, 20 triples, 13 homers, 281 TB, 104 RBI, and a 496 SA. Patsy Dougherty led the hitting department with 107 runs, .331 BA and 35 steals.

The first modern day World Series was played in 1903. The Boston Pilgrims, pennant winners of the American League and the Pittsburg Pirates from the National League played in a series which was best of nine games. Hank O'Day and Thomas Connolly worked that first modern World Series. The Pilgrims defeated the Pirates 5-3.

1904

In 1904 the height of the mound was built to be 15 inches higher than the baseline level.

Although the first World Series had been a success, the rowdyism more prevalent in the National League raised its ugly head. Johnson prevailed upon the American League owners to have the stands patrolled. The rowdyism was driving away paying customers. Players, managers and fans were expected to behave. However, there was one man who constantly challenged Johnson's authority. John McGraw, the manager of the upstart Baltimore Orioles team continued with his contentious ways. When McGraw refused to stop the constant abuse of the umpires, Johnson suspended him. McGraw never forgave him, and he returned to the National League where he became manager of the New York Giants, and continued managing for another 31 years.

The infield fly rule was further amended to not include a bunted ball as an infield fly. The Chicago White Stockings changed their nickname to the White Sox. The Pittsburg team added an "h" to their city's name to be known as the Pittsburgh Pirates.

The New York Giants, trying to get over a lackluster year in 1903, made up for it by winning 106 games in the 1904 schedule. The Chicago Cubs were in second by a distance of 13 games.

Joe McGinnity copped league highs in several categories—35 wins, .814 WP, nine shutouts, five saves, and a 1.61 ERA. Christy Mathewson was chasing him with 33 wins and striking out 212 batters—another league record. Here's a plus that any team would like to have. In the early days of baseball, some baseball players discarded their first names and replaced it with a nickname. Luther Taylor because he could not speak, was dubbed "Dummy," it certainly did not mean he was stupid. So Dummy Taylor led the Sox pitching with 21 wins. He also had five shutouts, struck out 138 and had a low 2.34

ERA.

A combination of batters drove the offense with Mike Donlin's .329 BA and .457 SA, George Brown scored 99 runs and peppered 168 hits, Sam Merles' 28 doubles and 47 stolen bases and Art Devlin's 62 walks.

The Boston Red Pilgrims, a perennial favorite in the American League, won that pennant again. This time with 95 wins. The New York Highlanders, a new team in 1903, played a tight season, but lost by 1.5 games.

Cy Young again lead the Sox with 26 wins. Bill Dinneen with 23 wins and Jesse Tannhill with 21 were not far behind. Young, however won league honors by pitching 10 shutouts.

Five of the Sox's offense were provided for by Patsy Dougherty, 53 runs, 33 hits; Jimmy Collins had 33 doubles; Buck Freeman, 19 triples, 7 homers; Chick Stahl a .366 BA and Kip Selbach, 48 walks.

No World Series was played in 1904 because the New York Giants refused to play the Boston Pilgrims. When McGraw won the National League pennant in 1904, he took great pleasure in his revenge not only toward the American League, but Ban Johnson as well.

Rube Waddell

George Edward Rube" Waddell was born on October 12, 1876 in Bradford, Pennsylvania and was a dominant southpaw pitcher for 13 years. He pitched for the Louisville Colonels (1897, 1899). the Pittsburg Pirates (1900-01) and Chicago Orphans in the National League and the Philadelphia Athletics (1902-07) and the St. Louis Browns (1908-10) in the American League. He was a dominant strikeout pitcher, having an excellent fast ball, sharp breaking curve, a screwball and great control. He led the league in strikeouts for six consecutive years for the Athletics (1902-07).

When he was young he threw rocks at birds at the family farm which accounts for his excellent control as a pitcher. He did not attend school very often, but was considered to be very literate. He strengthened his arm by working at mining and drilling, which also helped in his conditioning. He played with several area teams, but he would leave in the middle of games to go fishing. He had a penchant for leaving games in progress to chase fire engines. His erratic behavior irritated his different managers and teammates, when he pitched in the majors causing many teams to release him. His childlike behavior has been assessed by baseball historians who believe that he was faced with many mental problems during his life. He was an alcoholic most of his adult life.

 In 1903, Waddell struck out 302 batters and in 1904 whiffed 349 more. No other pitcher since then had stuck out 300 batters for two straight seasons, until Sandy Koufax did that in 1965 (382) and 1966 (317).

 He caught pneumonia when he helped save Hickman, Kentucky from a flood in 1912. He was later diagnosed with tuberculosis and died on April 1, 1914. He was elected into the Baseball Hall of Fame in 1946.

1905

The Doubleday Myth

 Albert Spalding, a successful pitcher and Henry Chadwick, a sportswriter from England were found to be in constant verbal skirmishes concerning Spalding's affirmation that baseball was an American game, and was invented by an American, in the United States. Spalding had pitched for the Boston Red Stockings in the upstart National Association and the Chicago White Stockings in the new National League from 1866 to 1878 and boasted a pitching record of 252 wins and only 12 losses.

 Chadwick asserted that baseball was a lot like Rounders that he had played in the Mother country of his youth. Let's look at the game of rounders and see how it might compare to baseball.

Rounders

Rounders was a game that was played in England, and now in Ireland, with slightly different rules. There were six positions in the field: the batters box (no home plate), the bowler's (pitcher's) box, and four posts (bases). At each base there was a post which was driven in the ground. First, second and third post were situated where todays baseball bases were, but fourth base was behind third base. All posts were the same distance apart. When a player reached the fourth base a point was scored. If there was a runner on second when there were three outs, a half-point was scored. There were three outs before the defensive team came to "bat." The bowler (pitcher) threw underhand to each batter from about 50 feet. A ball bowled (pitched) to the batter between his head and knees was considered a "good" ball. Anything bowled outside the batter's box was considered a "bad" ball. Three strikes and the batter was out. There was no base on balls. If a bad ball was caught it was not an out, nor would a bad ball hit be put out at first post. Five innings constitute a game.

Since no one else could solve the problem of baseball's origin, both Henry Chadwick and Albert Spalding concurred that they would submit it to an impartial committee. Since these men on the committee were very astute, they really did not have any time to spend on the issue of baseball being an invented American game. Spalding submitted a request in the Beacon Journal in Akron, Ohio for information about baseball's American beginnings. Abner Graves, a former Cooperstown, N.Y. resident wrote to the editor in which he claimed that Abner Doubleday, who lived in Cooperstown in 1839, had invented the game of baseball. Based on the evidence that Graves had given in his letter, it then was established that baseball was an American game.

In England and Ireland, this game of ball and bat evolved to become rounders. However, when it is played in America, some of the rounders rules begin to change. When adults play this game of baseball, as the game evolved, it is supposed that it was invented in America. Many men who played the game in the nineteenth century met together in general grocery stores or barbershops of that era.

Spalding wrote the report in 1905 and it remained on an obscure shelf until it was found in the mid 1930s. When many of the baseball greats were retiring from baseball, an appropriate museum was being investigated. Lo and behold, someone found Spalding's report and decided that Cooperstown would be the site of Baseball's Hall of Fame. Further evidence disclosed later was that Graves would have been five years old in 1839 and not a participant in a baseball game. Despite this information, work to establish the National Baseball Hall of Fame was continued in Cooperstown.

This author in consultation with a West Point official recently said that in 1839, Doubleday was still an underclassman and would either have been at West Point or at his family farm near Auburn, New York and was not eligible to be somewhere else.

Ty Cobb

Ty Cobb was born on December 18, 1886 in Narrows, Georgia, which was then a rural community. Soon Ty's parents William and Amanda Cobb moved their family to Reynolds, a nearby community. At an early age, Ty became fascinated with the game of baseball. Ty could never please his father in anything that he did. Baseball was not any different. But Ty wanted to be a baseball player. He played with the local semi-pro team, but his father was still adamant about him playing baseball. Before Ty left to play professional baseball, his father had a stern admonition, "don't come home a failure!" Those words haunted him for the rest to his life.

Ty was impatient about playing in the major leagues. He set about promoting himself by sending postcards to the famed Grantland Rice, editor of the Atlanta Journal. Each card promoting his great talents was signed with a bogus name. Soon Rice wrote a column about a player named Ty Cobb who had multiple talents to play baseball. Soon, Ty was invited to the Detroit Tigers in 1905.

    Back in Reynolds, a terrible family tragedy occurred. His father, believing that his wife was unfaithful, one night went to see if there was someone in his wife's bedroom and silently went outside her window. She, thinking it was an intruder, shot him. Ty was devastated. He was angry that his father would never see him playing baseball. That anger permeated his personality for the rest of his life. He played baseball with an explosive fervor. Later in his career, Cobb attributed his playing ability: "He said, "I did it for my father. He never got to see me play, but I knew he was watching me, and I never let him down." Cobb amassed many awards during his career, culminating with the best lifetime batting average of .366. No one ever surpassed him. Despite his many abilities, he was ahead of his opponents, and even his teammates. He honed his running ability by attaching an ankle bracelet made with lead pieces which he wore before each game. The effort to run with them on increased his running speed after he had taken them off. Although he had considerable speed, he was ferocious when stealing a base. Before each game he would file the cleats on his spikes in front of the dugout before each game in full view of his opponents. None of them were brave enough to tag him out on a steal. He claimed a record of 892 lifetime steals, until Rickey Henderson claimed that record with 1,406 of his own. Cobb was elected to the first Baseball Hall of Fame class in 1936.

    The Washington Senators changed their name to the Washington Nationals in 1905.

    The New York Giants won the National League pennant in a big way winning 105 games. Runner-up Chicago Cubs missed the mark by nine games.

Christy Mathewson led the pitching staff with 31 wins followed by Leon "Red" Ames 22, and Joe McGinnity with 21. Mathewson also pitched eight shutouts, a league high.

Mike Donlin with a .356 BA was the leader on offense, scoring 124 runs, with 216 hits, 31 doubles, 16 triples, seven homers and 300 TB.

In the American league the Philadelphia Athletics won the pennant with 92 games, while the Chicago White Sox finished two games behind.

Rube Waddell led the pitching staff with 27 wins, followed by Eddie Plank with 24, while Al Orth and Andy Conkley won 18 each.

Harry Davis seemed to lead the offense with 93 runs, 173 hits, 47 doubles and 8 homers. Topsy Hartland had a OBP of .408 and receive 128 bases-on-balls.

Nap Lajoie, the Cleveland playing manager, excelled by hitting in 31 straight games.

When McGraw's Giants won the pennant in 1905, he agreed to play the Philadelphia Athletics. The previous year, when he refused to play the American League winner, the Boston Pilgrims, that move penalized his players by depriving them of $1,000 which was about half of their regular salary.

In the best of seven World Series games, the New York Giants (NL) defeated the Philadelphia Athletics (AL), 4-2. Christy Mathewson performed exceedingly well by pitching and winning games one, three and six as the Giants beat the Athletics handily.

1906

Billy Evans, at 22-years old, became the youngest person to umpire in the major leagues.

The Chicago Cubs took first place in The National League like a Nor'easter storm winning 116 games, while the New York Giants, in a slump all season, ended up 20 games behind.

Mordecai Brown, Jack Pfiester. Ed Reulbach and Cal Lungren were the mainstays of the Cubs pitching staff. Besides winning 26 games, Brown had the league's high mark for ERA at 1.04. Pfiester won 20, Relbach 19 and Lungren 17. Harry Steinfelt led the Cubs in hitting. He had 176 hits, 27 doubles, 232 TB, 83 RBI, .327 BA and a .430 SA shared with Frank Chance, the playing-manager who had .430 SA too. Chance also had 103 runs scored, .419 OBP, Frank Schulte had 13 triples.

The cross-town American League rivals, Chicago White Sox won their pennant, by a 93-58 record. The New York Highlanders were in second place by only three games.

Frank Owen and Nick Altrock led the pitching staff. Owen with 22-13 and Altrock with 20-13. However Doc White had the greatest .750 WP with a 18-6 record. Ed Walsh with 17-13 record pitched 10 shutouts and struck out 177 batters. Fielder Jones as a playing manager collected 83 walks and a .346 OBP. Second-baseman Frank Isbell led the White Sox hitting as he peppered 153 hits including 11 triples, had 193 TB,, and stole 37 bases. Shortstop George Davis hit 26 doubles, had 80 RBIs and a .355 SA. Center fielder Ed Hahn scored 80 runs.

The Chicago White Sox (AL) won the 1906 World series defeating the Chicago Cubs (NL), 4-2.

Christy Mathewson

Christy Mathewson grew up in Factoryville, PA and played baseball when he was only 14 years old. When he was 19 he played in the minor leagues with a pitching record of 21 wins and only two losses. In his first year with the New York Giants he was not very successful and was returned to the minors. He eventually was returned to the Giants, and in 1905, he pitched three shutouts, and won 373 games. He served in the U.S. Army during WW I and was injured in a gas attack practice. He pitched for the Giants from 1907 to 1916. He was traded to the Cincinnati Reds in 1916 where not only pitched, but served as their manager until 1918. He died on October 25, 1935 from Pneumonia associated with his gas attack earlier. He was elected to the first Hall of Fame class in 1936.

1907

Walter Johnson

    Appearances can be deceiving as Hall-of-Famer Ty Cobb found out. Cobb said that he first saw Johnson on August 2, 1907 nearing the end of the baseball season. Cobb said, "He was a tall . . . galoot about twenty with arms so long that they hung far out of his sleeves." At least that was what Cobb thought. It was common place to make fun of and harass a rookie. "Washington Senators manager Joe Cantillion," according to Cobb, "had found a rube he was going to pitch in that game." But, Cobb and the rest of the Detroit Tigers team were more than surprised at the rookie's pitching. In his first at bat, Cobb was astonished to see something whiz past him and he said "We couldn't touch him."
    Johnson's side arm delivery blinked the ball past all those Tigers' batters on that day. In those days they didn't have any devices to measure speed, but a munitions factory device for measuring ballistics measured Johnson's fast ball as moving 134 feet per second and calculated it at 91.36 miles per hour.
    Johnson was born at a rural farm four miles west of Humboldt, Kansas. He was the second oldest child of his six-child family. Soon after his fourteenth birthday, his family moved to Olinda, A small town in Orange county, California. Johnson split his time among playing baseball, working in nearby fields and going horseback riding, He attended Fullerton Union High School, where he struck out 27 batters in a 15-inning game against Santa Ana High School. At the age of 19, he signed a contract with Washington in July 1907. Johnson pitched for the Washington Senators from 1907 to 1927, winning 417 games, an is only second in wins to Cy Young, who had 511. From 1913-1916 he

led the American League in wins. In 1913 he had the highest winning percentage of .837 and up to that time struck out a total of 313 batter and a high 11 shutouts. He had a career high of 110 shutouts and up to that time struck out the most batters at 3509. Johnson was among the five players to be enshrined in the National Baseball Hall of Fame in 1936.

Christy Mathewson of the New York Giants led the NL with 24 wins, eight shutouts and struck out 178 batters.

The Chicago Cubs captured the National League pennant in 1907 while winning 107 games, while the Pittsburg Pirates were in second place, 17 games behind. Orval Averall led the Cubs pitching staff with 23 wins, followed by Mordecai Brown, 20 and Carl Lundgren,18 and Ed Reubach 17. Pitchers with league highs were Reubach .800 WP and Jack Pfeister's 1.14 era, with 14 wins. Harry Steinfelt hit 25 doubles and had 70 RBI while second-baseman Johnny Evers stole 46 bases.

The Detroit Tigers won the American League pennant winning 92 games in a close race as the Philadelphia Athletics were runner-up at 1.5 games behind.

The Sox had two 20 game-winners with Ed Killen and "Wild" Bill Donovan. Donovan also captured the leagues highest WP with .862. George Mullen had 20 wins while striking out 246 batters. Ty Cobb's and Sam Crawford's hitting were more than the rest of the league's pitchers could handle. Cobb had 212 hits, 5 homers, 283 TB, 118 RBI, .350 BA, .380 OBP, .468 SA. and 49 steals. Crawford scored 102 runs, 24 doubles and 17 triples. Davy Jones had the most walks for the Tigers with 60.

The Chicago Cubs (NL) defeated the Detroit Tigers (AL), 4-0 and one tie.

1908

Several changes were made in 1908: pitchers were prohibited from soiling a new bat, shin guards were introduced, and the sacrifice rules were adopted.

The Merkle Blunder

On Monday, September 21, 1908, the New York Giants were scheduled to meet their long-time rival the Chicago Cubs. The Giant's first baseman Fred Tenney was injured so manager John McGraw replaced him with rookie Fred Merkle who only played 38 games that year. Both teams were tied for first place and winning the game was critical. The game proceeded to the ninth inning and both teams were tied at 1-1. After pinch hitter Mose McCormick was on first, there were two outs. Merkle hit a single in right field driving McCormick to third. With the two runners on first and third, shortstop Al Birdwell was up, and the first pitch he lined was past Cubs second-baseman Johnny Evers. As McCormick arrived to score, the home-town crowd all rushed into the field, believing that the game was over, with the Giants beating the Cubs, 2-1. Merkle had not touched second base yet, and with the maniacal crowd swarming him on all sides, he retreated to the clubhouse. Evers noted that Merkle had not touches second and was frantic to get the ball so he could claim a force-out at second, creating the third out and nullifying the apparent winning run. Somehow, Giant coach Joe McGinnity, the Giant third-base coach, knew what Evers was up to, and got possession of the ball and summarily threw it into the stands. Two Cubs players ran into the stands to get the ball.
A happy fan was leaving with his trophy. They attacked and wrestled the ball from him, throwing it to Joe Tinker, who was just outside the stands. Tinker threw it to Evers, who with the ball in his possession, jumped up and down on the bag to get the attention of head umpire

Hank O'Day. O'Day recognized that Merkle was out for failing to touch second. In the 16 years playing in the majors, Fred Merkle never lived down the fact that he was the goat of the Giants 1908 season.

Two days elapsed, when National League president Harry C. Pulliam declared the game to have been tied and, if both teams were tied at the end of the season, there would be a one-game playoff to determine the pennant winner. They were tied then and when the twos team met, the Cubs defeated the Giants,4-2. The Cubs beat the Detroit Tigers and beat them 4-1. It was the last World Series the Cubs won until 108 years later, in 2016.

Honus Wagner

The Pittsburg Pirates were mixed up in the 1908 cluster. They were essentially tied with the Giants with identical 98-56 records. Honus Wagner was the backbone of the team and could play any position except catcher and Giants manager John McGraw said that he wished that Honus was one of his players. Wagner was one of the five players who were inducted in the first induction to the Baseball Hall of Fame on February 2, 1936.

He was one of nine children to be born to his parents in Carnegie, Pennsylvania. He dropped out of school when he was 12 to help his father and brothers in the coal mines. In his free time, he and his brothers played sandlot baseball where they developed their skills.

Three of his brothers were good enough, so they could play professional baseball too. Honus' older brother Albert 'Butt" Wagner had a brief major league career and asked his manager to try out Honus when they were short of players. In his first year, Honus played for five different teams. Ed Barrow from the Atlantic League liked Honus' playing skills and signed him to a contract in 1896. Barrow recommended him to the Louisville Colonels. At first the Colonels were hesitant to sign Wagner because of his awkward figure, but signed him to a contract. By the end of the season, he batted .318. Following the

1899 season, the National League cut the Colonels along with three other teams. Barney Dreyfus, owner of the Colonels took many of his players with him to Pittsburg. From 1891 to 1911, the Steel City, now known as Pittsburgh, was spelled without the "h" ending. Many baseball card collectors believe that the 1908 card with Honus' picture was incorrectly spelled. But for that time, it was not.

While he played for the Colonels and Pirates, he was considered the best shortstop of the National League, he was also considered the best second-baseman, best third-baseman, outfielder, and first baseman as well. When he played for the Colonels, he won a throwing contest by throwing the ball an incredible 403 feet.

Honus claimed the National League batting title eight times, slugging average five times and led the league in steals for five years.

When he retired in 1918, he had amassed 3,418 career hits. It took St. Louis' Stan Musial 45 years to surpass Honus' hits title in 1953. After retirement, Wagner served as a baseball coach for the Pirates from 1933 to 1952. He was one of the first five selected into the National Hall of Fame. He passed away in 1955.

The American League Boston Americans (sometimes called the Pilgrims) changed their name to the Boston Red Sox in 1908.

The Chicago Cubs again captured first place in the National League with 99 wins, squeezing by the Pittsburg Pirates by one game.

Mordecai Brown powered the Cubs to the pennant with 29 wins, nine shutouts, five saves, 123 Strikeouts and a 1.47 ERA. Johnny Evers was "on fire" as he led the team with his hitting. He scored 83 runs, .300 BA, .402 OBP, 66 walks and 36 steals. Shortstop Joe Tinker added his bit with six home runs and 68 RBI.

Christy Mathewson led the NL with 37 wins, 11 shutouts, had five saves, completed 34 games, pitched in 56, with 390 innings pitched, 259 strikeouts, 1.43 ERA.

The Detroit Tigers won the American League pennant with 90 wins, a mere half game ahead of the Cleveland Naps.

Ed Summers won 24 games followed up by Bill Donovan's 18 and George Mullen's 17. Donovan also had six shutouts, five saves. 143 strikeouts and a 2.08 ERA.

Ty Cobb had a great year as he had 188 hits, 36 doubles, 20 triples, 276 TB and .475 SA. He also lead the league with 108 RBI and .314 BA. Teammate Matty McIntyre scored 105 runs and had a .392 OBP and 83 walks.

During the season Hal Chase of the New York Highlanders had a hitting streak of 33 games.

The Chicago Cubs (NL) again defeated the Detroit Tigers (AL), 4-1 in the 1908 World Series. The Cubs never won another World Series until they won again 108 years later in 2016.

1909

The Boston Red Stockings of the National League changed their name to the Boston Doves.

The Pittsburg Pirates, finished the season by winning 110 games, just 6.5 games ahead of the Chicago Cubs.

Howie Camnitz won 25 games and earned the league title for WP at .806. He also had six shutouts, three saves, 133 strikeouts and a 1.62 ERA. Lefty Leifield added 19 wins for the Pirates.

Honus Wagner and Fred Clarke each scored 100 runs. His 39 doubles was a league high. Wagner also had 201 hits, 19 triples, ten home runs, 308 TB, .354 BA, .415 OBP and .542 were the best for the team. Clarke's 80 walks was the league's top mark.

Christy Mathewson led the NL with .806 WP and a 1.14 ERA.

The Detroit Tigers was the 1909 American pennant winner at 98 games. The Philadelphia Athletics were second, 3.5 games behind.

George Mullen, the Tigers ace pitcher had league highs in wins (29) and WP (.784). Ed Summers also notched 19 wins.

Ty Cobb was their best hitter, scoring 116 runs, 216 hits, nine home runs, 296 TB, 107 RBI, .377 BA, .431 OBP, .517 SA and 78 stolen bases. Sam Crawford hit 35 doubles and 14 triples, while Donie Bush walked 88 times.

The Pittsburg Pirates (NL) defeated the Detroit Tigers (AL) in the 1909 World series, 4-3. The 1909 World Series first experienced the use of four umpires to call the games.

Two of United States President Theodore Roosevelt's sons, Kermit and Quentin, played baseball on a regular basis, but Teddy Roosevelt did not like the game of baseball. He considered it to be a mommy-coddle game. He went to see his sons' team play a local team on White House grounds — his sons' team won the contest 23-4. President Theodore Roosevelt received the first United States presidential pass ever issued by Major League Baseball, and it was actually made of 14 kt gold. It is doubtful that he ever used it.

Grantland Rice Scolding President Teddy Roosevelt

Most sports fans are aware of Grantland Rice's poem about winning and losing which was included in his poem Alumnus Football: "For when the One Great Scorer comes/To mark against your name,/ He writes – not that you won or lost –/But how you played the Game."

Rice, a prominent sports writer of his day, was upset that a sitting President did not like baseball (he was a football buff). Rice wrote a piece of prose called "A Tip to Teddy" published in Baseball Magazine in 1909.

A Tip to Teddy

"That's the only job for you, take your tip now, Theodore. Think of how your pulse will leap when you hear the angry roar. Of the bleacher gods in rage, you will find action there, which you've hunted in vain, in the Presidential chair. Chasing mountain lions and such, catching grizzlies will seem tame. Lined up with a jolt you'll get in the thick of some close game, choking angry wolves to death as a sport will stack

up raw, when you see Kid Elberfield swinging for your under jaw. When you hear Hugh Jennings roar, 'Call them strike you lump of cheese!' Or McGraw kicking at your shins and knees."

1910

The umpire organizational chart was established in 1910. The plate umpire was designated as the umpire-in-chief and all the other umpires were designated as field umpires.

In 1910, a cork center was added to the official baseball. The Chicago Cubs seemed to be in a league all their own as the captured the National League pennant winning 104 games, while second place New York Giants remained 13 games behind.

Mordecai Brown continued as ace for the Cubs with 25 wins, six shutouts, seven saves, 143 strikeouts and an 1.86 ERA. King Cole with a 20-4 record captured the league's highest .833 WP. Bob Beacher scored 95 runs while Solly Hofman, Frank Schulte and Johnny Evers provided most of the offense. Hofman had 16 triples and 86 RBI, .325 BA, and .461 SA. Schulte had 10 homers and 257 TB. Evers had a .413 OBP and 108 walks.

Christy Mathewson led the NL with a 1.99 ERA.

The Philadelphia Athletics scored 102 wins for the American League pennant in 1910, but the New York Highlanders remained in second place, 4.5 games off the pace.

Jack Coombs in pitching 31 wins and winning 13 games by Highlanders' shutouts and was league-high in those categories. Chief Bender (23), Morgan Scott (18) and Ed Walsh (18) all contributed in the quest for the 1910 title.

Second-baseman Eddie Collins had a great year with 188 hits, 81 RBIs, .324 BA, .382 OBP and 81 steals. Danny Murphy made his presence known with 28 doubles, 18 triples, 244 TB, and .436 SA.

Addie Joss was an outstanding pitcher, playing for the Cleveland Naps from 1902-11. He won 20 or more games for four seasons. He won 27 games in 1907 and had the lowest American League ERA of 1.59 and later in 1908 reduced that AL ERA to 1.16. In 1910 he had a terrible secret because he was suffering from meningitis. He died the following spring. His teammates who were afraid that the owner would not give them a day off for the funeral, simply skipped town. After Joss' death, his teammates wanted to stage what we would call today an all-star game. All the great stars came including Walter Johnsion, Ty Cobb, Smoky Joe Wood and Napoleon Lajorie. The game raised $12,931, but it's success only raised more anxiety among the players. They had no pensions, job security or grievance procedures which might have been accepted by the baseball owners. They established a baseball fraternity which had two goals: to rid baseball of the hated reserve clause and gain a larger share of the profits. The owners ignored them, but gave momentum to a new proposed Federal League.

The Philadelphia Athletics (AL) defeated the Chicago Cubs (NL), 4-1 in the 1910 World Series. Chicago Cubs manager Frank Chance became the first person ejected from a World Series game by umpire Thomas Connelly for protesting a home run call.

1911

The Brooklyn Superbas of the National League changed their name to the Brooklyn Dodgers. The Boston Doves of the National League changed their name to the Boston Rustlers.

The first unofficial MLB All-Star game was called The Addie Joss Benefit game and was held on July 24, 1911 at Cleveland League Park. The park existed from 1891 to 1946. The American League All-Stars played against the Cleveland Naps. The American League All Stars won 5-3.

The New York Giants won the National League pennant for 1911, winning 99 games, while the second place Chicago Cubs dropped to 7.5 games back.

Christy Mathewson led his team winning 26 games. Rube Marquard and Doc Crandal won 24 and 15 games respectively. Marquard had league highs with winning percentage (.774) and strikeouts with 237 K's.

Larry Doyle led the Giant's attack scoring 102 hits, 25 triples, 13 homers, 377 TB, .97 OBP and .527 SA. Some of his teammates provided additional punch including Bud Herzog's 33 doubles, Chief Meyers' .332 BA and Josh Devore's 61 steals.

The Philadelphia Athletics team was the standard bearer in 1911 American League winning 101 games. Detroit Tigers were in second place, 13.5 games behind, but their best player, Ty Cobb had a 40 game hitting streak, which up to that time was the longest hitting streak.

Jack Coombs' and Chief Bender's pitching were the league highs in two categories: Coombs with 38 games and Bender with a .773 WP. Eddie Plank had 23 wins, six shutouts and a 2.10 ERA.

The A's third baseman Frank "Home Run" Baker showed that he could do more than hit homers. He hit 11 homers, 42 doubles, 301 TB, 115 RBI and .508 SA. Eddie Collin chipped in with a .365 BA and a .450 OBP.

The Athletics (AL) defeated the Giants (NL) in the 1911 World Series. 4-2, as Chief Bender notched two wins, striking out 20. Frank Baker was hot hitting two round-trippers, two doubles and had five RBI. Jack Barry had seven hits and four doubles. The Boston Rustlers of the National League change their name to the Boston Braves. Bill Dinneen was umpire in the 1911 World Series. Dineen is one of the few baseball players who later had become a MLB umpire.

1912

In 1912, both the American and National Leagues had 10-man staffs as two of them worked games with two reserves.

United States President Howard Taft was a frequent visitor to the Washington Senators baseball games. Legend says that his presence at a game in 1912 was responsible for the seventh inning stretch in all baseball games. It appears that when he was seated during one game, his 350 pound body had trouble remaining seated, so before the seventh inning, he got up and stretched. All the fans there followed their president and got up too, and stretched!

That year, the New York Giants won the National League pennant with a 103-45 record. The Pittsburgh Pirates, who were runners-up fell ten games behind. Rube Marquard received the league's winning crown with 26 big wins, while whiffing 175 batters. Christy Mathewson had 23 wins and 134 strikeouts.

Larry Doyle led the Giants offense with 184 hits, 34 doubles, 263 TB, 91 RBIs and scored 98 runs. Three others who helped with the Giants offense were Red Murray, Fred Snodgrass, Chief Meyers and Fred Merkle. Murray sliced 20 triples, Snodgrass stole 43 bases and walked 70 times, Chief Myers sported a .358 BA, .441 OBP and .477 SA, while Merkle hit 11 homers.

The Boston Red Sox were successful in being victorious in winning the American League pennant with 105 wins. Their closest pursuer was the Washington Senators who trailed the Sox by 14 games.

Smoky Joe Wood was really hot that year with 34 wins and only 5 losses and a .876 WP, both of which were tops in the National League. Rookie Hugh Bedient won 20 games with only 9 losses. Tris Speaker monopolized the Sox hitting in almost all categories: 136 runs, 222 hits, 53 doubles, 10 home runs, .383 BA, .464 OBP, .567 SA, 82 walks and 52 stolen bases. In two categories, lefty Larry Garner hit 18 triples and Duffy Lewis had 109 RBI. Speaker also had a 30-game hitting strek during the season.

The 1912 World Series was tightly played as the Red Sox (AL) edged the Giants (NL) 4-3, including a tie. Joe Wood had a 3-1 record in the series striking out 21 Giants. He had a low 0.50 ERA and only gave up one earned run.

The Sox third baseman, Larry Gardner had five hits including a home run, double and triple and drove in five runs despite a .179 BA.

1913

The New York Highlanders change their name and were called the New York Yankees. The Brooklyn Dodgers of the National League change their name back to the Brooklyn Superbas for one season.

The New York Giants captured the National League title in 1913 as the Philadelphia Phillies fell behind by 12.5 games.

Christy Mathewson led the Giants pitching staff winning 25 games. Not far behind were Rube Marquard's 23 and Jeff Tesereau's 22 wins. Marquard was also the league's strikeout leader, whiffing 151 batters. George Burns was the driving force behind the winners with 173 hits, 37 doubles and theft of 40 bases.

The American League winner was the Philadelphia Athletics team winning 96 games. The Washington Senators, their closest competitor missed by 6.5 games.

Although the A's pitching was good with Chief Bender winning 21, Eddie Plank 18 and Bullet Joe Bush 15, the offense carried the team to the top.

In the offensive duo were Frank "Home Run" Baker and Eddie Collins. Baker had 190 hits, 34 doubles, 12 home runs, 278 TB, 117 RBI, .493 SA while Collins' scored 125 runs, had a .345 BA, .441 OBP, 85 walks and 55 steals.

In the 1913 World Series between the Giants (NL) and the Athletics (AL), Philadelphia won 4-1. The A's offense relied on Baker and catcher Wally Schang who both had 7 RBI and one homer. Eddie Collins had 8 hits including 2 triples. Chief Bender won two games during the series, but gave up 19 hits. The Giants were outhit by the A's by a 46-33 count.

1914

The Brooklyn Dodgers of the National League changed their name to the Brooklyn Robins in 1914 to honor their manager, Wilbert Robinson.

The Boston Braves won the National League title with 94 wins and 59 losses. The New York Giants dragged behind in second place by 10.5 games. The Boston team was called the "Miracle Braves" because on July 4 they had been in last place.

The Braves Dick Rudolph won 26 games including six shutouts while teammate Bill James also won 26 games, striking out 150 batters adding a 1.90 ERA. James also set a league high for the best winning percentage with .788.

Their hitting wasn't great despite winning the league crown. However, Joe Connolly hit 28 doubles and a .494 SA. Johnny Evers, formerly from the Cubs, collected 87 walks.

Meanwhile, the American league pennant winners were the Philadelphia Athletics winning 99 games. Their highly touted pitching staff was Chief Bender, Bob Shawkey and Eddie Plank, but they were all off their usual games that year. Bender had a 17-3 record, seven shutouts and a .850 WP. Plank and Shawkey each had 15 wins as Plank added 110 strikeouts.

The "Miracle" Boston Braves (NL) continued their dominance over their opponents whitewashing the Philadelphia Athletics (AL), 4-0 in the 1914 World Series.

The Federal League

The Federal League of Baseball, commonly known as the Federal League, started operation in 1914, even though it was organized in 1913. It was established by John F. Powers as a third major league and operated for two seasons. The league allowed players to avoid the restrictions of the Reserve Clause. This caused the competition to raise the cost of players' salaries—a foreshadowing of what is now free agency.

There were eight teams in the Federal League. They were Baltimore Terrapins, Brooklyn Tip-Tops, Buffalo Blues, Chicago Whales, Indianapolis Hoosiers (transferred to Newark Peppers in 1915), Kansas City Packers, Pittsburgh Rebels and St. Louis Terriers.

Interference by the other two leagues caused the Federal League to fold after the 1915 season. It was the last serious attempt to create a third major league until the abortive Continental League in 1960.

The Indianapolis Hoosiers were the pennant winner in the Federal League's during the 1914 season finishing 88-65. Chicago Whales were a close second only 1.5 games behind, Cy Falkenberg won 25 games for the Hoosiers, pitching nine shutouts, struck out 226 batters, finishing with a 2.22 ERA.

Benny Kauf scored 129 runs, slapped 211 hits, including 44 doubles, 305 TB, .447 OBP, .534 SA, walked 72 times and stole 75 bases. Tommy Emmons hit 15 triples while Frank LaPorte had 107 RBIs.

1915

Colonel Jacob Ruppert

Jacob Ruppert, Jr is best known as the owner who bought Babe Ruth's player contract from the Boston Red Sox in 1919 to play for the New York Yankees. Ruppert attended school in New York City. When he graduated from high school, he was eligible to attend Columbia College (over the years Columbia became a University), but he opted to work in his father's, Jacob Sr.'s brewery. After his father's death Ruppert became the owner and president of the brewery. He served in the United States Army during the Spanish-American War and later became a U.S congressman. In 1915, together with millionaire Tillinghast

Huston, they purchased the New York Yankees baseball team. In 1919 he purchased the contract of Babe Ruth from the Boston Red Sox who had hit 29 home runs, the highest number of homers up to that time.

Often, outstanding players and managers are remembered, once they have retired. But on rare occasion and team owners may be accorded such accolades. In 1915 Yankee owner Jacob Ruppert began to become a owner who wanted to win. He and his partner Tillinghast Huston became owners of the now fabled team. In 1917, American League president Ban Johnson told Ruppert that he should try to hire Miller Huggins, who was the St. Louis Cardinals manager in 1915.

Huston was away in Europe when Huggins was hired. Huston's choice was Wilbert Robinson, the Brooklyn Dodgers manager since 1913. Huston disliked Rupert's choice, which eventually resulted in his selling his share of the team to Ruppert in 1922. Huggins success in New York from 1916 to 1929 highlights Huggins talent. Ruppert owned the team until 1938 when he passed away. He was also elected to the Hall of Fame in 2013.

The Cleveland Naps of the American League changed their name to Cleveland Indians.

The Philadelphia Phillies were the National League's pennant winner with 90 wins. The second place Boston Braves finished seven games back.

The Phillies' Pete Alexander was the league's best pitcher with 31 wins, .756 WP, 241 K's and 1.22 ERA. Erskine Mayer won 21.

Gavvy Cravath was the Phillies hottest batter scoring 89 runs, hit 24 homers, 255 TB, 115 RBIs, .510 SA and 86 walks. An offensive player who contributed was Fred Lundrus who hit 36 doubles and batted .315.

The Boston Red Sox won the top spot in the American League in 1915 by 101 games. The Detroit Tigers, the Sox biggest rival finished 2.5 games behind.

Smoky Joe Wood, a usually a top-notch pitcher, was only able to win 15 games but won the league winning percentage .750 crown. Woods' 1.49 ERA was his team's best. Rube Foster and Ernie Shore had identical 19-8 records and Shore also had five shutouts and struck out 152 batters. Babe Ruth at age 20 had a 15-8 record and a .315 BA.

Tris Speaker led the Sox offense scoring 108 runs, 176 hits, 25 doubles, 13 triples and 25 stolen bases. Harry Hopper hit 13 triples.

In the Federal League, the Chicago Whales in 1915 won the pennant with a record of 86-66, .566 WP on a 152-game schedule. They were virtually deadlocked with the St. Louis Terriers whose record was 87-67, .565 WP. Chicago was declared the winner by one percentage point. Included in this clotted mess was the Pittsburgh Rebels, only half-game behind the other two.

The Whales pitcher George McConnell had a 25-10 record., striking out 151 batters and a 2.20 ERA. Mordecai Brown who jumped from the National League's Chicago Cubs to the Whales had a 17-8 record and a 2.09 ERA. Several players contributed to the Whales offense: Dutch Zwilling hit 32 doubles, 13 round-trippers, 242 TB and 94 RBIs. Les Mann hit 19 triples. William Fischer had a .329 BA and a .449 SA while Max Flack stole 37 bases.

The Phillies won their first World Series game in 1915, by a 3-1 score, but lost the next four by close scores to the Boston Red Sox, 2-1, 2-1, 2-1 and 5-4.

Rube Foster won two games and struck out 13 batters. Harry Hooper had seven hits and two homers while Duffy Lewis had a triple, eight hits and five RBIs. The Phillies' Fred Luderus had seven hits, two doubles and a home run.

In the 1915 World Series, the Boston Red Sox (AL) defeated the Philadelphia Phillies (NL), 4-1.

1916

The Brooklyn Robins captured the 1916 National League pennant winning 94 games. The Phillies having won the year before were a close second, 2.5 games behind.

Jeff Pfeffer won 25 games including six shutouts and a 1.92 ERA. Zack Wheat led the Robins batters with 177 hits, 32 doubles, nine home runs and 73 RBI. He also had league highs with 262 TB, and a .461 SA. Jake Daubert had a .316 BA and a .371 OBP.

The Boston Red Sox in 1916 won 97 games in copping their second straight pennant, two full games ahead of the Chicago White Sox.

The Sox's 21-year-old Babe Ruth notched 23 wins and 107 K's. His nine shutouts and 1.75 ERA were both tops in the American League. Larry Gardner's .308 BA and Harry Hooper's 80 walks led the Red Sox offense.

In the 1916 World Series, Larry Gardner's two home runs and seven RBIs led the Boston Red Sox (AL) to a 4-1 win over Brooklyn Robins (NL) to win in the series, Babe Ruth broke into the win column striking out four batters. Ernie Short won two games for the Sox and struck out nine.

Rogers Hornsby

Rogers Hornsby was born in Winters, Texas on January 5, 1896. He was the youngest child to be born in his family and when he was two years old, his father died from undisclosed causes. He started playing with the St. Louis Cardinals in 1915 and was with them until 1926, when they played against the New York Yankees in the World Series, winning 4-3. Hornsby was difficult to get along with and not well liked by his teammates. He did not drink, smoke or attend movies, but had an addiction to gambling on horse races all his life.

At the end of the 1926 season, Frankie Frisch of the New York Giants, said he was quitting baseball because of problems with Giants manager, John McGraw. So that the Giants would not lose anything by Frisch's being traded to the St. Louis Cardinals, the Giants received

Rogers Hornsby in the trade. While he was with the Giants, he became the interim manager while McGraw was incapacitated with medical problems. Hornsby's animosity-driven temperament showed up again in his new role. He insisted that the players follow his fielding procedures. When the players objected and said that McGraw told them to play a different way, Hornsby said, "You'll do it my way, not McGraw's!"

His usual disposition was probably the cause of his having limited tenure with all the teams that he played for. After the one-season with the Giants, he played with the Boston Braves in 1928. His contract was sold to the Chicago Cubs in 1929, with whom he played until 1932. He was re-signed with the St. Louis Cardinals in 1933. He was released part-way through the season and was picked up by the neighboring St. Louis Browns. He stayed with the Browns until 1937.

Hornsby accumulated several life-time marks at the end of his playing career: 2,930 hits, 301 home runs, .358 batting average and the National League MVP, twice. Several times during his playing career, he was a playing-manager. He died on June 5, 1963 in Chicago. He was elected to the National Baseball Hall of Fame in 1942 and the St. Louis Cardinals Hall of Fame in 2014.

1917

In 1917, earned-run statistics and definitions were added to the rules.

The New York Giant's won the 1917 National League crown by winning 98 games. The Philadelphia Phillies were runners-up, 10 games behind.

Ferdie Schupp led the Giants pitching with 21 wins and losing only 8 to earn the league's .750 winning percentage title. He also struck out 147 batters, pitched 6 shutouts and a 1.75 ERA. Pol Perritt had a 17-8, .708 win record.

Three different players who earned the National League's high marks were George Burns who scored 103 runs and 75 bases-on-balls as Dave Robinson hit 12 homers and Heinie Zimmerman drove in 102 runs. Burns also had team marks with 180 hits, 248 TB, .380 OBP, .412 SA and 40 steals.

The Chicago White Sox captured the American League flag with 100 wins as the Boston Red Sox trailed behind by nine games. Eddie Cicotte, the Sox knuckle-ball pitcher, topped the league with 28 wins and a 1.53 ERA and pitched in 49 games. Cicotte also pitched seven shutouts.

Joe Jackson and Eddie Collins each scored 91 runs. Jackson hit 17 triples while Collins had 89 walks, a .389 OBP and 53 stolen bases.

During the season Detroit Tigers scrappy outfielder Ty Cobb had a 35-game hitting streak.

The Chicago White Sox (AL) were victorious over the New York Giants (NL) in the 1917 World Series, 4-2.

1918

Prior to the beginning of the Major League baseball season when it appeared that so many major league players were involved in fighting the Great War, the baseball owners decided to cut the season to 130 games.

World War I Battle Fatalities

Two major league baseball players lost their lives during World War I. Captain Eddie Grant was killed by an explosive shell in the Argonne Forest in France on October 5, 1918 and Sergeant Robert "Bun" Troy died of his wounds two days later in an evacuation hospital on October 7, 1918.

Grant played at third base for the Cleveland Naps (1905), Philadelphia Phillies (1909-10), Cincinnati Reds (1911-13) and the New

York Giants (1913-15), He batted .249, had 844 hits and stole 153 bases.

Troy was a pitcher who played for the Detroit Tigers pitched his only game on September 15, 1912.

The Chicago Cubs were crowned National League pennant winners as they won 84 games while its closest competitor, the New York Giants trailed behind by 10.5 games.

Their best pitcher Hippo Vaughn gained league leadership with 22 wins and striking out 148 batters. Vaughn also led the Cubs with eight shutouts and a 1.74 ERA. Claude Hendrix added 20 wins for the Cubs. Lefty Tyler chimed in with 19 winners.

Max Flack scored 74 runs and walked 86 times. Charlie Hollocher knocked out 161 hits, a league high, and had 202 TB and 26 stolen bases. Les Mann hit 27 doubles while Fred Merkle had 65 RBIs.

The American League's Boston Red Sox won the pennant in 1918, winning 75 games while the Cleveland Indians chugged behind by 2.5 games.

Carl Mays, a submarine pitcher, had 21 wins, including eight shutouts and 114 strikeouts.

Harry Hooper scored 81 runs, hit 13 triples and stole 75 bases. Babe Ruth in his first year as an outfielder hit 26 doubles, 11 home runs, 66 RBI and a .555 SA.

The Boston Red Sox (AL) were winners in the 1918 World Series over the Chicago Cubs (NL), 4-2.

1919

The Cincinnati Reds won the National League pennant by winning 96 games. The New York Giants, the usually dominant team in the National League, missed the pennant by nine games.

Slim Sallee won 21 games for the Reds, but Dutch Ruether who won 19 had highest winning percentage in the league with a .760

record. Teammate Hod Eller also won 19, but recorded seven shutouts and struck out 137 batters.

Outfielder Edd Roush led the Reds hitting with 149 hits, 217 TB, 71 RBIs and a .321 BA Heinie Groh scored 79 runs, had a .392 OBP and .431 SA.

The Chicago White Sox, in winning the 1919 American League pennant with only 88 wins were 3.5 games better than the league runner-up Cleveland Indians.

Eddie Cicotte, the Sox knuckleballer, was the best pitcher in the league winning 29 games and a .806 WP. with Lefty Williams' support winning 23 games and striking out 125. Shoeless Joe Jackson led the offense with 181 hits, 14 triples, 261 TB, 96 RBIs, .351 BA, .422 OBP and .506 SA. Buck Weaver scored 89 runs and Eddie Collin stole 33 bases, a league mark.

The Black Sox Scandal

Major League Baseball in 1919 reached a crisis that it might not have ever recovered from. The crisis stemmed from greed involving many people connected to the game of baseball and some outside of the game.

Gamblers have always tried to influence the game or any game so the result would be in their favor. Owners, since the game became professional and much money was involved, were greedy. They tried to make more money for themselves by restricting the players ability to play for another team, so they could make more money for themselves.

The Reserve Clause was a contributory problem because it had been effect since 1879, which stated that a player must continue to play for the team that signed him and did not allow the player to sign with other teams, because they might have had more benefits or more money to offer him.

The Black Sox Scandal might never have happened if Chicago

White Sox owner Charles Comiskey had not been imbued with greed. During the White Sox season, when it appeared that his knuckleball pitcher Eddie Cicotte was on his way to lead the Sox to the World Series, owner Charles Comiskey offered Cicotte a $10,000 bonus if he would win 30 games.

When the team had only two weeks left in the season, Cicotte won his 29th game. It certainly was possible that if Cicotte were to pitch another game, that he would have reached that goal of winning his 30th game and ultimately win the $10,000 bonus which Comiskey promised him. After winning the twenty-ninth game, the next day Comiskey ordered manager Kid Gleason to bench Cicotte to ostensibly save him for the World Series.

Cicotte did not "buy into the idea" that he was only being benched so he could pitch better in the series. He was not too happy with that decision. From that day on a conspiracy was been developed where he and several other players would plan to lose the 1919 World Series.

A few days before the series, Shoeless Joe Jackson found $5,000 in a roll left on his bed. He didn't want to throw the World Series, so he wanted to give it to the owner. Comiskey did not want the money.

It was planned that by "throwing" (lose on purpose), the conspiring players and the gamblers would make money. This is how the first game of the series began: Cicotte, in the bottom of the first inning hit the lead off hitter, Morris Rath with the second pitch, which was the prearranged signal that the "soon to be thrown series" was on. In the fourth inning Cicotte gave up a two-out triple to the opposing pitcher, Dutch Ruether. The Reds scored five times. Then Cicotte was replaced as the Reds won the first game 9-1. The Sox's Dickie Kerr, who was not in on the fix, won two games in the series.

Ultimately the Cincinnati Reds (NL) won the 1919 series beating the Chicago White Sox (AL), 5-3. Unlike today's series when the winner must win the best of seven, from 1919 to 1921 the winner played in the best of nine series.

The betting conspiracy between the players and gamblers accomplished two things—the permanent banning from baseball of the eight players involved (Eddie Cicotte, Claude "Lefty Williams, Shoeless Joe Jackson, Oscar "Happy" Felsch, Swede Risberg, Buck Weaver and Arnold "Chic" Gandil, and the establishment of the first baseball Commissioner, Judge Kenesaw Mountain Landis.

Shoeless Joe Jackson

Joseph Jefferson Jackson was born on July 16, 1887 in Pickens County, South Carolina. When he was 10 he had an attack of measles which almost killed him. He was paralyzed and in bed for two months as his mother nursed him back to health. Since Education at that time was considered a luxury which his family could not afford, he was an illiterate for the rest of his life.

When he was 13 he began playing for the local Brandon Mills baseball team. One day, according to Jackson, his new baseball shoes were hurting his feet creating a blister. He took them off to relieve the pain and played the rest of the game in his stocking-feet. For the rest of his life he was known as 'Shoeless Joe."

In 1908 he played for the Philadelphia Phillies, but had trouble fitting in with their baseball culture. In 1910 he was traded to the Cleveland Naps, playing in 20 games while he batted .387. In 1911 he set a rookie record batting .408, which as a rookie record still stands.

In 1915, he was traded to the Chicago White Sox. In 1917 he was part of the team when they won the World Series from the New York Giants when Jackson batted .307. In 1918 he worked in a shipyard for the World War I effort. He came back to play in 1919. He batted .351 during the season and he hit .375 in the World Series when the Sox threw the series to the Cincinnati Reds. He was one of the eight who were prevented from playing baseball again.

Many years later, Jackson owned a liquor store in Greenville, South Carolina and his old nemesis, Ty Cobb walked into the store. Joe acted like he didn't know Cobb. Cobb said, "Joe, don't you know me" Joe said, "Yes, I know you, Ty. But I didn't think that you wanted to talk to me after the 1919 scandal." Jackson died in Greenville on December 5, 1951 after trying to be accepted in the Baseball Hall of Fame as he accumulated a lifetime batting average of .356, second only to Cobb's .366 and two points behind Rogers Hornsby's .358.

On September 8, 1919, the National Baseball commission recommended that the 1919 World Series would be the best of nine games. Three years later, the number of series games reverted back to the best of seven games again.

There seemed to be a rush in completing baseball games on September 21, 1919. the Cubs beat the Boston Braves 3-0 in 58 minutes playing time, while it took the Brooklyn Robins only 55 minutes to defeat the Cincinnati Reds, 3-1. However, it took Slim Sallee of the Reds only 65 pitches to top Christy Mathewson's 69-pitch complete game against the Giants. They didn't need to count the pitcher's number of pitches in those days.

1920

The longest game by innings in Major League Baseball was a 1–1 tie in the National League between the Boston Braves and the Brooklyn Robins in 26 innings, at Braves Field in Boston on May 1, 1920. It had become too dark to see the ball (fields did not have lights yet and the sun was setting), and the game was considered a draw.

All of the players of the Black Sox, excluding McMullen who resigned at the end of the 1919 baseball season, continued to play during the 1920 Season. With the season having only two weeks remaining, it appeared that the Chicago White Sox might win again.

Judge Kenesaw Mountain Landis, First Baseball Commissioner

Kenesaw Mountain Landis was born in Millville, Ohio on November 20, 1866. His father had fought for the Union in the Civil War and in 1864 was wounded at the Battle of Kennesaw Mountain, a short distance from Marietta, Georgia. Why he would name his son Kennesaw Mountain is open to conjecture. (Landis always dropped one "n" in writing his name.)

Landis moved to Chicago where he earned a law degree. As a lawyer, he was appointed as a personal secretary to Secretary-of-State William Gresham. Gresham later died in 1893. Landis returned to Chicago, and 1905 was appointed by President Theodore Roosevelt as a Federal Judge. In 1907 he became famous by fining Standard Oil of Indiana $27 million for violating federal laws forbidding rebates on railroad freight tariffs. That verdict was soon overturned as Landis became known as a no-nonsense judge. It was in this tough-judge role that he was considered as the first baseball commissioner to deal with the Black Sox scandal of 1919.

A year after the Black Sox scandal, the baseball owners felt a need for a Baseball commissioner. The major league owners selected Judge Kenesaw Mountain Landis to serve as the first commissioner of major league baseball for life. Judge Landis, although he was not officially selected as the commissioner until 1921, banned all eight players considered to be part of the Black Sox Scandal. With the loss of all of those players, the Chicago White Sox threatened to win the American League pennant in 1920, but they were thwarted from winning it again. Two weeks before the end of the 1920 season, Landis went to work and suspended eight players for life. The Chicago White Sox lost the American League pennant to the Cleveland Indians by two games.

During the off-season the baseball owners elected their first Commissioner, Judge Kennesaw Mountain Landis to restore integrity to the game because of the 1919 scandal. On November 12, 1921, Judge Landis was selected as the first commissioner of baseball.

The Brooklyn Robins won the National league title in 1920 by winning 93 games, while the New York Giants finished in second place again, this time by nine games. Burleigh Grimes won 23 games and had a 2,22 ERA, he had the highest wining percent in the league with a .676 mark.

The Indians finally clinched the American League pennant winning 98 games while the Chicago White Sox who were playing well and looked like they might win it again, and had "the rug pulled out from underneath them" by Baseball Commissioner Kenesaw Mountain Landis' banning eight players in the Sox team, two weeks before the end of the season, and the pennant became a "walk off" for the Cleveland team.

Jim Bagby, Stan Coveleski and Ray Caldwell shouldered the Indians pitching. Bagby led the trio with 31 wins and a .721 WP in 48 games. Coveleski won 24 games, struck out 133 batters and posted a low 2.49 ERA. Caldwell added 20 wins.

Hall-of-Farmer Tris Speaker led his teams hitting bombardment with 214 hits, including 50 doubles, 310 TB, a .388 BA, .483 OBP, .562 SA and topped all scorers plating 137 runs. Elmer smith smash 12 homers while Larry Garner drove in 118 runs.

The First Baseball Fatality

Both the Cleveland Indians and the Chicago White Sox were 'neck and neck" in the standings when a terrible accident happened to their star shortstop Ray Chapman on August 17, 1920. Ray Chapman's temperament on the field and elsewhere was happy and friendly, He was a player who could be liked by everyone. In 1917 he had been recorded as having 67 sacrifices (a franchise record which was held until it was broken in 1980) and during his career he had 334 sacrifices. Chapman was so proficient in his fielding and batting that in 1915 the

Chicago White Sox wanted him in a trade, but the Indians refused, and Joe Jackson was traded instead.

On that fateful day, Carl Mays was pitching for the New York Yankees in a game that was played at the Polo Grounds. The Giants rented the Polo Grounds to the Yankees. Mays was asubmarine pitcher and in 1918 the New York Times claimed that "Carl slings the pill from his toes."

Chapman was leading off in the top of the fifth inning. The count was 0-1 and Cleveland was ahead 3-0. Chapman, who usually crowded the plate, huddled as usual over the plate. That day the skies were gray and overcast. The ball being used was almost dark, being scuffed up by dirt and tobacco juice. Mays threw the next pitch which was high and inside, but Chapman didn't move. He didn't see it. The ball hit him on the left side of his skull. Chapman although injured stood up and yelled to May, "It's not your fault, Carl. I'm Okay." Then he stumbled and fell. The next day he was dead. It took major league baseball over 51 years to use batting helmets, and luckily during that intermittent time, no other player had been killed by pitched balls.

In those days, preceding the accident, the American league baseball owners were complaining that many balls were being thrown out of the games, and they addressed their complaint to league president Ban Johnson. Johnson then instructed the umpires to keep the balls in the games as long as possible.

The Cleveland Indians (AL) won the 1920 World Series defeating the Brooklyn Robins (NL), 5-2. Bill Wambsganss, the Indian's second baseman executed an unassisted triple play in the fifth game of the nine-game series.

The Only World Series Unassisted Triple Play

Bill Wambganss, the Cleveland Indians' second baseman executed an unassisted triple play in the fifth game of the 1920 World Series. In that game with the Brooklyn Robins batting, thee were no out. Pete Kilduff was on second base and Otto Miller was on first. Clarence Miller hit a line drive which was caught by Wambganss as he was moving toward second base. He tagged the base for the second out, an Miller who had been running toward second not realizing that Wambganss had caught the ball was tagged out just before reaching second. It was the only time that an unassisted triple play was executed during a World Series game.

1921

Baseball Mud

The major leagues began the practice of rubbing mud on all baseballs to take away the shine. Through the years this practice has continued. It is assumed that the mud is retrieved from various places, but in 1950 it was in a secret place in southern New Jersey.

The mud is called Lena Blackburne Original Baseball Rubbing Mud and it comes from a secret spot in South Jersey off the Delaware River. Jim Bintliff, who owns Lena Blackburne Baseball Rubbing Mud, skims the top inch layer on the muddy riverbanks for collection and then puts the mud through screens to refine it before packaging it, aging it and shipping it to all the baseball teams in the MLB. Bintliff says the texture of his special mud is like chocolate pudding. The mud is applied because new baseballs are much too slick for pitchers to grip properly. Baseball ended up using Lena Blackburne's special mud because its fine-grain sediments properties added grip without scratching the leather and messing up a baseball's trajectory. The tradition of manually rubbing this special mud into baseballs, started in the 1950's and continues to this day.

George Herman "Babe" Ruth

George Herman "Babe" Ruth was credited with helping baseball to survive its black eye when he was sold by the Boston Red Sox to the New York Yankee's for $80,000. Ironically, Ruth was one of the first five baseball players to be inducted in the first 1936 ballot for the baseball Hall of Fame held in Cooperstown, N.Y. The other four were Detroit's Ty Cobb, Washington Senators pitching sensation, Walter Johnson, Pittsburgh Pirates shortstop Honus Wagner and New York Giants fadeaway pitcher Christy Matthewson. All of these all-star players deserved their Hall-of-Fame status as they were honored in Cooperstown. All were present except Matthewson who died in 1925, succumbing to the poisoned gas that overwhelmed him a few years after he fought for the United States in the First World War. His four-base drives created fan surges so they could see the "Great Sultan of Swat."

Babe had an ominous beginning. His father owned a bar and was unable to curb Babe's criminal leanings. He was sent to the St. Mary's Industrial Home for Boys in Baltimore, and learned how to play baseball for their team. He played every position even catcher. Being left-handed, he was the only left-handed catcher on any Baltimore boys' teams.

The New York Giants, unsuccessful the three previous years, finally won the National League Pennant winning 94 games, while their closest pursuer was the Pittsburgh Pirates falling behind by four games.

Art Nehf led the Giants pitching staff winning 20 games, but Phil Donahue who won 15 led the league with three shutouts.

In the hitting department, Frankie Frisch and George Kelly led the pack. Frisch scored 121 runs, had 211 hits including 17 triples and he stole 40 bases. Kelly hit 42 doubles, 23 home runs, 310 TB, 122 RBIs and 528 SA.

Their American League opponents across the river, the New York

Yankees won first place by winning 98 games. Try as they might, the World Series champion from the year before, the Cleveland Indians, ended up 4.5 games behind the Yankees.

Carl Mays led the Bombers at 27-5, .750WP. Waite Hoyt "blazed" a trail for the rest of the staff to follow, with 19 wins, which included 102 strikeouts.

Babe Ruth formed a hitting barrage with 177 runs scored, 44 doubles, 49 bombers, 457 TB, 171 RBIs, .378 BA, 512 OBP, 846 SA and 145 base-on-balls.

The Giants (NL) defeated the New York Yankees (AL), 5-3 in the 1921 World Series.

Ruth became the first baseball player in the live-ball era to start the cavalcade of baseball players who hit many home runs. In the dead ball era, Frank "Home Run" Baker received that moniker as he hit 30 home runs during the 1913-1915 seasons for Philadelphia Athletics. However another player hit more homers than Baker's 12 in 1911. Buck Freeman hit 25 four-baggers in 1899 for Washington's National League team. When Ruth hit 29 homers in 1919 for Boston Red Sox, they curtailed his pitching chores to only 17 games—his bat was needed every day.

When Ruth was sold to the Yankees in 1921 the Yankees ,finally won the National League Pennant winning 94 games, while their closest pursuer was the Pittsburgh Pirates falling behind by four games.

Art Nehf led the Giants pitching staff winning 20 games, but Phil Donahue who won 15, led the league with three shutouts.

In the hitting department, Frankie Frisch and George Kelly led the pack. Frisch scored 121 runs, had 211 hits including 17 triples and he stole 40 bases. Kelly hit 42 doubles, 23 home runs, 310 TB, 122 RBIs and 528 SA.

Their American League opponents across the river, the New York Yankees won first place by winning 98 games. Try as they might, the World Series champion from the year before, the Cleveland Indians, ended up 4.5 games behind the Yankees.

1922

Rogers Hornsby, the St. Louis Cardinals second baseman, had a 33 game-hitting streak during the 1922 season.

From the start in the season, it appeared that the two city teams were going to play each other at the end of the season. In the National League, the New York Giants captured the National League pennant winning 93 games. The Cincinnati Reds came alive after their absence in the forefront since 1919, but they faltered and finished seven games back.

Art Neft, always a favorite of manager John McGraw, led the Giants with 19 wins, but he also lost 13.

Dave Bancroft passed the other Giant hitters by scoring 117 times, 209 hits including 41 doubles. He received offensive help from George Kelly, Irish Meusel and captain Frankie Frisch. Kelly had stroked 17 four-baggers and 107 RBI, while Muesel hit 17 triples and 314 TB. Frisch was the team's best base stealer with 31 thefts.

The New York Yankees won the 1922 American League pennant by the "skin of their teeth', winning 94 games, just one game ahead of the St. Louis Browns.

The Yankee's pitching prowess was led by Bullet Joe Bush and Sam Jones. Bush won 26 games, but his .788 WP and Jones' 8 saves lead the league. Jones and Carl Mays formed one of the tandem twins in wins. They both had 13, while the other tandem of wining twins were Waite Hoyt and Bob Shawkey, both of whom had 19 wins.

Enter Babe Ruth who hit 35 round-trippers and had a .475 OBP, while Whitey Witt had the highest league walks with 89.

George Sisler, first baseman for the St. Louis Browns, had a 41 game-hitting streak.

The 1922 World Series went back to the best-of-seven winning format, but the New York Giants won again shutting out the losing New York Yankees (AL), 4-0. The two teams were also tied in the third game,

3-3, was called on account of darkness.

1923

The New York Giants again took the National League by winning 95 games, while the Cincinnati Reds fell 4.5 games behind.

The Giants did not have any 20-game winners, but Rosy Ryan and Jack Short both won 16. Only one game behind them was Hugh Quillan who had 15 winners.

Despite those low wins, the offense took over. Ross Youngs, captain Frankie Frisch and Irish Meusel pulled their team together with impressive hitting. Youngs, a favorite with manager John McGraw, led the team by scoring 121 runs, .412 OBP and drawing 73 walks. Frisch rattled the opposition with 223 hits and 311 TB. Meusel boosted the team with his slugging as he pounded 19 homers, driving in 125 runs.

The New York Yankees were no slouches as they won the American League flag with 98 wins as that left runner-up Detroit Tigers in the dust with 16 games behind.

The Yanks' pitching wasn't all that much better than their cross-town rival. Sad Sam Jones won 21, followed by Herb Pennock with 19, and Waite Hoyt's 17, but Pennock won the league title for his .760 WP.

Babe Ruth was to be the best hitter on the team as he led the "Bombers' scoring 121 runs, 205 hits, 45 doubles, and most importantly, hit 41 home runs. If that wasn't enough, he had 399 TB, 131 RBIs, a .393 BA, a .545 OBP and .764 SA.

The Giants felt confident that they would win the 1923 World Series against the Yankees as they did in 1921-1922. In 1923, the New York Yankees (AL) finally defeated the New York Giants (NL) 4-2 in the World Series.

1924

The New York Giants were successful in capturing the National League pennant winning 93 games, while the Brooklyn Robins were 1.5 games behind.

The Giants had no 20-game winners that year. Jack Bentley was their best pitcher with a 16-5 record followed by teammate Hugh McQuillan at 14-8 and a 2.69 ERA. The offense kept the Giants in contention all season, as Frankie Frisch scored 121 runs, 198 hits and 15 triples. George Kelly added with 37 doubles, 303 TB, and 136 RBIs (the league best) and Ross Youngs had a .356 BA, .441 OBP and walked 77 times.

The Washington Senators, in 1924, won their first pennant with 92 wins. The Yankees were hot on their trail, but petered out at the end of the season, finishing two games behind.

The American League recorded Senators ace Walter Johnson with highs with 21 wins, .767 winning percent and 2.72 ERA. His ERA beat out teammate Tom Zachary's 2.75. Zachary had 15 wins. Firpo Marberry, the team closer, had 15 saves, which was a league high too.

Sam Rice and Goose Goslin provided their team with league highs. Rice had 216 hits while Goslin excelled with 129 RBIs. Both players had team highs as Rice stole 24 bases, while Goslin contributed 17 triples and 299 TB. Rice also had a hitting streak of 31 games.

The Washington Senators players wanted to win their first World series for their aging Walter Johnson. The Senators (AL) defeated the New York Giants (NL) 4-3, in what proved to be a closely fought 1924 World Series.

1925

The new rule changes in 1925 were that the pitcher was allowed to use a rosin bag, and the minimum home-run distance was set at 250 feet.

Lou Gehrig

Henry Louis "Buster" Gehrig, most well known as Lou Gehrig was born in the Yorkville neighborhood of Manhattan of New York City on June 19, 1903. He was the second of four children born to Heinrick Gehrig and Christina Frock, however, all his siblings died in infancy.

Gehrig first gained national attention while in high school, the New York School of Commerce as his team opposed Chicago's Lane Tech High School in a game played at Cubs Park (now called Wrigley Field). In that game, his team was leading 8-6 in the top of the ninth, when Gehrig hit a grand slam out of the park. After he enter Columbia College (now called a university) he was signed by the New York Yankees to play for them in 1923.

Gehrig was known as a prolific port-side baseball hitter for the New York Yankees from 1923 to 1939. and because of his durability in playing 2,130 consecutive baseball games, he was called "The Iron Workhorse."

After playing in the minors, Gehrig became a member of the 1925 Yankees, playing as a utility first-baseman. On June 2 , he got his first break as a regular. Wally Pipp, the regular first-baseman was hit on the head two days before, from a wild throw during practice striking him in the temple. (There's some speculation that he was hit on the head trying to field a pop-up.) On June 2 when Pipp was supposed to play, he complained to manager Miller Huggins to take him out of the lineup that day. Miller Huggins put Gehrig in the game, and he continued there for 2,129 following games. Pipp, who lost his job to Gehrig, was traded the following year to the Cincinnati Reds.

After being dormant for several seasons in the National League, the Pittsburgh Pirates won the pennant in 1925. The New York Giants could not orchestrate a pennant, stumbling into second place, 8.5 games behind. The Pirates lacked an ace, but had three contributions from its pitching staff: Lee Meadows (19-10), Ray Kremer (17-8), Johnny Morrison (17-14) and Vic Aldridge (15-7). They all kept the Buc's winning until the end of the season.

Third-baseman Kiki Cuyler put on a one-man show in the Pirate's offensive drive, as he scored 144 runs, 222 hits, 43 doubles, 26 triples. 369 TB, .357 BA, .423 OBP and a .598 SA. However, there were a few of his teammates who had taken up the slack, as Glen Wright had 121 RBIs, Eddie Moore walked 73 times as Max Carey swiped 46 bases.

The Washington Senators, after winning the 1924 World Series, planned to repeat in 1925 . The Senators did capture the 1925 pennant by winning 96 games. Philadelphia Athletics' up and coming team, however, fell short as they finished 8.5 games behind. Walter Johnson still had a lot of his stuff as he was getting older, winning 20 games. Stan Coveleski won 20 games too. Goose Goslin was the hitting star scoring 116 runs, slugged 20 triples, 329 TB, 113 RBIs and 27 stolen bases.

The Washington Senators played well to compete in the 1925 World Series, but lost to the Pittsburgh Pirates in a nail-biter, 4-3.

1926

Three Men on Third

Since 1920, the Brooklyn Dodgers (then called the Robins) won a National league pennant, but were hapless as ever since, finishing each season in sixth place or lower in the standings. On August 15, 1926, the Dodgers haplessness reached a new level. That day, they played the

Boston Braves, a worse team than they were. In 1826 the Dodgers were in sixth place, the Braves in the seventh slot.

In the bottom of the seventh inning, the Braves were leading 1-0. To open the inning, shortstop Johnny Butler hit a single off Braves starter Henry Wertz. Catcher Henry DeBerry smashed a double to deep left field, scoring Butler, tying the score 1-1. Pitcher Dazzy Vance, in attempting a sacrifice bunt beat the throw to first. Next, Second-baseman Chick Fewster went to first, after being hit with a pitch. With a pitching change, reliever George Mogridge induced center-fielder Jake Jacobson to pop out. With the bases loaded, Babe Herman hit a drive near the right field wall. Braves right-fielder Jimmy Welsh looked like he was going to catch it, but Herman didn't think so, and thought he had a double or a triple. The other three runners weren't so sure, and they held their bases. As the ball dropped, DeBerry scored. As Vance was rounding third, third base coach, Tip O'Neill yelled for Fewster to hold up, but Vance thought he meant him, and he came back to third. Fewster did not hear him, or saw O'Neill's hands instructing him to stop at second, had his head down plowing for third. Soon there were two runners on third and Herman was rounding second, hoping for a triple. Braves third-baseman Zack Taylor was so excited that he thought that he needed to tag everyone out, forgetting that there was already one out. He tagged Herman before he reached third, and also tagged Vance, Fewster out, because Vance had reached third base first. and even. The umpire ruled that only Herman and Fewster were the only ones out and Vance was safe.

A few days later a fan was hurrying to Ebbets Field and another fan told him to hurry up because there were three runners on base. The late fan excitedly asked, "Which base?"

The St. Louis Cardinals captured the National League pennant in 1926 winning 89 games edging out the Cincinnati Reds by two games. That win total was the the lowest number of games in modern times to win the NL pennant. Pitcher Flint Rhem won a National League high of

20 games. Jim Bottomley led the Cardinals attack with 40 doubles, 19 homers and 305 TB. Lee Bell had 189 hits and a .518 SA. Ray Blades had a .409 OBP and had 62 bases-on-balls, while Taylor Douthit had 23 stolen bases.

In the American League, the New York Yankees won the pennant, winning 91 games. The Cleveland Indians came close, but remained three games behind.

The Yankee's pitching staff had three stalwarts in Herb Pennock, with 23 wins, Urban Shocker at 19, and Waite Hoyt trailing at 16.

Even though Lou Gehrig hit 47 doubles and 20 triples, Babe Ruth dominated the Yanks' offense, scoring 139 runs, 47 home runs, 365 TB, .372 BA, .516 OBP, .737 SA. and walked 144 times. But 1926 was Gehrig's break-out year when he batted .313, hitting 16 home runs.

After two years absence from the World Series, the New York Yankees (AL) worked hard to be in the 1926 Series, but to no avail, as they lost to the up-and-coming St. Louis Cardinals (NL), 4-3.

Frankie Frisch

Frankie Frisch was a switch-hitting second baseman who played for the New York Giants (1919-26), and the St. Louis Cardinals (1927-37).

Frisch was born on September 9, 1898 in the Bronx section of New York City. He attended Fordham Preparatory School, graduating in 1916. He continued by attending Fordham University where he starred in baseball, basketball, football and track. His exceptional speed earned him the title of 'The Fordham Flash.

When Frisch played for Giants, manager John McGraw made him team captain because of his leadership abilities. That title supposedly being an asset had some emotional liabilities. Every time the team lost due to player errors, McGraw, rather than dress down the offending player instead "balled out" Frisch. He endured these singular harassments by McGraw for a long time, and found them to be too intolerable. At the end of the 1926 season he told McGraw that he was quitting and would not play for him the following season. Even though he had quit, Frisch could not play for any other team because of "The Reserve Clause." McGraw was able to arrange for Frisch to be traded to the St. Louis Cardinals for Rogers Hornsby.

Later Frisch managed the Cardinals from 1933-38, the Pittsburgh Pirates, 1940-46 and the Chicago Cubs from 1949-51. Frisch was a very talented baseball player. He was a three time All-Star (1933-35), a four-time World Series champion (1921, 1922, 1931 and 1934). He was NL MVP in 1931, three time NL stolen base leader and member of the St. Louis Cardinals Hall of Fame.

He had a lifetime batting average of .316, still highest for a switch-hitter, 2880 hits, 1532 runs, 194 home runs, 1244 RBIs and 419 stolen bases. He was inducted in the National Baseball Hall of Fame in 1947. He died in Wilmington, Delaware from injuries receive a month earlier in a car accident in Ekton, Maryland.

Two other former Giants' Hall-of-Famers Mel Ott (1958) and Carl Hubbell (1988) also died from injuries from car accidents.

1927

The Pittsburgh Pirates captured the National League pennant in 1927, after an absence of one year, winning 94 games. St. Louis Cardinals, the 1926 winner, was unable to keep up with the Pirates, falling 1.5 games behind.

Carmen Hill led the Pirates pitching staff with 22 wins, while teammate Ray Kremer had 19.

The Waner brothers led the Pirates' attack as Lloyd scored 133 runs, and Paul had 237 hits, 42 doubles, 18 triples, 342 TB, .341 BA, 131 RBI. .380 BA, .437 OBP, .549 SA and walked 86 times.

The New York Yankees in the American League won 110 games for the pennant, while knocking out the Philadelphia Athletics who trailed by 19 games. The 1927 Yankees' season wins was the record until the Cleveland Indians won 111 in 1954.

In 1927 Babe Ruth hit a record 60 home runs. The record lasted until 1961 when Roger Maris hit 61. Ruth dominated several offensive categories too--158 runs, .486 OBP, .373 BA and 137 bases-on-balls. Earl Combs and Lou Gehrig provided the rest of the Yankee's punch. Gehrig hit 52 doubles, 447 TB, 175 RBI and 373 BA. Combs had 231 hits and 23 triples.

The New York Yankees and their "Murderers Row" players defeated those pesky Pittsburgh Pirates (NL), 4-0 in the 1927 World Series.

1928

In 1928, the St. Louis Cardinals bounced back after a year's absence from the National League pennant chase scoring 95 wins. The New York Giants returned for the run for the title, but ended up two games behind.

The Cardinals had three "big arms" in Bill Sherdel (21 wins) and Jesse Haines (with 20). Jim Bottomley again led the Cardinals' attack with 123 runs scored, 20 triples, 31 homers, 362 TB and 136 RBIs. Teammates Chick Haley hit 46 doubles while Taylor Douthit walked 84 times.

The New York Yankees won the American League pennant totaling 101 games, fending off the Philadelphia Athletics that were only 2.5 games behind.

Lou Gehrig took some of the offensive brunt off of Babe Ruth as he cracked 210 hits, 47 doubles, .374 BA and .467 on base percentage. Ruth only hit 54 home runs that year, scoring 163 runs, 380 TB, 142 RBIs, .709 SA and 137 walks. Center-fielder Earl Combs added 21 triples.

In 1928, the New York Yankees (AL) avenged their 1926 loss to the St, Louis Cardinals (NL) by whitewashing them by a 4-0 score.

1929

The Chicago Cubs gained the National League pennant in 1929 by winning 98 games. In second place were the Pittsburgh Pirates who were 16.5 games behind.

Pat Malone and Charlie Root both had league leading season highs. Malone led the league with 22 wins including five shutouts and 166 strikeouts. Root peaked for his .760 winning percentage and his appearance in 43 games. Guy Rush highlighted the team's pitching with eight saves.

The team had a few league high offensive players in five categories. Rogers Hornsby had three for scoring 156 runs, 409 TB and .670 SA. Hack Wilson had 159 RBI and Kiki Cuyler stole 43 bases. Wilson and Hornsby shared in hitting 39 homers each. Hornsby also led the team with a .380 BA, .489 OBP and 87 walks.

The Philadelphia Athletics (AL), with 104 games won copped the American League pennant as the rest of the league fell very far behind. The New York Yankees fell behind by 18 games.

George Einshaw led the league as he pitched in 44 games, winning 24 games. Lefty Grove had seven saves as he struck out 170 batters.

The Philadelphia Athletics, who had been absent from the World Series for 16 years, returned to the big stage by decisively defeating the Chicago Cubs (NL) 4-1.

The Beginning of Team Jersey Numbers

The New York Yankees in 1929, had the best fielding averages and were the first team to place numbers on the backs of their baseball jerseys. Owner Jacob Ruppert said that the Yankees were the first team to have numbers because it would identify their favorite players for the fans, and those numbers would be printed on the fans' scorecards.

Most fans knew that Babe Ruth's number was 3, but the fans weren't aware that the other player's number in the batting order were the same as their batting-order number. Center-fielder Earl Combs was number 1, short-stop Mark Koenig was number 2, then Ruth's number 3, Lou Gehrig was number 4, left fielder Bob Muesel was number 5, second-baseman Tony Lazzeri was number 6, Leo Durocher, who alternated at short-stop with Koenig, was number 7.

It's a puzzle why third baseman Gene Robinson was number 22. In his last year with the Bombers in 1929, because he had the best .966 team-fielding average and a decent .296 batting average.

1930

The St. Louis Cardinals won the 1930 National League championship totaling 92 games. The Chicago Cubs finished in second place two games behind.

"Wild Bill" Hallahan and Hi Bell were the leagues best players in these categories: Hallahan for striking out 177 batters and Bell for saving eight games. Hallahan also won 15 games. Frankie Frisch hit 46 doubles and Chick Hafey had a .652 SA.

The Philadelphia Athletics finished on top of the 1930 American League winning 102 games. The second place Washington Senators finished eight games out.

Lefty Grove was brilliant as he topped six categories as being tops in the league. They were 28 wins, .848 WP, 209 strikeouts, 2.54 ERA, nine saves and pitching in 50 games.

Al Simmons was the league's best in scoring 152 runs, and peppering 211 hits, 16 triples, 392 TB, 166 RBIs and a .708 SA. Teammates Jimmie Foxx hit 37 homers and .429 OBP, while Max Bishop received 128 base on balls.

The Philadelphia Athletics (AL) returned to the World Series in

1930 defeating the St. Louis Cardinals (NL), 4-2.

1931

After two years of inconsistent field managers, Chicago Cubs manager Joe McCarthy was selected as manager. He served in that role until 1946. When he was hired by Ed Barrow, then Yankee president, McCarthy established his "ten commandments" to his team for the player's success in the majors.

They were "(1) Nobody ever became a ball player by walking after a ball, (2) you will never become a .300 hitter unless you take the bat off of your shoulder, (3) a fielder who throws behind a runner is 'locking the barn after the horse is stolen, (4) keep your head up and you may not have to keep it down, (5) when you start to slide, SLIDE!, (6) He who changes his mind, may not have to change a good leg for a bad one, (7) always run them out, you can never tell, (8) Do not quit. (9) try not to find too much fault with umpires and (10) a pitcher who hasn't control, has nothing."

The St. Louis Cardinals copped the 1931 National League pennant winning 101 games while the New York Giants finished 13 games behind.

Bill Hallahan won 19 games, twirled four saves and his strikeout total was a league highest with 159. Paul Derringer's winning percent of .692 was the highest in the league.

Chick Hafey's .349 BA was the leagues highest mark as was his .404 OBP. He also had a .569 SA. Sparky Adams hit 46 doubles while Frankie Frisch stole 28 bases.

The Philadelphia Athletics were the 1931 American League champion winning 107 games. The New York Yankees had a new manager, Joe McCarthy, to replace Miller Huggins, who had died in 1929, but the Bombers ended up 13.5 games out.

Lefty Grove had a blockbuster season to gain several league marks as he pitched 31 wins, four shutouts, 175 strikeouts and a 2.06 ERA.

George Earnshaw had 21 wins and 152 strikeouts.

Al Simmons led the Athletics' attack with 200 hits, 329 TB, 121 RBI, .39- BA, 444 OBP and a .641 SA. Jimmie Foxx slugged 30 homers while Max Bishop had 112 walks.

The Philadelphia Athletics (AL) tried to win the World Series for a third year, but they were thwarted by a much improved St. Louis Cardinals team (NL) who beat them by a close 4-3 score.

1932

The Brooklyn Robins of the National League changed their name to the Brooklyn Dodgers in 1932.

Lou Gehrig was the third batter in baseball history, and the first in the modern era to hit four home runs in a single game on June 3, 1932, Since Babe Ruth and he had been teammates, he always was designated to the shadows.

The newspapers dropped the ball in reporting Gehrigs four-homer game. It certainly was his opportunity to shine. One reason was that on that particular day long-time manager of the New York Giants, John McGraw had announced his retirement. The other reason was that the newspapers did not realize that hitting four homers in one game was a superlative achievement. It had been 36 years since Ed Delahanty, of the 1896 Phillies, accomplished that feat in Chicago. Another of Gehrig's achievements were thwarted again.

The Chicago Cubs won the 1932 National League pennant, winning 90 games. The Pittsburgh Pirates were runners-up and four games behind.

Lon Warneke won two league-best performances with his 22 wins and .786 WP. He also whiffed 106 batters and compiled a 2.37 ERA. Guy Bush and Charlie Root had won 17 and 15 wins respectively,

Billy Herman led the offense with 206 hits as Riggs Stephenson followed with 49 doubles.

The 1932 American League title was won by the new York Yankees with 107 wins. The Philadelphia Athletics, last year's World Series winner were unable to repeat in 1932, falling 13 games behind.

Lefty Gomez pitched 24 wins for the Yankees, but Johnny Allen had a league high winning percent of .810. Red Ruffing was the strikeout leader, whiffing 190 batters.

On the offensive side several players provided the Yankees with plenty of punch. Babe Ruth, although not quite as dominant as in earlier years, hit 41 circuit clouts and claimed league summits with a .489 OBP and 139 bases-on-balls. Ruth also led the team with a .661 SA. Lou Gehrig helped the "Bombers" with 208 hits, 370 TB, 151 RBI and a .349 BA. Earl Combs was the team's top scored plating 143 runs, Tony Lazzeri powdered 16 doubles and speedy Ben Chapman pilfered 38 bases.

The Chicago Cubs lost another World Series and they were unsuccessful again when the New York Yankees (AL) walloped them by a 4-0 score.

Babe Ruth's Called Shot

During the third game of the 1932 World Series, the Cubs were harassing Babe Ruth. In the fourth inning, Ruth came to bat. There were two balls and two strikes on him. He held up a finger, saying "That's one...that's two." Harnett, the Cubs catcher heard him say, "It only takes one to hit it," a time honored baseball phrase. Then Ruth waved his arm. Whether he was merely gesturing toward the Cub dugout or pointing toward the center field stands; no one knows for sure. Then he hit a home run and it wasn't just that he hit the home run. He hit the longest home run ever hit in Chicago to dead center field—a fairly rare thing. It was a tremendous home run—and it stunned the crowd. Ruth told a reporter later that he had said to himself, "You lucky bum." He said something to the Cubs first baseman, and then the second baseman as he was circling the bases, and he waved at the Cubs dugout.

Then United States president, Franklin D. Roosevelt was present and sitting just behind home plate. As Babe crossed home plate, Roosevelt put his head back, and laughed.

Charlie Root, the Cubs pitcher who threw the home run ball said that Ruth never pointed to the fence. "If he had, I would have put one in his ear, and knocked him on his a- -."

Lou Gehrig was no less certain that Ruth had called the shot—and said, "What do you think of the nerve of that big monkey. Calling his shot and getting away with it." Gehrig was the real hero of that game. He hit two homers, and during the series batted .529 , and scored nearly a quarter of the Yankee's runs, but he was cheated again by the "called homer."

1933

Bill Lee led the Cubs pitching staff with 20 wins and a .769 WP, both best in the league.

The first official All-Star Game was played at Chicago's Comiskey Park on July 6, 1933. The highlight of the game was Babe Ruth, who hit a two-run homer in the bottom of the third and made a stellar catch against the right field wall against the scoreboard. There were 36 players in that game, and 20 of them were later enshirined in the National Baseball Hall of. Fame. The American League defeated the National League 4-2.

The umpires for that first All-Star Game were Bill Klem, Bill Dinneen, Bill McGowan and Cy Rigler. The game was intended to be a one-time event. Its proceeds of $45,000 went for the benefit of disabled or needy Major League baseball players. The idea was posed by Chicago Tribute sports editor Arch Ward, and although it was designed as a benefit, its purpose was to overcome the public's dismal mindset during the "Great Depression."

The New York Giants finally found their niche after John McGraw's retirement in 1932, winning 91 games in 1933 to capture the National League pennant. The second place Pittsburgh Pirates could get no closer than five games from the top.

Screwball pitcher Carl Hubbell won three league summits with 23 wins, 1.66 ERA and having pitched in 45 games. Hal Schumacher won 19 games to help his team to reach the top.

Mel Ott, as manager, showed he could excel too! Ott scored 98 runs, had 103 RBI and received 75 free trips to first base. Ott was noted for his famous "foot-in-the-bucket" stance when batting, as he lifted his front foot before swinging at the pitched ball.

Bill Terry contributed to the offense with a .322 BA and a .375 OBP.

The New York Giants under the tutelage of first-year manager Mel Ott, managed 91 game wins for the 1933 National League crown. The Pittsburgh Pirates finished in second place only five games behind.

Screwball pitcher Carl Hubbell earned three league bests as he had 23 wins, a 1.66 ERA and for having pitched in 45 games. Teammate Hal Schumacher won another 19 games. Ott scored 98 runs, hit 23 homers, hit in 103 RBIs and he earned 75 free trips to first base. Bill Terry assisted in the offense with a .322 BA and a .375 OBP.

The Washington Senators took the 1933 American League pennant winning 99 games, but the second place New York Yankees remained seven games back.

General Crowder was the Senators most successful pitcher, winning 24 games. He shared that league title with Lefty Grove of the Philadelphia Athletics who also won 24 games. Crowder pitched in 52 games, tops in the league. Earl Whitehill won 22 games to help the Senators to the title.

The Washington Senators (AL), trying for their second franchise win in three tries were thwarted, and lost the 1933 World Series to the New York Giants (NL), 4-1.

1934

Dizzy Dean

    Dizzy Dean was born in Lucas, Arkansas on June 16, 1910 as Jay Hanna "Dizzy" Dean. Both Dizzy and his brother Paul sometime known as "Daffy," led a pitching staff which won the 1934 National League pennant. That year, Dizzy won 30 games and Paul won 19 games.
    Dizzy played for the St. Louis Cardinals in 1930, 1932-37, the Chicago Cubs from 1938-41 and the St. Louis Browns (AL) in 1947. He was an All-Star four times from 1934-37, a World Series champion in 1934, won the NL MVP in 1934, a two time wins leader in 1934-35, a four time strikeout leader (1932-1935) and elected to the National Baseball Hall of Fame in 1953.
    In the 1937 All-Star game Earl Averill of the American League Cleveland Indians hit a line drive toward the mound striking Dean's toe. When he was told that the bone was fractured, Dean said. "Fractured? Hell, the damn thing's broken." When Dean pitched again, he altered his pitching style so that he would not fall on the injured toe, causing him to injure his arm.
    He later was a baseball sports announcer and he infuriated teachers by saying "ain't"
and especially his describing a runner who "slud into third."
    He died in Reno, Nevada on July 17, 1974.

    The second annual All-Star Game was played at the Polo Grounds in New York City on July 10, 1934. The American league beat the National League again, 9-7.
    The National League pennant-winner was the St. Louis Cardinals, who won 95 games, just edging out the New York Giants by two games.
    Brothers Paul and Dizzy Dean were an awesome pitching duo for the Cardinals. Dizzy was best in the league with some pitching

performances like his 30 wins, .811 WP, 195 strikeouts and seven saves, He also had a team's best 2.66 ERA while brother Paul had 19 wins.

Ripper Collins took control of the Cardinals offense slapping out 200 hits, 40 doubles, 35 four-baggers, 368 TB, 128 RBI and a .333 BA. Joe "Ducky" Medwick helped as he scored 110 runs and hit 18 triples while short-stop Pepper Martin stole 23 bases.

The Detroit Tigers became the American League 1934 pennant champion by winning 101 games. The New York Yankees again settled for second place, only seven games behind.

The Tigers had a winning pitching crew with Schoolboy Rowe, Tommy Bridges and Eldon Auker having 24, 22 and 15 wins, respectively.

The "Bengals" had two hitters who stole the Tigers hitting show, Hank Greenberg and Charlie Gehringer. Greenberg had 356 TB, 139 RBIs and a .600 SA. Gehringer scored 134 runs, had 214 hits, 50 doubles and a .346 BA. Other teammates who contributed were Jo-Jo White who scampered to steal 25 bases and the eagle-eyed Mickey Cochrane who took 98 passes to first base.

The St. Louis Cardinals returned to the 1934 World Series stage by beating the Detroit Tigers, 4-3.

Goose Goslin, Detroit Tigers (AL) outfielder hit safely in 30 consecutive games.

1935

Hank Greenberg

Henry Benjamin "Hank" Greenberg (born Hyman Greenberg) was born on January 1, 1911, and played first base for the Detroit Tigers for 12 of 13 seasons. He was a power hitter and considered to be one of the sluggers during that time. He had a batting average over .300 for eight seasons. He was on an AL All-Star team for four seasons and an AL

MVP in 1935 as a first baseman, and in 1940 as a left fielder. He was the first major league player to hit 25 or more home runs in each league, with the Tigers and the Pittsburgh Pirates. He remains the AL record-holder as a right-handed batter with the most 183 RBIs in a single season. He played his last season in 1940 for the Pirates. As a Jewish player, he refused to play on the Jewish holiday, Yom Kippur. He was elected as the first batter of Jewish heritage to be inducted into the Baseball Hall-of-Fame in 1956. He died on September 4, 1986.

The third All-Star Game was played on July 8, 1935 at the Municipal Stadium in Cleveland, Ohio. Despite the dismay of the National League All-Stars. The American League won it three times in a row, winning 4-1.

The Chicago Cubs captured the National League crown in 1935, winning 100 games, while the previous year's World Series winner, the St. Louis Cardinals, languished in second place, four games behind.

Lon Warneke, Bill Lee and Larry French led the Cubs pitching staff. Warneke and Lee both won 20 games; Warneke pitched 4 saves and struck out 120 batters. Lee only lost six games and had a team high .769 WP. French ha 17 wins with four shutouts.

Augie Galen scored 133 runs, stole 20 bases and had 87 walks. Billie Herman, Ernie Lombardi, Stan Hack and Gabby Hartnet assisted in the offense. Herman collected 227 hits, 57 doubles and 317 TB. Lombardi season average was .343, Hack had a .406 OBP and Harnett's had a .545 SA.

The Detroit Tigers snatched the 1935 American league title winning 93 games. The New York Yankees for the third straight year, failing to win a title, got closer, and was only three games behind.

Tommy Bridges surged ahead of the pitching staff, winning 21 games and striking out 163, both league's best. Eldon Auker pitched the league's best .720 WP. Schoolboy Rowe won 19 games.

Hank Greenberg led most offensive categories with 203 hits, 46 doubles, 16 triples. 36 homers, 389 TB, 170 RBIs and .628 SA. Charlie

Gehringer plated 123 runs and had a .330 BA. Catcher Mickey Cochrane had a .452 OBP and 96 walks, while Jo-Jo White stole 19 bases.

The Detroit Tigers (AL), losers in last year's World Series, beat Chicago Cubs (NL), 4-2.

1936

The Philadelphia Phillies Chuck Klein was the fourth batter in Major League history to hit four home runs in a single game at Pittsburgh, in a 10-inning game, on July 10, 1936.

The National League Boston Braves changed their nickname to Boston Bees.

For the fourth All-Star Game, the National League players had a collective drive to win, and sure enough they squeaked by a 4-3 score past the American League at the Boston Braves Field on July 7, 1936.

The New York Giants won 92 games to win the 1936 National League crown, The St. Louis Cardinals were runners-up for the second straight year, and were five games out.

The Giant's best pitcher, Carl Hubbell won three league best titles by winning, 26 games, .813 WP and a 2.37 ERA. He also struck out 123 batters, while Frank Gabler pitched six saves.

The New York Yankees won 102 games in 1936 to cop the American League pennant. The Detroit Tigers, pennant winners the last two years, failed to repeat this year, falling dismally to 19.5 games behind. Although Red Ruffing led the Yankee pitchers with 20 wins, two other players were good enough for high league marks: Pat Malone had nine saves, and Monte Pearson had a high .731 WP. Lou Gehrig batted well enough to top the rest of the league, scoring 167 runs , .478 OBP, .596 SA and 130 walks. He also claimed team leadership in smashing 49 homers, 403 TB and 152 RBIs. Third-baseman Red Rolfe, shared a league high with Cleveland Indian's Earl Averill, where both hit 15 triples. Teammates Bill Dickey's .362 BA and Joe DiMaggio's 15 triples paced the team.

That July Babe Ruth, Ty Cobb, Christy Mathewson, Walter Johnson and Honus Wagner were elected as the first members of the National Baseball Hall of Fame.

The New York Yankees (AL) defeated the New York Giants (NL) in the 1936 World Series, 4-2.

1937

In January, Nap Lajoie, Tris Speaker and Cy Young were elected into the National Baseball Hall of Fame while Veterans Committee selected Morgan Buckeley (executive), Ban Johnson (executive), George Wright (executive), Connie Mack (manager) and John McGraw (manager).

The fifth annual classic All-Star Game was played at Griffith Stadium on July 7, 1937 as the American league continued their winning ways, defeating the National League, 8-3.

The New York Giants won the 1937 National League pennant, winning 95 games while the Chicago Cubs trailed by three games. Carl Hubbell, with his renowned screwball, led the league in winning 22 games, a .733 WP and striking out 159 batters as Cliff Melton added 20 wins. Mel Ott also gained league honors hitting 31 round-trippers and collecting 102 walks. Ott also led the Giants with 285 TB, 95 RBIs. .408 OBP and .523 SA. Teammate Dick Bartel hit 38 doubles.

The New York Yankees topped the American League with 102 wins as the Detroit Tigers could get no closers than 13 games. Lefty Gomez earned multiple league marks with 21 wins, six shutouts, 194 strikeouts and a 2.33 ERA. Joe DiMaggio, in his second season, chalked up several American League honors by scoring 151 runs, 46 homers, 418 TB and a .673 SA. Lou Gehrig had a couple league marks with a .473 OBP and a 127 walks.

The New York Yankees (AL) defeated the New York Giants (NL) in

the 1937 World Series, 4-1.

1938

The BBWAA elected Grover Cleveland Alexander into the National Baseball Hall of Fame while the Veterans Committee selected Alexander Cartwright (pioneer) and Henry Chadwick (pioneer).

The Chicago Cubs won the 1938 National League pennant with 89 wins as the Pittsburgh Pirates came close, only two games behind. Bill Lee was the top Cubs pitcher, snarling four National League honors with 22 wins, .710 WP, nine shutouts, and a 2.66 ERA. Teammate Clay Bryant earned one high league mark striking out 135 batters. Outfielder Stan Hack led the Cubs hitters, scoring 109 runs, slashing 195 hits and a .411 OBP.

The New York Yankees, the American League champs, won 99 games, leaving the Boston Red Sox 9.5 games behind. Red Ruffing and and Lefty Gomez collected three league honors between them. Ruffing had 21 wins and a .750 WP while Gomez had four shutouts. Joe DiMaggio led the Yankees by scoring 129 runs, hitting 32 triples, 32 homers, 140 RBIs and a .324 BA. Red Rolfe collected 196 hits while shortstop Frankie Crosetti stole 27 bases.

George McQuinn of the St. Louis Browns had a 34-game hitting streak in 1938.

The American League tried to cop another Classic All-Star win at Crosley Field, Cincinnati. on July 6, 1938, but they were rebuked, as the National League won, 4-1.

The New York Yankees (AL) defeated the Chicago Cubs (NL) in the 1938 World Series, 4-0.

Stan "The Man" Musial

In 1938, when Babe Ruth was in retirement, most people familiar with Stan Musial's past, when he started as a pitcher and eventually became an every-day player, waking everyone up with his hitting. No one ever thought that could happen again—where a left handed pitcher would covert to becoming an every-day player, whose bat spoke for him, like Ruth.

Musial was born in Donora, Pennsylvania on November 21, 1920. When he was 15, he joined the Donora Zinc semi-pro baseball team. In his first game, as a pitcher, he struck out 13 batters in six innings, all adults. When he was 17, the St. Louis Cardinals offered him a contract as a pitcher. He reported to the Class-D Williamson Red Birds in West Virginia. After graduating from high school in 1939, his skills improved as he had a 9-2 record, .435 ERA and a .352 BA. That batting average caught a few eyes—a hitting pitcher? He spent the 1940 season with another Class-D team, the Daytona Beach Islanders. Then he went under the tutelage of Manager Dickie. Kerr, who many could recalled as the only Chicago White Sox pitcher with two of the wins during the Black Sox Scandal in the 1919 World Seriesl. Luckily, he wasn't part of that ejected crew.

That season, Musial injured his arm, and in 1941, he was assigned to Class-C Springfield (Missouri) Cardinals. Due to his weakened arm he was designated to playing the outfield. During the first 87 games, Musial hit a league-leading .379 and was promoted to the Rochester Red Wings of the AAA International League.

He was observed due to his unique batting stance as he went into a crouch with his back squarely toward the pitcher. One of his teammates describe the stance "like a boy who would be peaking around the corner of a building to see if the cops were coming."

Musial was called up to the Cardinals. Musial had a .304 average during the 1944 World Series, against the neighboring St. Louis Browns.

He enlisted in the United States Navy during World War II, and served during 1944 and 1945. When he returned, he began playing first base and remained there until his retirement in 1963. He finished his career batting a lifetime .331, blasting 475 home runs. He was inducted into the National Baseball Hall of Fame in 1969. He died on June 19,

2013.

1939

In January the BBWAA elected Lou Gehrig, George Sisler, Eddie Collins and Willie Keeler into the 1939 National Basball Hall of Fame while the Veterans Committee selected Cap Anson, Buck Ewing , Al Spalding (executive) Candy Cummings (executive), and Charlie Cominskey (exective) .

Lou Gehrig's Farewell Speech

On July 4, 1939, Lou Gehrig Appreciation Day, Lou Gehrig uttered these famous words at a Home Plate Ceremony:
"Fans, for the past few weeks you have been reading about a bad break I got. Today, I consider myself to be the luckiest man on the face of the earth."
The vast gathering sat in absolute silence for the longest period than perhaps any baseball crowd in history, as they heard Gehrig deliver such an amazing speech as ever came from a ball park.
"I have been in ball parks for 17 years, and have never received anything but kindness and encouragement from you fans. Look at these grand men, which of you wouldn't consider it a highlight of his career just to associate with them, even for a day? Sure, I'm lucky. Who wouldn't considerate an honor to have known Jacob Ruppert? Also, the builder of baseball's greatest empire, Ed Barrow? To have spent the next six years with that wonderful fellow, Miller Huggins? Then to have spent the next nine years with that outstanding leader, that smart student of psychology, the best manager in baseball today. Joe McCarthy? Sure, I'm lucky!
"When the New York Giants, a team you would give your right arm to beat, and visa versa, sends you a gift—that's something! When

everybody down to the groundskeepers and those boys in the white coats, remember you with trophies—that's something! When you have a wonderful mother-in-law who takes sides with you in a squabble with her own daughter—that's something! When you have a mother and father, to work all of their lives, so that you can have an education and build your body—it's a blessing! When you have a wife, who has been the tower of strength and shown more courage than you dream existed—that's the finest I know!

So I close, in saying that I may have had a tough break, but I have an awful lot to live for."

Gehrig had been forced to retire as a player two weeks earlier due to his busy diagnosis with Amyotrophic Lateral Sclerosis, the disease that bears his name. But on this hot muggy day, he was being showered with kind words, and numerous gifts, one of which remained as a source of inspiration to his dying day. The event was held between a double-header with the Washington Senators, which were viewed by 61,808 fans. In December 1939, Lou Gehrig was elected into the National Baseball Hall of Fame. He died on June 2, 1941. Both Gehrig, and later in 1972, Roberto Clemente were elected by special elections.

The 1939 All-Star Game was played at Yankee Stadium, in New York City, but the American League All-stars wouldn't be denied that time, defeating the National League, 3-1.

A major league baseball game that was shown on television was a double-header played in Brooklyn on August 26, 1939 between the Cincinnati Reds and the Brooklyn Dodgers. Both games were televised by station W2XBS, New York City, using two cameras that alternated according to the play, Walter Lanier "Red" Barber was the announcer.

The Cincinnati Reds took the 1939 National League pennant winng 96 games, while runner-up St. Louis Cardinals trailed by 4.5 games.

Pitcher Bucky Walters earned three league honors with 27 wins, 137 strikeouts and a 2.29 ERA. Paul Derringer also won a NL mark with a .781 WP Two Reds' batters won two league marks too, as Billy Werber scored 115 runs and Frank McCormick peppered 209 hits. McCormick also had three team highs, with 41 doubles, 128 RBIs and 312 TB. Ival Goodman led in three categories hitting 16 triples, a .401 OBP and .916 SA. Catcher Ernie Lombardi provided the Reds with 20 powersmashing homers.

The 1939 American League champions were the New York Yankees with 106 wins, while the Boston Red Sox were a distant 17 games behind.

Red Ruffing had 21 wins and a league-high five shutouts. Closer Johnny Murphy also had a league-high 19 saves, as Lefty Gomez whiffed 102 batters. Red Rolfe and Joe DiMaggio shared high team offensive marks. Rolfe scored 139 runs, had 213 hits, 46 doubles and 321 TB. DiMaggio did his share with 30 homers, 126 RBIs, .391 BA and a .671 SA. Center-fielder George Selkirk was no slouch, as he added a .452 OBP, 12 stolen bases and 103 walks.

The New York Yankees (AL) defeated the Cincinnati Reds (NL) in the 1938 World Series 4-0.

1940

Joe DiMaggio

One of the most gifted baseball players in major league history was Joe DiMaggio. Joe was born Guiseppe Paolo DiMaggio Jr. on November 15, 1914, in Martinez, California. When Joe was a boy, he wasn't particularly interested in playing baseball. Often when his friends wanted him to play baseball, he would only play if they would give him something in return. Joe's brother Vince, who was two years older, arranged for a tryout for Joe with the Pacific Coast League San Francisco Seals.

In his first year with the Seals, at the age of 19, he batted safely in 61 games, a league record. He was called up to the Yankees in 1936, and retired in 1951. He was elected to the National Baseball Hall of Fame in 1955. After he retired, he was the spokesman for "Mr. Coffee," a popular decanter for making coffee which replaced the old standby coffee pot. He died on March 8, 1999.

A major league no-hitter, on opening day, was pitched on April 6, 1940 in Chicago, by Robert William Feller, of the Cleveland Indians, who retired 15 men in a row, from the fourth to the eighth inning, against the Chicago White Sox, defeating them 1-0.

On July 9,1940, the National Leaguers were ready to rock at the Sportsman's Park, in St. Louis, as they white-washed the Americans in a 4-0 shutout in the All-Star Game.

The Cincinnati Reds were the 1940 National League champions, as they won 100 games, while the second place Brooklyn Dodgers remained 12 games behind. Several Reds' pitchers had high league marks, including Bucky Walters, who had a 2.48 ERA. Reliever Jim Bagby saved seven games. Elmer Riddle had a .826 WP, and Johnny Van der Meir struck out 201 batters. Paul Derringer won 20 games, while Gene Thompson, Jr. had won 16. On the offensive side, Lonnie Frey stole 22 bases, a league high and he also walked 80 times. Billy Werber scored 105 runs, while Frank McCormick peppered 191 hits, including 44 doubles, 19 home runs, 298 TB and 127 RBIs. Catcher Ernie Lombardi sported a .319 BA, .382 OBP and a .489 SA.

The 1940 Detroit Tigers captured the American League pennant winning 90 games, while the second place Cleveland Indians missed out by only one game.

Two Tigers pitchers received high league recognition, as Schoolboy Rowe had a .842 WP and Al Benton saved 17 games. Bobo Newsom won 21 games, Rowe won 16, and Tommy Bridges struck out 133 batters. Two Tigers players had some of the league's best hitting performances: Barney McCosky had 19 triples, while Hank Greenberg had all the others—slicing 50 doubles, 41 homers, and had a .340 BA and .433 OBP. Second baseman Charlie Gehringer walked 101 times.

The Cincinnati Reds (NL) defeated Detroit Tigers (AL) in the 1940

World Series, 4-3.

1941

Joe DiMaggio of the New York Yankees, hit safely in 56 consecutive games from May 15 to July 17, 1941. In the last game, DiMaggio hit two line drive grounders at Cleveland third-baseman Kenny Keltner and in his final at bat, playing manager Lou Beaudreau fielded another line shot to throw out DiMaggio, to putting an end to his game-hitting string.

Ted Williams, of the Boston Red Sox, ended the 1941season, with a batting average of .406. He was the last .400 hitter in the majors.

The National League Boston Bees changed their nickname to Boston Braves.

In a barn-burner at Briggs Stadium in Detroit, the All-Star Game was close all the way, on July 8, 1941, as the Americans bested the Nationals, 7-5.

The Brooklyn Dodgers finally won the National League pennant in 1941, after 21 lean years, by copping 100 wins. Their last pennant was won in 1920, when they were called the Robins, then losing to the Cleveland Indians. The St. Louis Cardinals, who were on their necks all the way, screeched to second place, 2.5 games behind.

Both Whit Wyatt and Kirby Higby pitched league-high 22 wins for the Dodgers, while Higby also pitched in 48 games, also tops for the league. Pete Reiser, and Dolph Camilli shared in several different league high offensive categories. Reiser scored 117 runs, stoked 39 doubles, 17 triples, had a .343 BA, a 299 TB, and .558 SA. Camilli smacked 34 homers and had 120 RBIs. He and Joe Medwick had team batting marks---Medwick with 171 hits, Camilli with a .407 OBP and 104 walks.

The New York Yankees captured the 1941 American League pennant with 101 wins, while the Boston Red Sox fell behind by 17 games.

Lefty Gomez snatched a league high .750 WP as Johnny Murphy

saved 18 games. Joe DiMaggio stunned the whole world by hitting safely in 56 games, while earning league highs a he scored 125 runs while collecting 378 TB. He also excelled in the Yankees-best 193 hits, 43 doubles, 125 RBIs, .357 BA, .440 OBP and a .643 SA. Charlie Keller had 104 walks.

The New York Yankees (AL) defeated the Brooklyn Dodgers (NL) in the 1941 World Series, 4-1.

1942

The BBWAA in 1942 elected Rogers Hornsby into the National Baseball Hall of Fame.

The All-Star Game returned to the Polo Grounds on July 6, 1942, but the National leaguers hoping for a win were disappointed as the American Leaguers won for the seventh time, 3-1.

The Second World War drafted over 1,000 Major and Minor leaguers, and the drain of all this talent showed in the 1942 league campaigns.

The St. Louis Cardinals capture the National League title in 1942 winning 106 games, but the runner-up Brooklyn Dodgers stayed two games behind. Mort Cooper earned two high league marks for winning 22 games, and a low 1.78 ERA., but he also struck out 152 batters. Enos Slaughter led the Cardinals offense by scoring 100 runs, amassing 188 hits, including 17 triples, 13 home runs, 156 TB, 98 RBIs, .318 BA, .412 OBP, .494 SA and 88 walks. Shortstop Marty Marion hit 38 doubles and Johnny Hopp stole 14 bases.

In the American League the New York Yankees won 103 games while the Boston Red Sox struggled as they were nine games behind. Big Tiny Bonham won 21 games, but had a low 2.27 ERA. and six shutouts. Joe DiMaggio led the Yankees by scoring 123 runs and slicing 188 hits including 13 triples, 21 homers, 114 RBIs and 304 TB. Tommy Henrich hit 30 doubles, while second baseman Joe Gordon had a .322

BA. Charlie Keller sported a .417 OBP, .513 SA and 114 free trips to first base, while speedy Phil (Scooter) Rizzuto stole 22 bases.

The St. Louis Cardinals (NL) defeated New York Yankees (AL) in the 1942 World Series, 4-1.

1943

The All-American Girls Professional Baseball League was formed in the Chicago area in 1943, when Major League baseball was feeling the loss of 1,100 players, who had joined the United States Armed Forces during World War II. The league was organized by Philip Wrigley, owner of the Chicago Cubs. The teams were from the states of Illinois, Wisconsin, Michigan and Indiana.

Players who were first signed in 1943 were Clara Schillace, Ann Hamett, Edie Perlick and Shirley Jamison. There were four teams: the Kenosha Comets, Racine Belles, Rockford Peaches and South Bend Blue Sox. Other teams who eventually played in the league were the Milwaukee Chicks, Fort Wayne Daisies, Grand Rapids Chicks, Muskegon Lassies, Peoria Red Wings, Chicago Colleens, Springfield Sallies and the Battle Creek Belles. For several years, there was an All-Star team. This league was portrayed in a movie call, "A League of Their Own," directed by Penny Marshall. The league disbanded in 1954.

As many of the American Leaguers had gone off to war, the National Leaguers thought that their chances of winning the All-Star game at Shibe Park, Philadelphia on July 13, 1943 improved, but they were disappointed again, losing to the American League, 5-3.

The St. Louis Cardinals captured the 1943 National League pennant by winning 105 games as the hapless Cincinnati Reds fell a distant 18-games behind. The Cardinals pitching staff garnered two league highs, as Mort Cooper had a .724 WP and Howie Pollet snared a 1.75 ERA. Cooper also struck out 141 batters, as Max Lanier won 16 games.

The 1943 New York Yankees captured the American League pennant winning 95 games as the runner-up Washington Senators were a distant 13 games behind. Yankees Spud Chandler was the league's best pitcher winning 20 games (which he shared with Detroit Tiger's Dizzy Trout who also won 20) and a 1.64 ERA. Chandler also pitched five shutouts and stuck out 134 batters. Catcher Bill Dickey led the Yankees offensive attack with a .351 BA, .445 OBP and a .492 SA. Third-baseman Bill Johnson peppered 166 hits, while Nick Etton smashed 35 doubles, Johnny Lindell collected 12 triples and Charlie Keller had 31 fence-busters. Keller also connected with 269 TB and 106 walks as he added 107 RBIs. The New York Yankees (AL) defeated St. Louis Cardinals (NL) in the 1943 World Series, 4-1.

1944

The first baseball commissioner, Judge Kenesaw Mountain Landis who had served since 1921, had a heart attack at Forbes Field in Boston on July 11, 1944 while attending the All Star Baseball game. (He later succumbed to a seizure on November 25, 1944.) The National Leaguers finally got it together as they beat the Americans, 7-1 in the All-Star Game.

The BBWAA elected former commissioner Kenesaw Landis into the 1944 National Baseball Hall of Fame.

The two crosstown rivals of St. Louis, the Cardinals and the Browns, met each other at the World Series for the first, and only time in 1944.

The St. Louis Cardinals were the National League champions, winning 105 games. The second place Pittsburgh Pirates were unable to get into the mix, as they were left behind by 14.5 games.

Mort Cooper demonstrated that he was the league's best pitcher in shutouts, with seven. He also won 22 games, earning a 2.46 ERA.

Max Lanier added 17 wins, while striking out 141 batters, Ted Wilkes had the highest winning percentage, with a .810 mark. Jack Kramer struck out 124 swingers. Their offense captured four league-best categories monopolized by Stan Musial as he popped 197 hits, 51 doubles, .440 OBP and a .549 SA. He also did well in several team categories—scoring 112 runs, 14 triples, 312 TB, .347 BA and 90 bases-on-balls. Whitey Kurowski's 20 homers and Ray Sanders' 102 RBIs helped in the Cardinals pennant drive. George Caster received the top prize with a league-high 12 saves.

The St. Louis Browns captured the 1944 American League crown edging out the Detroit Tigers by only one game. Jack Kramer and Nels Potter lead the Browns pitchers as each won 19 games. Kramer also had a 2.49 ERA and struck out 124 batters. It was surprising that the greatest bulk of their offense was driven by shortstop Vern Stevens, who scored 91 runs, peppered 164 hits including 32 doubles, powdered 20 four-baggers, 248 TB, .462 SA, but most of all, had a league-highest 109 RBIs. Don Gutteridge drilled 11 triples and stole 20 bases. Mike Kreevich had a .301 BA, Milt Barnes claimed a .396 OBP and George Quinn had 85 free passes.

The St. Louis Cardinals (NL) defeated their cross-town rivals the St. Louis Browns (AL) in the 1944 World Series, 4-2.

1945

On July 10, 1945, the Veterans Committee inducted Dan Brouthers, Ed Delahanty, Jimmy Collins, Hugh Duffy, Fred Clark, Hughie Jennings, Jim O'Rourke, Roger Bresnan, King Kelley and Wilbert Robinson (manager) in the National Baseball Hall of Fame. .

Albert "Happy" Chandler, Second Baseball Commissioner

Albert Benjamin "Happy" Chandler was selected as Major League Baseball's second commissioner in 1945. Chandler was born in Corydon, KY, on July 14, 1898. He served as U.S. Senator, and was a two-term governor of Kentucky. He was frequently called the "players' commissioner." He served as Commissioner from April 24, 1945 to July 15. 1951, a six-year term.

Chandler boasted of many achievements which secured the baseball institution of our country. Shortly after assuming his office, he was challenged by multimillionaire Jorge Pasquel, who attempted to establish the new Mexican League to be part of Major League Baseball. He attempted to secure the talents of many major league players by offering them salaries up to triple amounts they were then paid. Chandler's response was to threaten those players, who jumped into the Mexican League with a five-year suspension.

In 1947, Chandler threw his support behind Brooklyn Dodgers owner, Branch Rickey's attempt to break the color barrier, with his signing of Jackie Robinson. He also threatened to suspend Philadelphia Phillies manager Ben Chapman for his racially insensitive taunts against Robinson. He further supported National League president Ford Frick's threat, to indefinitely suspend any St. Louis players, who proposed to sit out games against the Dodgers.

Chandler suspended Dodger's manager Leo Durocher for one year for "unpleasant incidents" including suspicious ties with gamblers. That year, during the World Series, Chandler placed two alternate umpires from the sidelines to work along the two baselines.

Chandler used money raised from the leagues' World Series radio broadcast contract to establish a players pension fund.

In 1949, Chandler negotiated a new seven-year contract with the Gillette Razor Company and the Mutual Broadcasting System, for radio-rights to the World Series, and funneled the proceeds into the Players Pension Fund. He repeated submitting the proceeds from 1950 as well.

Chandler was the third baseball commissioner to be elected into the National Baseball Hall of Fame in 1982.

Players Who Jumped to the Mexican League in 1945

Twenty-one players jumped to the Mexican League in 1945. Only 14 returned, when the ban was lifted in 1947. The players who jumped were Ace Adams, Alex Carrasquel, Bobby Estrella, Moe Franklin, Harry Feldman, Danny Gardella, Roland Gladu, Chili Gomez, George Hausman, Chico Hernandez, Lou Klein, Max Lanier, Sal Maglie, Fred Martin, Rene Montequez, Luis Olomo, Robert Ortiz, Mickey Owen, Nap Reyes, Adrian Zabola and Roy Zimmerman.

Jackie Robinson signed to play for the Brooklyn Dodgers in 1945 on a minor league contract. He was the first African-American to play in the major league baseball leagues in over sixty years. He played for the Dodger's minor league club the Montreal Royals.

In the midst of the Second World War, its ending was in doubt. Harry Truman, who became United States president in April, with the untimely death of FDR, asked the public to make many sacrifices. To follow the President's lead, the Major League owners, as a group, decided that they needed to sacrifice by not having the All-star game in 1945. The group realized that there would be a public outrage for canceling the game. Early in the season, there was a possibility that the season could not be played. Both the fans and the league owners knew that the sacrifice was to cancel the All-Star game. Since the game was scheduled to take place at Fenway Park in Boston, it was decided to postpone the game, and for it to be played at that location in 1946. As luck would have it, the war was ended in August of 1945. Ford Frick, then president of the National League, estimated that by canceling the All-Star game, there would be significant savings with approximately 500,000-less passenger miles spent.

There were 11 players who would have been selected in the 1945

All-Star game, who were never selected to play in any other All-Star game that was played after that one. They were Mike Tresh, catcher, Chicago White Sox; Ken O'Dea, catcher, St. Louis Cardinals; Nick Etten, first base, New York Yankees; Eddie Mayo, second base, Detroit Tigers; Oscar Grimes, third base, New York Yankees; Goody Rosen, outfield, Brooklyn Dodgers; Russ Christopher, pitcher, Philadelphia Athletics; Steve Gromek, pitcher, Cleveland Indians; Red Barrett, pitcher, St. Louis Cardinals; Hal Gregg, pitcher, Brooklyn Dodgers and Hank Wyse, pitcher, Chicago Cubs.

Replacement games were decided to be scheduled as a series of exhibition games, instead, which did not require the use of many passenger miles. The reason for scheduling these was to raise money for the American Red Cross and War Relief efforts. The games included the New York Yankees vs. the New York Giants, at the Polo Grounds, the Chicago Cubs vs. the Chicago White Sox at Comiskey Park, the Cincinnati Reds vs. the Cleveland Indians at Cleveland Stadium, the Brooklyn Dodgers vs. the Washington Senators at Griffith Stadium, the St. Louis Cardinals vs. the St. Louis Browns at Sportsman Park, the Philadelphia Athletics vs. the Philadelphia Phillies at Shibe Park. The Detroit Tigers vs. the Pittsburgh Pirates at Forbes Field (which ended up being canceled) and the Boston Braves vs. the Boston Red Sox at Fenway Park. Neither the fans nor players considered the exhibition games very satisfying.

The Chicago Cubs won 98 game as they capture the National League crown. The erstwhile rival, the St, Louis Cardinals were only three games behind. Hank Wyse, one of those pitchers who missed out on being in the All-star game received the honor of pitching his team in the World Series with 22 wins, but Ray Prim with but 13 wins capture the league best 2.40 ERA. Stan Hack led the Cubs in so many categories during the 1945 season when he scored 119 runs, spread his 193 hits, walked 99 times, and stole 12 bases. Phil Cavarretta had a league high .355 BA, hitting 34 doubles, had 249 TB, a .449 OBP and a .500 SA. Andy Pafko hit 12 triples, driving in 110 runs while Bill Nicholson smashed 13 home runs.

In the American League, the Detroit Tiger capture the league crown winning a low 88 games, barely edging out the Washington Senators by 1.5 games. Hal Newhouser managed to lasso three league highs with 25 wins, 1.81 ERA and striking out 212 batters. Roy Cullenbine scored 80 runs hit 27 doubles, drove in 93 runs, had 102 walks, a .398 OBP, .451 SA and slammed 18 home runs. Rudy York collected 157 hits, but matched Cullenbine with homers as he hit 18 of his own.

Pete Gray, an amputee, completed a season playing for the St. Louis Browns.

The Detroit Tigers (AL) defeated the Chicago Cubs (NL) in the 1945 World Series, 4-3.

1946

On July 12, 1946, the Veterans Committee inducted Joe Tinker, Johnny Evers, Frank Chance, Jack Chesbro, Clark Griffith (executive), Joe McGinnity, Eddie Plank, Rube Waddell, Jesse Burkett, Ed Walsh and Tommy McCarthy into the National Baseball Hall of Fame.

Bill McKinley was the first graduate of the umpire's training school to reach the major leagues.

On July 9, 1946, the All-Star game was played in Fenway Park, as it was scheduled in 1945. The American leaguers gave their National counterparts quite a trouncing with a 12-0 rout.

There was a tie in the final standings in the National League in 1946, during the first week of October, involving the St. Louis Cardinals and the Brooklyn Dodgers, whose teams had tied on September 29. They both had identical records of 96 wins and 58 losses. The Cardinals won the best of three playoff series by 4-2 and 8-4 scores.

The St. Louis Cardinals, although they tied with the Dodgers, they eventually won 98 games, but the playoff losses left the Dodgers two games behind. The Cardinals Howie Pollet, rose to the top of the

National League by winning 21 games and earned a low 2.10 ERA. Murray Dickson was on top of the heap too, as he had a .714 WP. Stan Musial showed no mercy in collecting seven league high performance by scoring 124 runs, scattering 228 hits, including 50 doubles, 20 triples, 366 TB, a .365 BA, 73 walks and a .587 SA. Not to be undone, Enos Slaughter offered the league's best with 130 RBIs. Slaughter and Musial had team highs, as Slaughter hit 18 homers while Musial earned a .434 OBP.

The Boston Red Sox had an easier time in getting the American League pennant, because the Detroit Tigers couldn't quite catch up, causing them to fall behind by 12 games. Dave Ferris won 25 games and had a .806 WP, while Bob Klinger had saved nine games; both Ferris and Klinger had league highs. Johnny Pesky peppered the outfield with 208 hits, tops in the league. He also had a team high, rapping 43 doubles. Ted Williams had a league-high monopoly for the rest of the offense as he scored 142 runs, had 343 TB, a .497 OBP, .667 SA and 156 walks. He also had three team highs with 38 home runs, 122 RBIs and a .342 BA.

The Cardinals really handcuffed Ted Williams with a defense that they called the "Williams Shift" in the 1946 World Series. They knew that most of Williams hitting was done on the right side of the baseball field, therefore the infield and the outfield shifted their defensive positions toward that field. This procedure raised havoc on Williams' hitting as he finished the 1946 series with a measly .200 BA and only one RBI.

The St. Louis Cardinals (NL) defeated the Boston Red Sox (AL) in the1946 World Series, 4-3.

1947

The BBWAA elected Mickey Cochrane, Frankie Frisch, Lefty Grove and Carl Hubbell into the 1947 National Baseballl Hall of Fame.

In 1947, Jackie Robinson was the first African-American to sign with any major league baseball team in sixty years. He signed with the Brooklyn Dodgers on April 15, 1947 although he actually signed his contract in 1945, and during the 1946 season played with the Dodgers. A Triple A team in Montreal, Canada. Robinson became the benchmark for African-Americans to be accepted as a major league players.

Larry Doby was the first African-American to sign with the Cleveland Indians on July 5, 1947.

The New York Giants were the next team to sign not only one, but two African-American baseball players, Hank Thompson and Monte Irvin, on the same day, July 8, 1947.

It took the Boston Braves two years to show off their new African-American recruit, Sam Jethroe. Sam proved his worth while he played for the Montreal, then an International League team .

The 1947 All-Star Game was played at Wrigley Field in Chicago on July 8, 1947. The American League edged the National League in a pitchers' battle which was won by the American loop, 2-1.

Showing baseball games on television began on the 1947 World Series, in the opening game of that series, played on September 30, 1947 between the New York Yankees and the Brooklyn Dodgers at Yankee Stadium in New York City. The game was transmitted to three stations, WABD, WCBS and WNBT, in New York City, and all the outlets along the Eastern Seaboard. The series was co-sponsored by the Ford Motor Company and the Gillette Safety Razor company, costing them $65,000.

The Brooklyn Dodgers took six years to show that they deserved to represent the National League in 1947 by winning 84 games. The St. Louis Cardinals were good too, but they petered out at the end of the season, by five games. Ralph Branca won 21 games and struck out 148 batters, while Hugh Casey saved 18 games. Jackie Robinson was a sensation, as he scored 125 runs, had 175 hits and 252 TB. Robinson managed to tie two of his teammates in different categories. He tied Dixie Walker as they both hit 31 doubles, and with Pee Wee Reese as each hit 12 home runs. Reese and Robinson were tops in the league, as Robinson stole 29 bases and Reese walked 104 times. Walker led the team in a few areas—252 TB, 94 RBIs, .306 BA and a .415 OBP.

The New York Yankees won 97 games in 1947, as the American League champions, while the Detroit Tigers lagged hopelessly behind by 12 games. Allie Reynolds won 19 games, striking out 129 batters, but had a league high with a .704 WP. Always a good closer, Joe Page was tied for the most league saves with Ed Klieman of the Cleveland Indians. Both had 17 saves.

First baseman Tommy Henrich, "Mr. Dependable," was the best triples leader in the league with 13. He also had other top team marks, with scoring 109 runs, hitting 35 doubles and had 98 RBIs. Joe DiMaggio paced the team with 168 hits, 29 four-baggers, 279 TB, and a high .533 SA. George Quinn had a high .395 OBP, as teammate Snuffy Sternweiss walked 89 times and Phil "Scooter" Rizzuto stole 27 bases.

The New York Yankees (AL) defeated the Brooklyn Dodgers (NL) in the 1947 World Series, 4-3.

1948

The BBWAA elected Herb Pennock and Pie Traynor into the 1947 National Baseball Hall of Fame.

On July 13, 1948 the All-Star Game was played a the Sportsman's Park in St. Louis as the American League won its third straight game, defeating the National League 5-2.

The Chicago White Sox's Pat Seerey was the fifth batter in major league history to Hit four home runs in a single game in an 11-inning game in Philadelphia on July 18, 1948.

Larry Doby, the Cleveland Indians outfielder, was the first African-American to hit a home run in the 1948 World Series on October 9, 1948. Another African-American Satchel Paige, a premier Negro League pitcher, was 42 when he signed a contract with the Cleveland Indians on July 9, 1948. He was considered the best pitcher to come our of the Negro Leagues.

Since the Boston Braves were in the World Series in 1914, their fortunes in 1948, winning 91 games, was a long wait. In winning the National League championship. The St. Louis Cardinals finished in second place 6.5 games behind. Johnny Sain pitched a league high 24 wins, as he struck out 137 batters while earning a 2.60 ERA. Warren Spahn pitched 15 more wins.

Third baseman Bob Elliott had the highest number of issued walks at 131, but he also scored 99 runs, hit 23 homers, had 100 RBIs, .423 OBP and a .582 SA. Tommy Holmes help the Braves rise to the top, by spraying 190 hits, had 257 TB and a .325 BA. Earl Torgenson swiped 19 bases.

Phil Masi is best known for being involved in the worst umpiring call in the 1948 World Series, or any other World Series games. In game one, of the 1948 series, being played at the Braves Field in Boston, Braves Johnny Sain and Indians Bob Feller were engaged in pitching a scoreless baseball game. Feller walked the first batter, catcher Bill Salkeld. Since Salkeld was a very slow runner, manager Billy Southworth replaced him with another catcher, Phil Masi. The next batter, Mike McCormick, sacrificed Masi to second. Then Feller, intentionally walked the next batter, Eddie Stanky, who was then replaced by Sibby Sisti. Then, to everyone's surprise, including umpire Bill Stewart, Feller made a pickoff attempt, throwing to shortstop Lou Beaudreau covering second, as Masi slid into the bag. Feller knew he was out, and to everyone's surprise, especially the 40,135 fans, who were at the game. Stewart called Masi safe. Everyone knew that Masi was out, except umpire Stewart. Feller and Boudreau were incredulous, and the safe call was accepted, but questioned. Tommy Holmes, the next batter hit a single, driving Masi home with the only run of the game. When Masi was questioned after the game, if he was indeed out, Masi affirmed that he was safe. But in a few years before his death, Masi confessed that he was out.

The Cleveland Indians (AL) defeated the Boston Braves (NL) in the 1948 World Series, 4-2.

1949

The BBWAA elected Charlie Gehriinger into the 1949 National Baseballl Hall of Fame, while the Veterans Committee selected Mordecai Brown and Kid Nichols.

The only All-Star Game ever to be played at Ebbets Field in Brooklyn on July 12,1949, was the fourth straight win for the American League over the National League, 11-7.

The Brooklyn Dodgers claimed the National League pennant, winning 97 games while runner-up St. Louis Cardinals were edged out of first by one game. Don Newcombe won 17 games, striking out 142 batters and pitched five shutouts. Preacher Roe added 15 wins as Ralph Branca had 13, but he had the team's highest WP at .722.

Jackie Robinson lead all of the National League's batters with a .342 BA, but he also lead the Dodgers in other offensive categories with 203 hits, including 38 doubles and 12 triples, as well as 124 RBIs, 313 TB, 37 stolen bases, .432 OBP and a .528 SA. Duke Snider and Gil Hodges were a tandem-hitting-twins as they both smashed 23 four-baggers apiece. Pee Wee Reese scored 110 runs and had 116 bases-on-balls.

The New York Yankees squeezed past the Boston Red Sox by a slim game, winning 97 games to steal the American League 1949 pennant. Vic Raschi led the Yankee twirlers with 21 wins, followed by Allie Reynolds' 17 and Tommy Byrne's 15. Eddie Lopat pitched four shutouts, while Byrne struck out 129 batters.

Surprisingly, little Phil Rizzuto led most of the Yankee's stats as he scored 110 runs, peppered 159 hits, including 22 doubles, 226 TB and 18 swiped bases. Tommy Henrich added 86 walks, .416 OBP, 24 homers, and .526 SA. Yogi Berra contributed 91 RBIs.

The New York Yankees (AL) defeated the Brooklyn Dodgers (NL) in

the 1949 World Series, 4-1.

Baseball players were often concerned that some fans in their love for a baseball player, might hurt them. That scenario finally occurred on June 14, 1949. Ruth Ann Steinhagen, a deranged Chicago Cubs fan, decided to kill Eddie Waikus because he had been traded to the Philadelphia Phillies during the off-season. She had been angry, because he had "left her" to play for the Phillies. When the Phillies came to Chicago to play, she decided she would kill him for leaving her. The shooting was not successful, because Waikus survived. She was arrested, and in the court trial, she was deemed to be mentally insane, and was remanded to a mental institution for the rest of her life.

Jackie Robinson, the first African-American to play in the majors, received a Most Valuable Player Award for the National League on November 1, 1949. It is quite ironic, that the award was on a Judge Kenesaw Mountain Plaque. The irony is, when the entry of African-Americans into the majors was proposed, Judge Landis always vetoed the notion of them entering the realm of the white man.

1950

Yogisms

Yogi Berra, born Lawrence Peter Berra became a baseball icon and will remain that way as long as the game of baseball exists. As a manager, when his New York Mets were 9-1/2 games behind the Chicago Cubs, and exclaimed to his players when they were losing, that "It's not over until its over." That case was proven to be true, as the Mets advanced to the playoffs, and played in the World Series. Some other Yogisms are sure to make you smile: "When playing in high summer temperatures, he would say, "It isn't the heat, it's the humility." About other team's prowess, he'd say," The other teams could make trouble for you, if they win."

He'd philosophize about playing baseball, as he said, "Baseball is ninety percent mental, and the other half is physical"and "You don't have to hit the ball hard. If your timing is good it'll go." He seemed to have trouble with his math: When asked if he would like his pizza cut in four pieces or six, he said "I don't think that I'm hungry enough for six pieces of pizza, give me four pieces."

He attended school until the eighth grade, which might explain why some of his yogis ms were paradoxical or unreasonable, like, when asked why he wore baseball gloves, said "Because my hands are cold." and his retort to his being in a slump. said "I ain't in a slump, I just ain't hitting."

He failed to sign with the St. Louis Cardinals because his friend, Joe Gargiola was given a bigger bonus than was offered to him. He signed with the Yankees in 1943, before joining the U.S. Navy, to serve during World War II. He debuted with the Yankees, in in 1946 and played with them until 1962. He later becoming a coach, and manager for the Yankees, New York Mets, and coach of the Houston Astros. He was elected to the Hall of Fame in 1972, and he passed away on September 22, 2015.

Sam Jethroe was the first African-American to play for the Boston Braves on April 18, 1950. The National League won the 1950 All-Star Game in a squeaker, 4-3, over the American League, played on July 11, 1950 at Comiskey Park in Chicago.

The Brooklyn Dodgers' Gil Hodges was the sixth batter in major league history to hit four home runs in a single game, at the Boston Braves' Forbes Field on August 31, 1950.

The Philadelphia Phillies won their first National League pennant since 1914 by winning 91 games. The Brooklyn Dodgers were scrambling to win in 1950 as they slid two games behind the Phillies. Robin Roberts won 20 games and pitched five shutouts while closer Jim Konstanty saved 22 games. Both Roberts and southpaw Curt Simmons, each struck out 146 batters.

Eddie Waikus, recovering after being shot by a deranged fan the year before, was the Phillies best scorer, plating 102 runs. Del Ennis sprayed 185 hits, including 34 doubles, 328 TB, .311 BA and a .551 SA. Ennis and Richie Ashburn both had league leading performances with Ennis' 126 RBIs and Ashburn's 14 triples. Catcher Andy Seminick rounded out the offense with .406 OBP and 68 walks.

The New York Yankees were the 1950 American League champions, when they won 98 games, while runner-up Detroit Tigers finished three games behind. Vic Raschi in winning 21 games, was the league's best pitcher, and had a .724 WP. Allie Reynolds won 16 and struck out 160 batters. Closer Joe Page's saved 13 games. They were instrumental in the Yankees winning the pennant.

The New York Yankees (AL) defeated the Philadelphia Phillies (NL) in the 1950 World Series, 4-0.

1951

The BBWAA elected Jimmie Foxx and Mel Ott into the 1951 National Baseballl Hall of Fame.

Mickey Mantle

Mickey Mantle became the heir-apparent to Joe DiMaggio, as DiMaggio was nearing his retirement in 1951. DiMaggio had been "king of the roost" since he started playing for the Yankees in 1936. DiMaggio didn't enjoy sharing the outfield with the new rookie, playing right field. During the third game of the 1951 World Series, against the New York Giants. Willie Mays hit a high fly ball to right-center field. Mantle was hustling to get under it. DiMaggio yelled, "I got it kid." Mickey was trying to get out of DiMaggio's way, caught his foot in an outfield drainage pipe, injuring his own foot. He would never be the same after that injury. Mantle played center field after DiMaggio retired, roaming that position until 1966. His last two years with the Yankees, Mantle played first, while regular first baseman Joe Pepitone took his spot in center field.

Mantle was born in Spavinaw, Oklahoma on October 20, 1931. When he was four, the family moved to Commerce, a nearby town. Mickey's father had always been a fan of Mickey Cochrane, then catcher for the Detroit Tigers. That's how Mickey got his name. When he was playing for the Yankees, Mantle found out that Cochrane's real first name was Harold, and Mickey expressed a sigh of relief saying, "I guess my father did not know that, or I would have had problems being called "Harold." Mantle was a good athlete, playing football and basketball, as well as baseball in high school.

Mantle began his professional baseball career playing with the Baxter Spring Whiz Kids team playing shortstop. While playing for that team, Yankee scout Tom Greenwade observed him while he looked at another player, Billy Johnson. Mantle hit three home runs that game. Greenwade forgot about Johnson, and had his eyes on Mantle. The following year, Greenwade was there at Mantle's graduation, and signed him to a Yankee contract.

He first played for the Yankees of Independence, Kansas. He was soon promoted to the Class-C Joplin Miners of the Western Association League, where he batted .383, smashed 26 homers and had 136 RBIs, but had a terrible time fielding at shortstop.

He was invited to spring training, and manager Casey Stengel was so impressed with him, that he promoted him to the team, playing right field. He was moved to center field where his played, until 1967, when he played first base until 1968. Regular first-baseman, Joe Pepitone, then played center field for those last two years. Mantle was elected to the National Baseball Hall of Fame in 1974 and he died on August 13, 1995.

Willie Mays

Willie Mays was born in Westfield, Alabama on May 6, 1931. Mays played on multiple sports teams when at Fairfield Industrial High

School. He set a then-record of scoring 17 points in basketball, and kicked a 40 yard field goal while playing as a football quarterback. When he was 16, and still in high school, he played for the Chattanooga Choo-Choos during the summer. The following year, he played for the Birmingham Black Barons of the Negro American League, leading them to the 1948 pennant, but they lost to the Homestead Grays of the Negro National League, 4-1. He hit a .262, but it was his superb running and fielding that caught the eye of of most baseball scouts.

In 1951, the New York Giants signed him to a $4,000 contract. He was assigned to a Giants affiliate, the Minneapolis Millers, a Class AAA American Association team. He was called up to the Giants on May 24, 1951.

The United State Army drafted him in 1952 during the Korean War. While at Fort Estis, Virginia, he learned the basket catch from another outfielder, Al Fortunato. He played for the New York Giants from 1951, 1954-1957 and the San Francisco Giants from 1958 to 1972. He was traded to the New York Mets, playing there from 1972-1973. When he retired in 1973, he had amassed 660 home runs and a lifetime .302 BA. He was elected to the National Baseball Hall of Fame on January 23, 1979.

Minnie Minoso was the first African-American to play for the Chicago White Sox on May 1, 1951.

The National League defeated the American League, 8-3 in the All-Star Game played on July 10, 1951 at Briggs Stadium in Detroit.

The Baseball owners had changed their procedures in voting a new term for the Baseball commissioner from 51 majority to 75 percent majority. When the vote for commissioner Happy Chandler was completed, there were nine votes for him and seven votes against him, Chandler quipped, "In all my years in politics, this is the first time I lost with a majority vote."

Ford Frick, Third Baseball Commissioner

Ford Frick, the National League president from 1934 to 1951, was the choice of the major league owners. Ford had been a teacher, a sports writer for the New York American, and a commissioner from September 20, 1951 to November 16, 1965. When he was the National League president, he had a major role in establishing the National Baseball Hall of Fame, honoring the best players in Baseball History.

As Commissioner, he stopped the threat of a players' strike to integrate the major leagues, as he faced the threat of the major leagues having their anti-trust exemption revoked by Congress. Frick was elected to the Baseball Hall of Fame in 1970.

Since major league games were initially televised, beginning with the 1947 World Series, they were viewed in black-and-white television. Beginning on August 11, 1951, televised games were viewed in color. The beginning event was a baseball doubleheader, being played at Ebbets Field, in Brooklyn. The visiting team was the Boston Braves, and they were televised on WCBS-TV of the Columbia Broadcasting System, with Red Barber and Connie Desmond as announcers.

The New York Giants and the Brooklyn Dodgers completed the National league 1951 season with identical 96-58 records. Those playoff games were played on October 1,2, 3, 1951. The Giants won game one, while the Dodgers won the second game. In the third game, the Dodgers were winning 4-2 in the ninth inning. In their half of the ninth inning, the Giants had runners on second and third, Pitcher Ralph Branca came in to relieve starter Don Newcombe. On the second pitch, Bobby Thomson hit a line drive into the left-field bleachers for a walk-off home run. It was called the "Shot heard around the world." But I doubt if anyone in China or India heard it.

During the season, Giants pitchers Sal Maglie and Larry Jansen, each had 23 wins, both league highs. Monte Irvin was the league's best

RBI leader with 121. Irvin also hit 11 triples. .312 BA and a .415 OBP. Shortstop Alvin Dark lead the team in scoring 114 runs and scattering 196 hits, including 41 doubles. The team's home-run leader was Bobby Thomson with 32 four-baggers, while second-sacker Eddie Stanky walked 127 times.

The New York Yankees collected 98 wins for the 1951 American League title, five games ahead of the Cleveland Indians. Yankee pitchers Vic Raschi and Ed Lopat each had 21 victories and four shutouts, but Raschi led the league in strikeouts with 164. Port-side hitter Yogi Berra came into his own, as he scored 93 runs, 161 hits including 22 doubles, 269 TB, 88 RBIs and a .492 SA. Hank Bauer and Gene Woodling had the same OBP, at .373, as Bauer had the highest .293 BA, while Woodling walked 62 times.

The New York Yankees (AL) defeated the New York Giants (NL) in the 1951 World Series, 4-2.

1952

The BBWAA elected Harry Heilman and Paul Waner into the 1952 National Baseballl Hall of Fame.

Emmett Littleton Ashford was the first African-American umpire to officiate in the Class C, Southwestern International League, as a substitute official, on February 20, 1952. Ashford later umpired in the American League on September 15, 1965. He umpired third base, in an opening game of the season, at Washington D.C., where the home team Senators were playing the Cleveland Indians on April 12, 1966.

The Nationals League edged the American League, 3-2 in an All-Star Game played at Schibe Park in Philadelphia on July 8, 1952.

The Brooklyn Dodgers took the National League pennant, winning 96 games, ahead of rival New York Giants by 4.5 games. Joe Black won 15 games, saving 15, and striking out 131.

Jackie Robinson scored 104 runs and led his team with a .308 BA.

The hitting of Duke Snider and Gil Hodges helped push the Dodgers to the top. Snider had 162 hits with 264 TB, while Hodges hit 27 doubles, 32 homers, 102 RBIs and a .500 SA. Short Stop Pee Wee Reese had the high league mark with 30 stolen bases.

The New York Yankees again captured the American League pennant in 1952, winning 95 games. The Cleveland Indians came close, but were two games behind. Yankees pitcher, Allie Reynolds was best in the league with a 2.06 ERA and in striking out 160 batters. Sluggers Mickey Mantle and Yogi Berra led the team's offense—Mantle hit 37 doubles, collected 291 TB, had a .311 BA, .394 OBP, 75 free trips and .530 SA. Berra scored 97 runs, hit 30 round-trippers and had 98 RBIs. Phil Rizzuto hit 10 triples and stole 14 bases.

The New York Yankees (AL) defeated the Brooklyn Dodgers (NL) in the 1952 World Series, 4-3.

1953

The BBWAA elected Dizzy Dean and Al Simmons into the National Baseball Hall of Fame in 1953, while in that same year, the Veterans Committee elected the following to the Hall: Chief Bender and Bobby Wallace, Ed Barrow (executive), Harry Wright (manager), and umpires—Bill Klem and Tom Connolly. Connolly and Klem were the first two umpires ever inducted into the Baseball Hall of Fame.

In 1953, a rule was passed where players were required to remove their gloves from the field, when it was their time to bat. It was enforced during the 1954 season. Another rule was passed, which stated that no equipment was to be left on the field.

Although Curt Roberts was the first African-American to play for the Pirates on April 13, 1954, Carlos Bernier was the first Hispanic-American to debuted with the Pirates on April 22, 1953. Bob Trice was the first African-American to play for the Philadelphia Athletics on September 13, 1953, and Ernie Banks was the first African-American to play for the Chicago Cubs on September 17, 1953.

The Boston Braves transferred their franchise to Milwaukee in 1953, to be called the Milwaukee Braves.

The National League defeated the American League, 5-1, in the All-Star Game, on July 14, 1953, played at Crosley Field in Cincinnati.

The Brooklyn Dodgers were making a habit of winning the National League pennant, and 1953 was no different as they won 105 games. The Milwaukee Braves were 13 games behind them. The Dodgers pitcher, Carl Erskine won 20 games, while striking out 187 batters, and pitched four shutouts. Billy Loes pitched 11 wins, but had a team high .786 WP. Three of his teammates had league high performances—Carl Furillo's .344 BA, Roy Campanella's 142 RBIs and Duke Snider scored 132 runs. Snider also had 198 hits including, 42 home runs and had a .627 SA. Other players did their share too! Jim Gilliam hit 17 triples and walked 100 times. Jackie Robinson had a .425 OBP and Pee Wee Reese stole 22 bases, while Snider and Furillo each hit 38 doubles.

The New York Yankees won 95 games, to take the 1953 American League title, but the Cleveland Indians fell 8.5 games behind them. Pitcher Eddie Lopat won 16 games, and had the lowest league 2.42 ERA. Whitey Ford, who won 18 games, struck out 110 batters. Vic Raschi in winning 16 games, had four shutouts.

Offensively, Mickey Mantle scored 105 times, while Gil McDougald scattered 154 hits, including 27 doubles. Yogi Berra carried the brunt of the offense, by hitting 27 homers, collected 283 TB, 108 RBIs and a .523 SA. Gene Woodling had a .306 BA, .429 OBP and walked 82 times.

The New York Yankees (AL) defeated the Brooklyn Dodgers (NL) in the 1953 World Series, 4-2.

1954

The BBWAA elected Bill Dickey, Rabbit Maranville and Terry into the 1954 National Baseball Hall of Fame.

Curt Roberts was the first African-American player to sign with the Pittsburgh Pirates, and Tom Alston signed with the St. Louis Cardinals on April 12, 1954. Nino Escalera and Chuck Harmon were the first African-American player to sign with the Cincinnati Reds on April 17, 1954. Carlos Paula was the first African-American player to sign with the Washington Senators on September 6, 1954.

Hank Aaron

Henry Aaron was born on February 5, 1834 in Mobile, Alabama. He attended Central High School, which did not have a baseball team. On November 20, 1951, baseball scout Ed Scott signed Aaron to play for he Indianapolis Clowns, a Negro American League team. He played shortstop for them, and was signed by the Boston Braves. Aaron set a new lifetime record, when he hit 755 home runs, breaking Babe Ruth's record of 714. Aaron was elected to the Baseball Hall of Fame in 1982.

The Milwaukee Braves' Joe Adcock was the seventh player in major league history to hit four home runs in a single game, at Ebbets Field, in Brooklyn on July 31, 1954.
The American League defeated the National League, 11-9 in the 1954 All-Star Game played at Municipal Stadium in Cleveland, on July 13, 1954.
The New York Giants were the 1954 National League champion by winning 97 games, while the Brooklyn Dodgers came up short, by five games. Johnny Antonelli pitched a .750 WP, Willie Mays the highest league average at .345, hitting 13 triples and .667 SA. Mays also scored 119 runs, 41 homers, 377 TB, 110 RBIs, and a .415 OBP. Don Mueller had a league mark by scattering 212 hits. He also hit 35 doubles as Bobby Thomson walked 90 times.
The Cleveland Indians had last won a World Series in 1948, and finally won the 1954 American League pennant by a record 111 wins. Many of the Indians were successful at gaining high league marks.

Pitchers Bob Lemon and Early Wynn tied for the best pitching mark at 23 games. Mike Garcia won 19, but also gained a league high of a .264 ERA. Two position players were also awarded high league marks as Larry Doby hit 32 homers and had 126 RBIs while Bobby Avila had a high .341 BA. Avila also scored the most runs at 112 and swatted 189 hits. Third baseman Al Rosen had a .412 OBP and a .506 SA., as Al Smith walked 88 times.

The New York Giants (NL) defeated the Cleveland Indians (AL) in the 1954 World Series. 4-0.

When the Indians appeared to be helpless against a powerful Giants team, Vic Wertz hit a drive in the first game to deep center field, which appeared to be an inside-the-park home run, but speedy Willie Mays trying to catch up to it, and with his back to everyone else, reached out, in desperation to make a basket catch, that stunned the Indians, including everyone else who witnessed it.

1955

On July 25, 1955, the BBWAA elected Joe DiMaggio, Gabby Hartnett, Ted Lyons and Dazzy Vance, while the Veterans Committee selected Frank "Home run" Baker and Ray Schalk into the National Baseball Hall of Fame.

The Philadelphia Athletics transferred their franchise to Kansas City, to be known as the Kansas City Athletics.

Elston Howard was the first African-American to sign with the New York Yankees, on April 14, 1955.

The National League squeaked by the American League, 6-5 at the 1955 All-Star Game, played at County Stadium in Milwaukee on July 12, 1955.

The Brooklyn Dodgers captured the 1955 National League pennant, by winning 98 games, as runner up Milwaukee Braves lagged 13.5 games behind.

Don Newcombe won 20 games, striking out 143 batters while Ed

Roebuck saved 12 games. Newcombe had the league's highest .800 WP as was Clem Labine who pitched in 60 games.

Duke Snider had the best league marks scoring 126 runs and had 136 RBIs. Snider also paced the Dodgers in most of the hitting categories, as he scattered 166 hits including 34 doubles, walked 104 times, had a .418 OBP and a 628 SA. Roy Campanella sported a .318 BA.

The New York Yankees copped their American League championship winning 96 games, while the Cleveland Indians, winners of the 1954 championship, came close, finishing three games behind.

There were no 20-game winners in the American League in 1955, but Whitey Ford had 18 wins, but he shared it with two other teams who had 18-game winners. They were Bob Lemon of the Cleveland Indians amd Frank Sullivan of the Boston Red Sox. Ford also struck out 134 batters and had five shutouts, while Bob Turley post 17 wins and six shutouts.

In the offense department, Mickey Mantle ranked as the league's best in home run hitter with 37. Mantle virtually dominated the Yankee offense scoring 121 times and had 158 hits, including 25 doubles, 316 TB, 113 walks, .431 OBP and .611 SA. He also shared the triples mark with Andy Carey, as both hit 11. Yogi Berra had 108 RBIs while Moose Skowron batted .319.

The Brooklyn Dodgers (NL) defeated the New York Yankees (AL) in the 1955 World Series, 4-3. The Brooklyn Dodgers World Series win mark was the first in franchise history, and would be the only one for the Dodgers franchise, since the club later moved to Los Angeles in 1958.

1956

On July 23, 1956. the BBWAA Elected Joe Cronin and Hank Greenberg into the National Baseball hall of Fame.

The National League beat the American League, 7-3 in the 1956 All-Star Game, played at Griffith Stadium, in Washington, D.C. on July 10, 1956.

The Brooklyn Dodgers managed to capture the 1956 National League pennant winning 93 games as they edged the Milwaukee Braves by only one game. Dodger Pitcher Don Newcombe, who won 27 games was the best in the league. He also had a WP of .794 only losing seven games, and also had five shutouts, striking out 139 batters.. Clem Labine also saved 19 games. Center fielder Duke Snider led the offense as he hit 43 home runs, a league high, and scored 112 runs, hit 33 doubles, 324 TB, 101 RBIs, .402 OBP, .598 SA and received 99 free passes. Second baseman Junior Gilliam, picked up the slack, collecting 178 hits, batting .300 and stealing 21 bases.

The New York Yankees added the 1956 pennant to their American League résumé, winning 97 games, while second place Cleveland Indians were nine games behind. Lefty Whitey Ford won 19 games, but his .760 WP and 2.47 ERA were the league's best marks. Mickey Mantle received three league batting awards hitting 52 home runs, 130 RBIs and a .353 BA. He Also contributed in other offensive ways, by scoring 132 runs, collecting 188 hits, 376 TB, .464 OBP, .705 SA, 112 walks and even stole 10 bases. Catcher Yogi Berra hit 29 doubles.

The New York Yankees (AL) defeated the Brooklyn Dodgers (NL) in the 1956 World Series, 4-3. The fifth game recorded a perfect game where no batter reaches first safely. Don Larsen who had pitched the second game, giving up six runs, and was removed, after pitching 1-1/3 innings, was the pitching artist in the fifth game, facing 27 batters without even one reaching first base safely. Larsen credited his use of a no windup delivery for his success. Sal Maglie, lost for the Dodgers, and the 27th and last batter, to face Larson was Dale Mitchell who tried to hold up on the last strike, but umpire Babe Pinelli called him out. After the game, Larsen said that his control was so perfect that he never before had such control over his pitches.

1957

In 1957, the Veterans Committee elected Sam Crawford and Joe McCarthy (manager) into the National Baseball Hall of Fame.

California, got its first two Major League teams in 1957, as the New York Giants and the Brooklyn Dodgers moved out west, and respectively, became the San Francisco Giants and the Los Angeles Dodgers.

John Kennedy was the first African-American to sign with the Philadelphia Phillies on April 22, 1957.

The American League edged the National League, 6-5 in the 1957 All-Star Game, played at Sportsman Park, in St. Louis on July 9, 1957.

The Milwaukee Braves, installed as a transferring franchise in 1953, finally emerged as the 1957 National League champion, winning 95 games, while runner-up the St. Louis Cardinals was eight games behind. Braves southpaw Warren Spahn was ranked as the top winner in the league with 21, while Bob Buhl, with 17 wins, struck out 18. Hank Aaron, the heir-apparent, to Babe Ruth's 714 lifetime home run record, was cited by the league with 44 homers and 132 RBIs. Aaron's hitting very much dominated the Braves as he added 118 runs scored, had 198 hits, 369 TB and .600 SA. Third-baseman Eddie Mathews hit 28 doubles, had 90 walks but shared triples totals with teammate Bill Bruton with nine each.

The New York Yankees copped the American League crown with 98 wins, while runner-up Chicago White Sox, could do no better than being eight games behind. Tom Sturdivant won 16 games, but he and Bobby Schantz lassoed high league honers—Sturdivant with 19 saves (starters in those days sometimes were used as relievers), and Schantz with a low 2.45 ERA. Mickey Mantle again led the parade of hitters for the Yankees, as he scored 121 runs, had 173 hits including 28 doubles, 34 four-baggers, 315 TB, 95 RBIs, .365 BA, .512 OBP, .665 SA, 145 Walks and 16 stolen bases. Gil MacDougald and Hank Bauer squabbled to see who would hit the most triples as each got nine.

The Milwaukee Braves (NL) defeated the New York Yankees (AL) in the 1957 World Series, 4-3. The Braves pulled an upset Series win, not by top pitchers Warren Spahn and Bob Buhl, but 30-year-old Lew Burdette, the Braves number three pitcher. He won all three of his starts by defeating Bobby Schantz, 4-2 in game two, Whitey Ford, 1-0 in game 5 and 1956 World series perfect game pitcher, Don Larsen in game 7, 5-0, to win it all.

1958

No one was elected to the National Hall of Fame in 1958, because the Veterans Committee said that no candidate received 75 per cent of the vote.

Ossie Virgil, Sr. was the first African-American to sign with the Detroit Tigers on June 6, 1958.

The American League slid by the National League, 6-5 in the 1958 All-Star Game, playing at Memorial Stadium in Baltimore, on July 8, 1958.

The Milwaukee Braves in their second consecutive National League pennant, won 92 games, while second place Pittsburgh Pirates were eight games behind. Warren Spahn was the Braves ace pitcher, and his 22 wins were the league's highest mark. Lew Burdette, last World Series best pitcher, had 20 wins. Joey Jay had a low 2.14 ERA. Hank Aaron also led the Braves attack that year, scoring 109 runs, scattering 196 hits, including 34 doubles, a 328 TB, 95 RBIs, .328 BA and 546 SA. He and Frank Torre had the same .386 OBP. Eddie Mathews hit 31 home runs and collect 85 walks.

The New York Yankees qualified as the American League titlist, winning 92 games, while their closest competitor, the Chicago White Sox, lagged behind by 10 games. The two best pitchers in their individual league categories were Bob Turley with 21 wins and Whitey Ford with a low 2.10 ERA. Mickey Mantle's 42 home runs was the leagues' best. Mantle also scored 127 runs, while he sliced 158 hits,

307 TB, 97 RBIs, .443 OBP, .592 SA, 129 walks and stole 18 bases.

The New York Yankees (AL) defeated the Milwaukee Braves (NL) in the 1958 World Series, 4-3.

1959

The Veterans Committee in 1959 elected Zach Wheat to the National Baseball Hall of fame. The Cleveland Indians' Rocky Colavito was the eighth player in major league history, to hit four home runs in a single game, at Baltimore on June 10, 1959.

Pumpsie Green was the first African-American to sign with the Boston Red Sox on July 2, 1959. He finished what Jackie Robinson started—Robinson was the first African-American to play in the majors, and Green was the last. The Red Sox were the last team to hire an African-American player.

The National League won the 1959 All-Star Game defeating the American League, 5-4 at Forbes Field, in Pittsburgh, on July 7, 1959. The fans liked the All-Star game played in July, and another All-Star Game was played a month later, at the Memorial Coliseum in Los Angeles. This 27th All-Star Game was won this time, when the American League defeated the National League, 5-3 on August3, 1959.

The Los Angeles Dodgers were the National League champion, as they won 88 games, while the Milwaukee Braves finished two games behind. The Dodgers' Don Drysdale struck out the most batters in the league, at 242. Drysdale also shared the team lead for shutouts with Roger Craig at four. Craig also had the lowest ERA at 2.06. Charlie Neal, Duke Snider, Wally Moon, Junior Gilliam and Gil Hodges shared a few offensive honors. Neal scored 103 runs, scattered 177 hits, including 30 doubles, 11 triples, and had 286 TB. Snider drove in 88 runs, had a .308 BA and .535 SA. Moon sported a .394 OBP , Gil Hodges hit 25 four-baggers, while Junior Gilliam collected 96 walks and pilfered 23 bases.

The Chicago White Sox captured their first American League pennant since the disastrous Black Sox Scandal in 1919, winning 94 games, while the Cleveland Indians were five games behind. The Sox pitchers collected two league honors as Early Wynn won 22 and Turk Lown saved 15 games. Second-baseman Nellie Fox won several team honors, as he scored 98 runs, rifled 191 hits, including 34 doubles. He also had 243 TB, a .306 BA and a .380 OBP. Sherm Lollar hit 22 homers, gathered 84 RBIs and a .451 SA. Shortstop Luis Aparicio stole 56 bases, while Jim Landis had 78 free passes.

The Los Angeles Dodgers (NL) defeated the Chicago White Sox (AL) in the 1959 World Series, 4-2.

The Continental League

People in many large cities were still waiting for a Major League franchise. By 1960, Branch Rickey, among others, started to formulate plans for a new major league, which would be called the Continental League. There were many cities that wanted a major league team, and their impatiences were wearing thin. Unlike the previous third leagues, like the Players League (1890) and the Federal League (1914-1915), the Continental League wanted to have a place in Major League Baseball. Its formulation was announced in 1959, and its proposed schedule of play was designed to be introduced in 1961. The League was disbanded, without playing a single game. It was a concession by William Shea, as part of his negotiation with Major League Baseball, to expand and incorporate at least eight new teams. On August 2, 1960, the Continental League formally disbanded.

1960

No one was elected to the National Hall of Fame in 1960, because the Veterans Committee said that no candidate received 75 per cent of the vote.

Since fans liked two All-Star Games played in 1959, two were also scheduled in 1960. The first game was won by the National League, which defeated the American League, 5-3, played at Municipal Stadium, in Kansas City, Missouri on July 11, 1960.

The fans were so excited to see all the baseball stars in the second game, only two days later from the first one, when the National League whitewashed the American League 6-0. That game was played at Yankee Stadium, in New York City, on July 13, 1960.

The National League pennant champion was the Pittsburgh Pirates, who won 95 games, but second place Milwaukee Braves only finished seven games behind.

The Pirates Vernon Law won 20 games while Bob Friend notched 18 wins. Law had a .690 WP and pitched three shutouts while Friend also had a 3.00 ERA, four shutouts, and striking out 183 batters. Third baseman Don Hoak scored 97 runs and walked 74 times. Dick Groat peppered 186 hits and a .371 OBP. Bob Skinner hit 33 doubles while stealing 11 bases. Dick Stuart hit 23 homers and had a .479 SA. Future Hall-of-Famer Roberto Clemente sported a .314 BA while collecting 761 TB.

The 1960 New York Yankees continued their habit of winning American League pennants. This time, with 97 wins, while runner-up Baltimore Orioles fell eight games behind. Art Ditmar won 15 games, while Whitey Ford pitched four shutouts. Ralph Terry struck out 92 batters and Bobby Schantz saved 11 games. The two "M" twins, Mickey Mantle and Roger Maris, provided offensive leadership as both had league highs—Mantle for 40 home runs and Maris for 112 RBIs. Mantle also scored 119 runs, and .399 OBP, had 111 walks and even swiped 14 bases. Maris also had a .581 SA. Moose Skowron and Tony Kubek added their support: Skowron with hitting 34 doubles and a .309 BA, while Kubek contributed 155 hits.

The Pittsburgh Pirates (NL) defeated the New York Yankees (AL) in the 1960 World Series, 4-3. In the seventh and deciding game of the 1960 World Series, Bill Mazeroski blasted a walk-off homer to win the game, 10-9, and the series, before 36,683 euphoric Pittsburgh fans. The Yankee loss precipitated the firing of aging manager Casey Stengel.

1961

The Veterans Committee elected Max Carey and Billy Hamilton to the National Baseball Hall of Fame in 1961.

Willie Mays of the San Francisco Giants was the ninth player to hit four home runs in a single game on April 30, 1961.

During the 1961 season, the American league expanded to ten teams, while the National League maintained the usual eight-team loop. In the expansion by the American League, Los Angeles was awarded an expansion franchise, and became known as the Los Angeles Angels. The Washington Senators transferred their American League franchise to Minnesota, and then was known as the Minnesota Twins.

Another set of twin All-Star Games was also scheduled for 1961. The first All-Star game was scheduled for Candlestick Park in San Francisco on July 11, 1961. The National League won a tight game from the American League, by a 5-4 score.

The second All-Star Game was scheduled across the country, at Fenway Park in Boston, on July 31, that was a tie 1-1 game, called at the end of nine innings due to rain.

The Cincinnati Reds won 93 games in taking the 1961 National League pennant. Los Angeles Dodgers were eight games behind. Joey Jay shined as the best league pitcher in two categories, with 21 wins and four shutouts. Jay shared the same number of wins with Warren Spahn of the Milwaukee Braves who also won 21 games. Jays' teammate, Jim O'Toole also had 19 wins. O'Toole and Jay also shared in each having four shutouts, tops in the league.

Vada Pinson ignited the Reds offense with 208 hits, a league high. He also hit 34 doubles and a .343 BA. Frank Robinson contributed with 37 triples, 32 four-baggers and .411 OBP, but led the league with a .611 SA.

Meanwhile, in the American League, the New York Yankees collected 109 wins to capture the title. A stone's throw behind them, was the Detroit Tigers at eight games out. Luis Arroyo copped league honors with 29 saves , a 2.19 ERA, and in pitching in 65 games.

Mickey Mantle, usually the best in most hitting categories, had some help from Roger Maris in 1961. Mantle peppered 163 hits, as both he and Roger Maris had 16 doubles apiece. Mantle also had a .317 BA, a .448 OBP, a .687 SA, swiped 12 bases and 126 walks. Maris scored 132 runs, and 366 TB. He also shared a league high 141 RBIs with Jim Gentile of the Baltimore Orioles who also had 141 RBIs.

Maris, in his second year with the Yanks, broke Babe Ruth's single season 60-homer record, by hitting 61 big ones. He and Mantle were neck-and-neck with home runs, until Mantle became injured late in the season, and he finished with 54 round-trippers. Other offensive contributions were credited to Bobby Richardson's 173 hits, and Tom Kubek's 38 doubles. A early form of a batting helmet was used in 1961 by the Yankees.

A note on Maris' record: There were those who stated that Maris' record was accomplished in a 162-game season, where Ruth hit his during a 154-game season in 1927. Among those who claimed that Maris' record was different was Baseball Commissioner Ford Frick. He insisted that an asterisk be placed after Maris' record, to show the two differences. That asterisk was implemented then, but was removed by Baseball Commissioner Fay Vincent on September 4, 1991 in consultation with the Committee for Statistical Accuracy.

The New York Yankees (AL) defeated the Cincinnati Reds (NL) in the 1961 World Series, 4-1.

1962

The BBWAA elected Bob Feller and Jackie Robinson to the National Baseball Hall of Fame in 1962 as the Veterans Committee selected Edd Roush and Bill McKechnie (manager) .

The National League added the New York Mets and the Houston 45s so that both leagues now had ten teams. The lineup of both leagues continued until end of the 1968 season.

John "Buck" O'Neil was the first African-American to serve as coach in the major leagues. He was hired to serve as a coach as one of six coaches for the Chicago Cubs on May 29, 1962. Previously, he had served that club in several different capacities.

The National League defeated the American League in the first All-Star Game of that year, 3-1, at D.C. Stadium in Washington, D.C. on July 10, 1962.

The second 1962 All-Star Game was won by the American League, as they defeated the National League 9-4, at Wrigley field In Chicago on July 30, 1962.

The San Francisco Giants were awarded the 1962 National League pennant after winning 103 games. Los Angeles Dodgers were "breathing down their necks," finishing one game behind.

Jack Sanford, the Giant's ace, won 27 games. Billy O'Dell also won 19 games, including two shutouts, while striking out 195 batters. Stu Miller's 19 saves and his pitching in 59 games were the league's highest marks. Willie Mays claimed league summits, for 49 homers and 382 TB. He also led the Giants scoring 130 runs, hit 36 doubles, 141 RBIs, .615 SA and walked 78 times. Orlando Cepeda led spreading 191 hits, while Felipe Alou had the best team BA with .316.

The New York Yankees won three American League pennants in a row, by winning 96 games. The Minnesota Twins chasing the Yanks most of the season, ended five games behind them.

The Yankees' Ralph Terry was the league's best pitcher, chalking up 23 wins. Terry also whiffed 176 batters. Marshall Bridges had 18 saves, while appearing in 52 games.

Bobby Richardson lead the Yankees attack, scoring 99 runs, amassing 209 hits, including 38 doubles. Roger Maris swatted 33 four-baggers and had 100 RBIs. Mickey Mantle had a .486 OBP, .605 SA and 100 walks. The New York Yankees (AL) defeated the San Francisco Giants (NL) in the 1962 World Series, 4-3.

1963

In 1963, the Veterans Committee elected Sam Rice, Eppa Rixey, John Clarkson and Elmer Flick to the National Baseball Hall of Fame.

Elston Howard was the first African-American to win the Most Valuable Player Award for the American League in 1963.

Major League Baseball went back to having only one All-Star Game on July 9, 1963, as the National League beat the American League 5-3 at Municipal Stadium in Cleveland.

The Los Angeles Dodgers captured the National League pennant with 99 wins, as runner-up St. Louis Cardinals trailed behind by six games.

Sandy Koufax was the league's best pitcher as he won 25 games, struck out 305 batters and had a 1.88 ERA. Koufax also shared that win-record with Juan Marichal of the San Francisco Giants who also had 25 wins. Teammate Don Drysdale won 19, but also lost 17, striking out another 251 opponents. Ron Perranowski had league marks for a .842 WP and for pitching in 69 games.

The Dodgers offense was led by speedy Maury Wills, who scored 83 runs, had 159 hits, 19 doubles and 44 walks. Frank Howard socked 28 homers, while Tommy Jones earned a .326 BA.

The New York Yankees continued to extend their string of American League pennants, to four as they won 104 games. Their closest competitor was the Chicago White Sox, who were 10.5 games out of first place. Whitey Ford won 24 games while striking out 189 batters. Jim Bouton won 21 games while pitching six shutouts. Closer Hal Reniff saved 18 games.

Bobby Richardson had a league high in slashing 209 hits. Tom Tresh scored 91 runs, hit 28 doubles, claimed a .371 OBP and walked 83 times.

The Los Angeles Dodgers (NL) defeated the New York Yankees (AL) in the 1963 World Series, 4-1.

1964

1964 had the largest number of inductees, as BBWAA elected Luke Appling into the National Baseball Hall of Fame, while the Veterans Committee selected Red Farber, Heinie Manush and Burleigh Grimes, Tim Keefe, John Walsh and Miller Huggins (manager).

On July 7, 1964, the National League beat the American League in the All-Star Game, 7-4 at Shea Stadium in New York City.

The St. Louis Cardinals were the National League victors, as they won 93 games, edging the Philadelphia Phillies, by only one game.

Ray Sadecki won 20 games for the Cardinals, while Bob Gibson had 19 wins, whiffed 246 swingers and earned a 3.01 ERA.

Curt Flood and Ken Boyer both spearheaded the Cards attack-- Flood, with his 211 hits and Boyer's league-leading 119 RBIs. They both led their team in other offensive categories: Flood's .318 BA; Boyer scoring 100 runs, 30 doubles, 10 triples, 25 round-trippers, .367 OBP, .489 SA and 70 free trips to first.

The New York Yankees were led by the quotable Yogi Berra to corner the American League pennant, winning 99 games, beating the Chicago White Sox by one game. Jim Bouton pitched six shutouts. Whitey Ford led the Yankee pitching staff with 17 wins,, eight shutouts and a 2.13 ERA. Al Downing, with his blazing fastball, struck out 219 batters, a league-high mark.

Mickey Mantle led the "Bombers" scoring with 92 runs, hit 35 homers, 111 RBIs, 99 walks and a .591 SA. Mantle's .426 OBP , was the best in the league. Bobby Richardson had 181 hits while Elston Howard hit 27 doubles and earned a .313 BA.

The St. Louis Cardinals (NL) defeated the New York Yankees (AL) in the 1964 World Series, 4-3. At the conclusion of that World Series, the New York Yankees fired their manager, Yogi Berra, and hired the Cardinal's winning manager, Johnny Keane.

1965

On July 26, 1965 the Veterans Committee elected Pud Galvin to the National Baseball Hall of Fame.

The National League continued having a four-game win streak, as they defeated the American League in the All-Star Game, winning by a slim 6-5 margin, at Metropolitan Stadium in Bloomington, Minnesota on July 13, 1965.

William Eckert, Fourth Baseball Commissioner

In August 1964, longtime commissioner, Ford Frick announced his intention to retire the following year. Retired Air force Lieutenant General William "Spike" Eckert was named Commissioner of Baseball, on November 17, 1965. He was selected from a list of over 150 names. The owners wanted someone from outside the game, who would be respected by Congress. Eckert knew little about the sports business, or about the game.

The owners installed Lee McPhail, as a more qualified candidate, as Eckert's assistant. They also hired Joe Reichler, a career sports writer, to head public relations. Eckert knew nothing about baseball as a industry, and at times, he failed, in circumstances which required his leadership.

Eckert brought an understanding of business and bureaucracy to the position. His quiet demeanor helped with the perception that he was ill-equipped to handle the array of head-strong owners, and the demands of an emerging player's' union.

Five deputies were chosen to help run the commissioner's office in public relations, broadcasting, player affairs, amateur baseball and the administration for the office. The General's style didn't seem to be in tune to the job he inherited. Eckert left office on February 4, 1969, when the incoming commissioner, Bowie Kuhn, took office.

The Los Angeles Dodgers captured the National League pennant, winning 97 games. Runner-up San Francisco Giants were edged out by two games. Sandy Koufax was almost perfect in garnering an assortment of high league marks with 26 wins, .765 WP, 2.04 ERA and 382 strikeouts. Koufax's strikeouts set a new season record for left-handers, wiping out Rube Waddell's 349 strikeout mark, for the Philadelphia Athletics in 1904. Koufax also had eight shutouts. Maury Willis set the offensive tone for the Dodgers, scoring 92 runs, slapping 186 hits and stealing 94 bases. Willie Davis had a .609 OBP while Lou Johnson had a .391 SA.

The Minnesota Twins grabbed the American League pennant, since transferring the Washington Senators franchise to the Twin Cities in 1961, by winning 102 games. The Chicago White Sox could do no better than second as they slipped seven game behind the winners. With their pennant won, they also gathered nine league marks. Mudcat Grant claimed three of those for pitching, as he won 21 games, and added a .750 WP and six shutouts. Zoilo Versalles captured four of the leagues high summits, as he scored 126 runs, hit 45 doubles, 308 TB, but in capturing 12 triples, he had to share the same number with Carl Yastrzemski, of the Boston Red Sox, who also hit 12 triples. Tony Oliva, pulling two of those league-highs, scattered 185 hits and won a .321 BA. Oliva had three team highs, with 98 RBIs, .384 OBP and a .491 SA. Versalles also stole 27 bases.

The Los Angeles Dodgers (NL) defeated the Minnesota Twins (AL) in the 1965 World Series, 4-3.

1966

Marvin Miller and the Baseball Players Union

There have been owners for professional baseball teams since the Nineteenth Century, and it always has been a struggle for the players to get the respect that they need to play baseball. Even though most baseball players play the sport for their love of the game, the owners, in their greed, have consistently over the years, treated their players as chattel. All players want to be treated as people, whereas the owners look at them as things. The Reserve Clause was first implemented by the owners in 1879. At that time, they felt that it was necessary to prevent their players from jumping to other teams, usually after every season, but sometime in the middle of a season. The Reserve Clause was established so that any player who was originally signed by a team became the property of that team as long as they played professional baseball. The players, through the years, have always felt like they were slaves.

    The first group of players, who decided to organize, was started in the 19th Century by Montgomery Ward. Ward, and many others after him, formed different player organization, but they seemed to lack the power to change anything. Unfortunately, most players lack the ability to get anything done. In 1922, Congress passed a bill which protected the major leagues, while favoring the Reserve Clause, to protect the major leagues.

    In 1966, that all changed. Marvin Miller was elected executive director for the Players Union. In the spring of that year, he visited MLB spring training camps. The player seeing his talent to help them, elected him.

    In 1938, he graduated from New York University, with a degree in economics. Miller was able to control the players into an action which helped them in their wages and personal rights. The players' strikes in 1981 and 1994 gained great gains for the players, He was succeeded by Donald Fehr in 1985, who later stepped down in 2009. The next Executive Director was Michael Weiner, who died on November 21, 2013. The union is now directed by Tony Clark, who is the only former player to serve in that position.

    The Milwaukee Braves National League franchise was transferred to Atlanta in 1966, and became known as the Atlanta Braves.

Emmett Ashford became the first African-American umpire to work in the American League after 14 seasons in the minors.

Busch Stadium, in St. Louis, was the site of the All-Star game as the National League squeaked by the American League, 2-1 on July 12, 1996.

The Los Angeles Dodgers captured the National League pennant in 1966, for the second straight year, as they won 95 games. They barely got by the San Francisco Giants who were 1.5 games back. Sandy Koufax continued his dominance in the senior loop by grabbing four of the five pitching league high marks. He had 27 wins, including five shutouts, 317 strikeouts and a 1.73 ERA. The remaining high league mark went to Phil Regan, who saved 21 games. Willie Davis led the hitting and scoring attack, plating 74 runs, had 177 hits, 31 doubles and 253 TB. Ron Fairly had the best .288 BA, .380 OBP and .484 SA while Jim Lefebre swatted 24 circuit clouts and 74 RBIs, as Wes Parker trotted to first 69 times.

The Baltimore Orioles gained the American League pennant in 1966 winning 97 games as the Minnesota Twins remained nine games behind the pace. Jim Palmer won 15 games while closer Stu Miller saved 18 games. In the Orioles offense, one would think that it was a one-man show, as Frank Robinson showcased his high league performances when he scored 122 runs, hit 49 home runs, had a 367 TB, 122 RBIs, displayed a .316 BA, .415 OBP and .637 SA. He also had a few team high-hitting, marks with 182 hits, 35 doubles and 87 walks.

The Baltimore Orioles (AL) defeated the Los Angeles Dodgers in the 1966 World Series, 4-0.

1967

On July 23, 1967, Red Ruffing was inducted into the National Baseball Hall of Fame by the BBWAA vote in January, while executive Branch Rickey and Lloyd Waner were installed in the Hall, by the Veterans Committee who selected them in February.

The National League continued its winning ways, by sneaking by the American League, in the All-Star Classic, 2-1, played at Anaheim Stadium, in Anaheim, California on July 11, 1967.

The St. Louis Cardinals won the National League 1967 pennant. Dick Hughes won 16 games including three shutouts, Steve Carlton won 14, but struck out 168 batters and Joe Hoerner saved 15 games. Lou Brock captured two league leading performances with 52 stolen bases, and scoring 113 runs, which he share equally with home-run hitter Hank Aaron, of the Atlanta Braves, who also scored 113 runs. Orlando Cepeda had another league high with 111 RBI and team highs for, hitting 37 doubles, 25 home runs, 325 TB, .403 OBP and a .524 SA. Curt Flood was the team's best hitter, batting .335.

The Boston Red Sox finally won their first American League pennant in 21 years, with a 92- game mark. Jim Lonborg earned two league high marks for winning 22 games and striking out 246 batters. Carl Yastrzemski was the league's best offensive player in seven categories: 112 runs, 189 hits, 121 RBIs, .328 BA, .421 OBP, .622 SA, but in the last one, his 44 home runs, he had to share with Minnesota Twins' Harmon Killebrew, who also had 44 round-trippers. Yastrzemski also had team highs, with 31 doubles and 360 TB.

The St. Louis Cardinals (NL) defeated the Boston Red Sox (AL) in the 1967 World Series, 4-3.

1968

Joe Medwick was inducted into the National Baseball Hall of Fame on July 23, 1968 when he was elected by BBWAA in January. The Veterans Committee inducted Kiki Cuyler and Goose Goslin into the Hall in February.

The National League, over the years, continued to get better in the All-Star Classic, but in 1968, it was great. On July 9, 1968 at the Astrodome in Houston, they shutout the American League, 1-0.

The Kansas City Athletics, American League franchise, was

transferred to Oakland, and were known as the Oakland Athletics, and sometimes were called the A's.

The St. Louis Cardinals, in 1968, captured the National League pennant, winning 97 games. Runner-up San Francisco, finished nine games behind. Bob Gibson captured three league marks: 13 shutouts, 1.12 ERA and striking out 268 batters. Joe Hoerner saved 17 games. Lou Brock received high league marks in three categories: 46 doubles. 14 triples and 62 stolen bases. Brock also had team highs in scoring 92 runs, 276 TB and .418 SA. Curt Flood had 186 hits, .301 BA and .339 OBP.

Denny McLain sparked the Detroit Tigers in winning the American League pennant by delivering 31 wins, the highest number of wins since Pete Alexander won 33 in 1916 for the Philadelphia Phillies. The Tigers won 103 games, while the Baltimore Orioles, their closest competitor, were left behind by 12 games. Beside the most pitching wins, McLain also pitched a high .838 WP, best in the league. Dick McAuliffe, scored 95 times, another league high. He also hit 29 doubles, 10 triples and walked 82 times. Jim Northrup scored 153 runs, spread 153 hits and had 90 RBIs. Completing the team hitting, Willie Horton slammed 36 round-trippers, 278 TB, .285 BA and .543 SA.

The Detroit Tigers (AL) defeated the St. Louis Cardinals (NL) in the 1968 World Series, 4-3.

1969

The BBWAA inducted Waite Hoyt and Stan Coveleski into the National Baseball Hall of Fame on July 28, 1969, elected in January, while the Veterans committee inducted Roy Campanella and Stan Musial into the Hall.

Bowie Kuhn, Fifth Baseball Commissioner

Bowie Kuhn became the fifth baseball commissioner in 1969. His time as commissioner was marked by a labor strike (1981), owner disenchantment and the end of the reserve clause.

He suspended numerous players for involvement in drugs and gambling. He suspended Denny McLain for involvement in a bookmakers operation, and later, because McLain carried a gun. He barred Willie Mays (1979) and Mickey Mantle (1983) from baseball, because of their involvement in casino promotion. They were later reinstated by Kuhn's successor Peter Ueberroth in 1985.

Curt Flood

On October 7, 1969, the St. Louis Cardinals traded Curt Flood and six other players to the Philadelphia Phillies. He refused to go, based on the Phillies poor record, dilapidated stadium and racist fans.

He wrote to Commissioner Kuhn demanding that he be declared a free agent, but Kuhn refused based on the elements in the Reserve Clause. Flood filed a lawsuit against Kuhn and MLB. He likened the Reserve Clause to slavery. The Supreme Court sided with MLB. Flood sat out the 1970 season, but was traded to the Washington Senators in the American League, who was in last place. He only played in 13 games that year.

An infrequent rule change which did not happen that often, occurred in 1969, as the strike zone was reduced from the armpits to the top of the knees, and the mound height was changed, reducing it from a height of 15 inches to 10 inches. It has been speculated that the reduce mound rule was changed because Bob Gibson had earned a 1.12 ERA in in 1968, that many thought to be extremely low.

After the 1968 season, the Major League Baseball Players' Association and the owners concluded the first collective bargaining agreement in Major League Baseball history, but the owners refused to increase the players pension agreement.

The Association felt that the television agreements with major league baseball, had tremendously increased, but the owners still balked at increasing the pension benefits. In response to the owners refusal, the Association decided to boycott Spring Training in 1969. When this occurred, the owners still refused, because they all lost money on Spring Training anyway. The television networks did not want to televise minor league baseball players participating in Spring Training. In that response, Commissioner Bowie Kuhn pressured the owners to accede to a pension increase. All the players. then returned to their spring training sites.

Willie Davis, of the Los Angeles Dodgers, completed a 31-game hitting streak in 1969.

Kansas City, Missouri received an expansion franchise to play in the American League, and known as the Royals. The franchise was given to Kansas City to replace their earlier Athletics franchise which was moved to Oakland.

The Montreal Expos and the San Diego Padres were selected to receive National League franchises in 1969.

The American League continue to struggle with losing many All-Star Games, and the 1969 edition which played on July 23, 1969 was no different. The National League won this time 9-3 at the All-Star game played at R.F.K Memorial Stadium in Washington, D.C.

In the National League, the New York Mets defeated the Atlanta Braves, 3-0. At the World Series, the Baltimore Orioles played the New York Mets. The Mets beat the Orioles, 4-1.

The World Series since 1903 was the best of seven, except for three years from 1919 to 1921 in which the series was the best of nine. Why the two major leagues went to the best of nine and later to continue the best of seven, is unknown.

The first year of a divisional playoff was 1969. The New York Mets won the Eastern Division of the National League, in the best of five series and defeated the Atlanta Braves, 3-0. In the American Division Series, Baltimore Orioles won over the Minnesota Twins 3-0. The New York Mets were established as an expansion team in the National

League in 1962, but in 1969 the team captured the league with 100 wins. The team had many bad seasons when established, and in 1969, were called "The Miracle Mets." The Chicago Cubs were their closest competitor falling eight games behind.

The Met's Tom Seaver captured two league highs by pitching 25 wins and having a .781 WP. He also struck out 208 batters. Tommy Agee scored 97 runs, hit 26 home runs and collected 262 TB. Cleon Jones spread 164 hits, including 25 doubles, .422 OBP. The Baltimore Orioles won 109 games as they claimed the American League East division title. The Detroit Tigers, trying to overcome their deficit, still finished 19 games behind. Mike Cuellar won 23 games for the Orioles, while Jim Palmer poster a 2.39 ERA and Eddie Watt saved 16 games. Frank Robinson scored 111 runs, a .417 OBP, walked 88 times and posted a .308 BA. Boog Powell hit 37 home runs, 298 TB and had 121 RBIs and a .559 SA. Paul Blair scattered 178 hits and stole 20 bases as Dave Johnson hit 34 doubles.

When the National and American Leagues were the only two leagues, it was comparatively easy for the playoff match ups, because the first place team in each league played each other in the World Series. That continued until 1969, when each league was divided as East and West teams, and each league then had 12 teams each. The National League added Montreal Expos and the San Diego Padres while the American loop had two new teams, The Seattle Pilots and the Kansas City Royals.

Then the real playoffs began with the winner of each division playing one another. The winner would be declared the pennant winner of its league in the best of seven games.

In 1969, the Baltimore Orioles (E) beat the Minnesota Twins (W), 3-0 for the America League pennant. The New York Mets (E) defeated the Atlanta Braves (W), 3-0, for the National League championship.

The New York Mets defeated the Baltimore Orioles in the 1969 World Series, 4-1.

1970

Lou Boudreau was elected to the National Baseball Hall of Fame in 1970 by BBWAA, while the Veterans Committee selected Earl Coombs, Jesse Haines and Executive Ford Frick to the Hall.

Milwaukee was awarded an American League expansion franchise to be known as the Milwaukee Brewers. With the bankruptcy of the Seattle Pilots franchise, it was transferred to Milwaukee, as an American League team during which they remained until 1998, when they were transferred to the National League.

The National League had trouble in recent years in putting the American League away in the All-Star Game, they now did just that at Riverfront Stadium in Cincinnati on July 14, 1970, when they barely won 5-4, topping the American League.

The Cincinnati Reds won 102 games to win the West Division, of the 1970 National League. Runner-up Los Angeles Dodgers didn't stand a chance, as they slid 14.5 games behind in second place. Jim Merritt won 20 games for the Reds while while Wayne Granger claimed the league's high mark with his 35 saves. Pete Rose, Bobby Tolan and Johnny Bench gained four top league spots. Rose collected 205 hits, which he shared his top spot with Billy Williams of the Chicago Cubs, who also had 205 hits. Tolan captured his high by pilfering 57 bases while Bench copped two highs with 45 homers and 148 RBIs. All of these league winners also had team highs: Rose scored 120 runs and hit 37 doubles, as Bench collected 355 TB. Although first-baseman Tony Perez did not collect any league highs, he had several team highlights with a .317 BA, .405 OBP and a .589 SA.

The American League East Division championship was claimed by the Baltimore Orioles. They had the league's top pitchers, with 24 games each, but they also had to share their title with the Minnesota Twins' Jim Perry who also had 24 wins. Those Orioles pitchers were: Mike Cuellar, who hit the jackpot that year, as he also had the league's highest .750 WP, Jim Palmer, who pitched five shutouts, struck out 199 batters and had a 2.71 ERA.

An assortment of players contributed to the Orioles drive for the pennant: Don Buford scored 99 runs and drew109 walks. Brooks Robinson had 168 hits including 31 doubles. Boog Powell slammed 35 homers, 114 RBIs, .417 OBP, .549 SA and 289 TB , while Paul Blair stole 24 bases.

In the second year of the division playoffs, the Baltimore Orioles (E) defeated the Minnesota Twins (W), 3-0 for the American League championship. The Cincinnati Reds (W) beat the Pittsburgh Pirates (E), 3-0 for the National League title, 3-0,

The Baltimore Orioles (AL) defeated the Cincinnati Reds (NL) in the 1970 World Series, 4-1.

1971

In 1971, the Negro Leagues Committee elected one of their African-American players, Satchel Paige, who deserved to be in the National Hall of Fame. The Veterans Committee inducted the following: Dave Bancroft, Jake Beckley, Chick Hafey, Harry Hooper, Joe Kelley, Rube Marquard and George Weiss (executive).

The American League finally won an All-Star Game, defeating the National League 6-4 on July 13, 1971 at Tiger Stadium in Detroit.

The Pittsburgh Pirates earned the National League East Division title by winning 97 games. St. Louis came close, but they were three games back. Dock Ellis won 19 games, Steve Blass pitched five shutouts and Dave Guisti save 30 games, the league's best. Willie Stargell dominated the Pirate offense as he scored 104 runs, hit a league high of 48 homers, had 321 TB, 125 RBIs, 83 walks, .401 OBP and a .628 SA. Roberto Clemente scattered 178 hits and had a .341 BA, while Al Oliver hit 31 doubles.

Baltimore won the East Division crown of the American League winning 101 games. Another also-ran team, the Detroit Tigers were runner-up, a distant 12 games away.

Dave McNally won 21 games, and was cited by the league with a high .808 WP, while Jim Palmer struck out 184 batters and claimed a 2.68 ERA. Offensively, Don Buford had the highest run total for the league at 99, 89 bases-on-balls and 15 stolen bases, while Brooks Robinson slapped 166 hits. Frank Robinson powdered 28 homers and had a .510 SA. Merv Rettenmund had a .318 BA and a .424 OBP.

In the National League playoffs, the Pittsburgh Pirates (E) beat the San Francisco Giants (W) to win the pennant, 3-1. In the American League playoffs, the Baltimore Orioles (E) defeated the Oakland Athletics (W), 3-0.

The Pittsburgh Pirates (NL) defeated the Baltimore Orioles (AL) in the 1971 World Series, 4-3.

1972

Buck Leonard and Josh Gibson were selected by the Negro Leagues Committee to be inducted into the 1972 National Hall of Fame. The BBWAA selected Yogi Berra, Sandy Koufax and Early Wynn, while the Veterans Committee chose Lefty Gomez, Ross Youngs and Will Harridge (executive).

Roberto Clemente

Roberto Enrique Clemente Walker was born on August 18, 1934, at Barrio Anton, Carolina, Puerto Rico. He played his first game on April 17, 1955, and played 18 seasons for the Pittsburgh Pirates. He was the first Hispanic-American to play in the major leagues. He was inducted into the National Hall of Fame in 1973. His untimely death set a precedent, which allowed a candidate to be eligible for induction into the Hall. In that new precedent, an person who had been deceased for at least six months, would be eligible. Clemente, on December 31,

1972, was traveling to Nicaragua to deliver aid to the poor when the plane he was in, crashed.

The Washington Senators American League franchise was transferred to Arlington TX, and known as the Texas Rangers.

Two of the Senators minor league teams in Burlington, Vermont and Geneva, New York in 1972, continued to be called by the their "Senators" logo because the transfer of the Senators was not finalized for those two teams.

Bernice Gera

Since the demise of the All American Girls League, it wasn't until 1972 that a woman wished to become a baseball umpire. Her name was Bernice Gera. She had been active in woman's rights and decided that she would like to become an umpire.

Mrs. Gera wanted to be an umpire, and she took the necessary steps to become one. She attended an umpire school in Florida in 1967, and was able to execute all the requirements to become one.

The National Association of Baseball Leagues refused to accept her as an umpire. They stated that she had to be a certain height and weight to be accepted. No leagues would hire Mrs. Gera. After appealing to the courts, she was allowed to officiate in the New York-Penn league.

She was assigned to umpire a game at McCullen Stadium in Geneva, New York, on June 25, 1972, as Auburn Twins were playing the Geneva Senators in a New York-Penn League game.

Since the Geneva team had recently been aligned with the Washington Senators. When the franchise was moved to Texas, no provision had been made to change the Geneva logo from Senators to Rangers.

In the fourth inning, Gera called Terry Ford, an Auburn player, safe at second, during a double play. Almost immediately, she called him out. Auburn manager, Nolan Campbell came onto the field to question her reversed call. He stated that her first mistake was in putting on an umpire's uniform, and her second mistake was in blowing the call. She ejected him, but she decided to resign which she did between games of the scheduled double header. She was scheduled to umpire behind the plate for the second game. At the conclusion of the first game, she went into the general manager's office and announced that she was quitting. As she left the park, a car was waiting for her as she left the area.

Speculation was that her goal was not to be an umpire, but to prove that a woman could do it. It appeared the her umpiring skills were spotty, and when some photographers seem to have been too close to the first base line, she had the authority to have them moved, but she asked the plate umpire to move them instead. It brought to question, if she really passed the umpiring field requirements, or was she merely passed to get rid of her.

The Cincinnati Reds dominated the National League to win the West division by 94 games in the West Division. The Houston Astros were the closest runner-up at 10.5 games back. Clay Carroll, the Red's closer, had the highest league saves count at 37. Gary Nolan won 15 games and had a low 1.99 ERA. Joe Morgan, Pete Rose and Johnny Bench collected five high league marks. Morgan scored 122 runs and .419 OBP, while Pete Rose snared 198 hits. Bench hit 40 home runs and 125 RBIs, Morgan walked 115 times and stole 58 bases, while Rose had a .307 BA.

The Oakland Athletics (sometimes called the A's) garnered 93 wins in winning the American League West Division, while the Chicago White Sox trailed by 5.5 games. Catfish Hunter won 21 games, had a 2.04 ERA and had the league high .750 WP, and Rollie Fingers saved 21 games. Joe Rudi and Bert Campaneris were recipients of high league performances, Rudi spread 181 hits and nine triples, while Campaneris stole 52 bases. Rudi also scored 94 runs, hit 32 doubles, sported a .305

BA and had 288 TB. Mike Epstein blasted 28 four-baggers, while Sal Bando had 77 RBIs and 78 base-on-balls.

In the National League playoffs the Cincinnati Reds (W) beat the Pittsburgh Pirates (E) to win the pennant, 3-2. In the American League playoffs, the Oakland Athletics (W) defeated the Detroit Tigers (E), 3-2.

The Oakland Athletics (AL) defeated the Cincinnati Reds (NL) in the 1972 World Series, 4-3.

The 1972 MLB All Star game was played at the Atlanta Stadium on July 25 as the National League defeated the American League, 4-3.

1973

The Negro Leagues committee elected Monte Irvin to the 1973 National Baseball Hall of Fame. The BBWAA selected Warren Spahn and Roberto Clemente (Clemente was chosen in a special election). The Veterans Committee chose George Kelly, Mickey Welsh and Billy Evans (umpire).

The National League continued their old winning ways defeating the American League, 7-1 in the All-Star Game. The win proved to be the beginning of a string of ten future game wins. The site that year was Royals Stadium in Kansas City, Missouri on July 24, 1973.

The New York Mets grabbed the National League East Division in 1973 to win 82 games barely eking out the St. Louis Cardinals by 1.5 games. Tom Seaver won 19 games, but received recognition from the league, for 251 strikeouts and a low 2.08 ERA, while closer Tug McGraw had 25 saves. Felix Millan put on quite a show with his performances, when he scored 82 runs, scattered 185 hits and finished with a .295 BA. Rusty Staub wasn't too bad either, as he hit 36 doubles, collected 246 TB, 76 RBIs, .361 OBP and received 74 walks. John Milner cracked 23 homers and a .432 SA.

The Oakland Athletics had 94 wins, as they captured the 1973

American League West Division. The runner-up Kansas City Royals were six games behind. The A's had a hot pitching staff as Ken Holtzman and Catfish Hunter notched 21 wins apiece and Vida Blue had 20. Hunter also qualified for a league high with a .808 WP. Blue also struck out 158 batters.

Reggie Jackson paced the offense with his performances. Jackson was a high league man with 99 runs scored, slamming 32 four-baggers and 117 RBIs, while Sal Bando hit 32 doubles and 295 TB. Gene Tenace had a .391 OBP and walked 101 times as Billy North stole 53 bases.

In the National League playoffs the New York Mets (E) beat the Cincinnati Red (W) to win the pennant, 3-2. In the American League playoffs, the Oakland Athletics (W) defeated the Baltimore Orioles (E), 3-2 to win the American League crown.

The Oakland Athletics (AL) defeated the New York Mets (NL) in the 1973 World Series, 4-3.

1974

The Negro Leagues Committee elected Cool Papa Bell to the National Baseball Hall of Fame in 1974. The BBWAA selected Whitey Ford and Mickey Mantle. The Veterans Committee chose Jim Bottomley, Sam Thompson and Jocko Conlan (umpire).

The National League handed a 7-2 loss to the American League, in the All-Star Game played at Three Rivers Stadium in Pittsburgh on July 23, 1974.

The Los Angeles Dodgers won 102 games to capture the 1974 National League West Division. During the season, the Cincinnati Reds was a constant competitor, but at the season's end, they finished four games behind. Two pitchers on the Dodgers team qualified for high league performances. Mike Marshall had 21 saves, while Andy Messersmith had 20 wins, but he had to share those wins with Phil Niekro, of the Atlanta Braves, who also had 20. Jim Wynn scored 104 runs, hit 32 home runs, walked 108 times, had a .387 OBP and a .497 SA. Steve Garvey scattered 200 hits, including 32 doubles, had 301 TB and 111 RBIs. Bill Buckner sported a .314 BA and Davy Lopes stole 59 bases.

In the American League, the Oakland Athletics won 90 games to cop the West Division.

The runner-up Texas Rangers were only five games behind. Catfish Hunter had two league best marks. One was a low 2.49 ERA and the other was having won 25 games, but he shared that mark with Ferguson Jenkins, of the Texas Rangers, who also won 25. Reggie Jackson paced the A's offense, scoring 90 runs, hitting 29 homers, a 396 OBP and a .514 SA. Joe Rudi, Gene Tenace and Bill North were cited for high league marks: Rudi had 39 doubles and 287 TB, Tenace with 110 walks and North for his 59 stolen bases. Rudi also collected 174 hits and a .293 BA, while Sal Bando had 103 RBIs.

In the National League playoffs, the Los Angeles Dodgers (W) beat the Pittsburgh Pirates (E) to win the pennant, 3-1. In the American League playoffs, the Oakland Athletics (W) defeated the Baltimore Orioles (E), 3-1.

The Oakland Athletics (AL) defeated the Los Angeles Dodgers (NL) in the 1974 World Series, 4-1.

1975

The Negro Leagues Committee selected Judy Johnson to the 1975 National Baseball Hall of Fame. Earl Averill, Bucky Harris and Billy Herman were chosen by the Veterans Committee, and the BBWAA elected Ralph Kiner.

In the annual All-Star Game, the National league defeated the American League, 6-3 at County Stadium in Milwaukee, on July 15, 1975.

In 1975, Cincinnati was the National League West Division

champion, winning 108 games. The Los Angeles Dodgers lagged behind, by two games. Gary Nolan won 15 games, but Don Gullet had a league high of .789 WP, as he only lost four games. Closer Will McEnaney saved 15 games. Both Pete Rose and Joe Morgan had league highs in multiple categories. Rose scored 112 runs and 47 doubles, while Morgan earned a .471 OBP and collected 132 walks. Rose also scattered 210 hits and 286 RBIs, while Morgan's team-high was in stealing 67 bases. Johnny Bench helped in hitting 28 homers and a .519 SA.

The Boston Red Sox finally captured the American League East Division, winning 95 games, as their closest opponent, the Baltimore Orioles were 4.5 games behind. Luis Tiant won 18 games and struck out 142 batters. Dick Drago saved 15 games. Freddy Lynn captured three league summits as he scored 103 runs, hit 47 doubles and had a .566 SA. Lynn also had 175 hits, 299 TB, 105 RBIs and a .405 OBP. Jim Rice was the Sox's home run hitter, as he popped 22 of them.

In the National League playoffs, the Cincinnati Reds (W) beat the Pittsburgh Pirates (E), to win the pennant, 3-0. In the American League playoffs, the Boston Red Sox (E) defeated the Oakland Athletics (W), 3-0.

The Cincinnati Reds (NL) defeated the Boston Red Sox (AL) in the 1975 World Series, 4-3.

1976

Robin Roberts was elected by the BBWAA to the National Baseball Hall of Fame in 1976. The Negro Leagues Committee selected Oscar Charleston, as the Veterans Committee chose Roger Connor, Fred Lindstrom and Cal Hubbard (umpire).

Mike Schmidt, of the Philadelphia Phillies, was the tenth player to hit four home runs in a single game in Chicago on April 17, 1976, in a 10 inning game.

At the Veterans Stadium in Philadelphia, the National League won in the annual All-Star Game defeating the American League 7-1 on July

13, 1976.

The Cincinnati Reds climbed on top of the National League Western Division, for a second straight year, in winning 102 games, but the Los Angeles Dodgers remained 10 games behind. Rawley Eastwick was the best closer in the league, with 26 saves. Gary Nolan and Jack Billingham each won 15 games, while Pat Zachary notched 14. Pete Rose, George Foster and Joe Morgan notched top league performances. Rose scored 130 runs while spreading 215 hits, including 42 doubles. Foster had hit 121 RBIs as Morgan earned a .453 OBP and a .576 SA. The Reds also had high team successes: Rose for 299 TB, Foster's 29 home runs and Morgan's 114 free passes.

The New York Yankees captured the 1976 American League East Division, winning 97 games, while the Baltimore Orioles were also-rans at 10.5 games behind. Pitcher Sparky Lyle earned a high league mark, for saving 23 games as Ed Figueroa won 19 games. Dock Ellis and Catfish Hunter each won 17 games, as Hunter struck out 173 batters. There were two position players, who reached high league marks: Roy White in scoring 104 runs and Graig Nettles for smashing 32 circuit clouts, Chris Chambliss rifled 188 hits including 32 doubles and 283 TB. Thurman Munson had 105 RBIs, while Mickey Rivers sported a .312 BA and 43 stolen bases. Roy White had .379 OBP and 83 walks.

When Reggie Jackson became a new member of the New York Yankee team in 1976, one of his brash statements was that he was "the one that stirs the drink." In other words, he inferred that the Yankees success depended on him. This was a complete affront to catcher Thurman Munson, who was the captain of the team at that time. Of course, the New York sportswriters made hay with that comment, causing friction in the Yankee clubhouse.

In the National League playoffs, the Cincinnati Reds (W) beat the Philadelphia Phillies (E) to win the pennant, 3-0. In the American League playoffs, the New York Yankees (E) defeated the Kansas City Royals (W), 3-2.

The Cincinnati Reds (NL) defeated the New York Yankees (AL) in

the 1976 World Series, 4-0.

1977

The Veterans Committee elected Amos Rusie, Joe Sewell and Al Lopez (manager) to the National Baseball Hall of Fame in 1977, as the BBWAA chose Ernie Banks, and the Negro Leagues Committee selected Martin Dihigo and Pop Lloyd.

Toronto, was awarded an American League expansion franchise to be known as the Toronto Blue Jays. Seattle was awarded an American League Expansion franchise called Seattle Mariners.

The American League lost in the annual All-Star Game, to the National League 7-5 at Yankee Stadium, New York on July 19, 1977.

The Los Angeles Dodgers kicked into their winning ways, topping the National League West Division with 98 wins, while the Cincinnati Reds ended up on the back burner, a whopping 10 games behind.

Tommy John won 20 games while Bert Hooton struck out 153 batters. Don Sutton had three shutouts and knuckleballer Charlie Hough had 22 saves. Reggie Smith scored 104 runs, had a .307 BA , .432 OBP, .576 SA and 104 walks. Steve Garvey swatted 192 hits, 33 round-trippers, 322 TB and 115 RBIs. Bill Russell hit 28 doubles, while Davy Lopes stole 47 bases.

The 1977 New York Yankees made it two in a row, as they corralled the American League East Division title, winning 100 games. The Baltimore Orioles were pressing all the way, but at the end they were 2.5 games out. Lefty Ron "the Louisiana Lightning" Guidry (Yankee announcer Phil Rizzuto tacked that "Louisiana Lightning" moniker on Guidry) won 16 games, pitching five shutouts, who had 176 strikeouts, while closer Sparky Lyle saved 26 games. Lyle was the player in the league with the most pitched games at 72. Graig Nettles scored 99 runs, hit 37 homers and collected 292 TB. Reggie Jackson popped 39 doubles, had 110 RBIs, a .375 OBP and a .550 SA. Mickey Rivers helped the offensive attack with 184 hits, while stealing 22 bases. Roy White was the recipient of 75 free passes.

In the National League playoffs, the Los Angeles Dodgers (W) beat the Philadelphia Phillies (E), to win the pennant, 3-1. In the American League playoffs, the New York Yankees (E) defeated the Kansas City Royals (W), 4-2.

The New York Yankees (AL) defeated the Los Angeles Dodgers (NL) in the 1977 World Series, 4-2.

1978

The BBWAA elected Eddie Mathews to the National Baseball Hall of Fame in 1978, as the Veterans Committee selected Addie Joss and Larry McPhail (executive).

The National League beat the American League in the All-Star Game, for the sixth straight time. This time it took place at San Diego Stadium, in San Diego, on July 11, 1978.

Pete Rose of the Cincinnati Reds, had a 44 game hitting streak in 1978.

The Los Angeles Dodgers captured the 1978 National League West Division winning 95 games, barely beating out the Cincinnati Reds who finished 2.5 games behind. Bert Hooton won 19 games while Tommy John had 17 and Don Sutton had 15 wins. Closer Terry Forster saved 22 games. Steve Garvey led the offense with a league-leading 202 hits, while he also hit 36 doubles, nine triples, 319 TB, 113 RBIs and a .316 BA. Reggie Smith smacked 29 homers, .392 OBP and a .559 SA. Davy Lopez scored 93 runs and stole 45 bases, while Ron Cey walked 96 times.

The New York Yankees took first place in the American League West Division, winning 100 games outlasting the Boston Red Sox by one slim game. Ron Guidry and closer Goose Gossage had three league-leading performances. Guidry had 25 wins and a 1.74 ERA, while Goosage saved 27 games. Guidry also pitched nine shutouts and struck out 248 batters as Ed Figuora contributed 20 wins. Willie Randolph scored 87 runs, had a .385 OBP, walked 82 times and stole 36 bases. Thurman Munson scattered 183 hits while Lou Piniella sliced 34 doubles and had a .314 BA. Graig Nettles popped 27 homers and had 270 TB. Reggie Jackson had 97 RBIs and a .479 SA.

In the National League playoffs, the Los Angeles Dodgers (W) beat the Philadelphia Phillies (E) to win the pennant, 3-1. In the American League playoffs, the New York Yankees (E) defeated the Kansas City Royals (W), 3-1.

The New York Yankees (AL) defeated the Los Angeles Dodgers (NL) in the 1978 World Series, 4-2.

1979

The BBWAA elected Willie Mays to the National Baseball Hall of Fame in 1979, while the Veterans committee chose Hack Wilson and Warren Giles (executive).

The Kingdome in Seattle was the site of the annual All-Star Game, as the National League edged the American League, 7-6 on July 17, 1979.

The National League East Division champions were the Pittsburgh Pirates, who won 98 games. The Montreal Expos for the first time was the runner-up, close behind by only two games.

Kent Tekulve had 31 saves, but had a league-leading appearances in 94 games--that's 96 percent of the won games. John Candelaria had 14 wins while Bruce Kison had 13 and Bert Blyleven chipped in 12, but had 172 strikeouts. Omar Moreno had a league high 77 stolen bases, but also scored 110 runs and slashed 196 hits including 12 triples. Dave Parker cracked 45 doubles, 327 TB, 94 RBIs and 67 bases-on-balls. Willie Stargell blasted 32 homers and had a .552 SA.

The Baltimore Orioles captured the 1979 American League East Division by winning 102 games. The Milwaukee Brewers were in second place by eight games. Mike Flanagan pitched a league-high 23 games and had five shutouts while striking out 190 batters. Dan Stanhouse had 21 saves. Ken Singleton scored 93 runs, hit 36 four-baggers, 384 TB, 111 RBIs, had a .409 OBP, .533 SA and received 109 walks. Eddie Murray spaced 179 hits including 30 doubles and had a .295 BA which he share with Singleton who also had .295. Speedy Al Bumbry stole 37 bases.

In the National League playoffs the Pittsburgh Pirates (E) beat the Cincinnati Reds (W) to win the pennant, 3-0. In the American League playoffs, the Baltimore Orioles (E) defeated the California Angels (W), 3-1.

The Pittsburgh Pirates (NL) defeated the Baltimore Orioles (AL) in the 1979 World Series, 4-3.

1980

The BBWAA elected Al Kaline and Duke Snider to the National Baseball Hall of Fame in 1980 as the Veterans Committee selected Chuck Klein and Tom Yawkey (executive).

The annual All-Star Game was played as the National League defeated the American League, 4-2 on July 8, 1980 at Dodge Stadium in Los Angeles.

The Philadelphia Phillies were the National League East Division champions winning 91 games while the Montreal Expos missed first place for the second straight year. This time by a single game. Both the pitching and the offensive players excelled with several league-leading counts. Steve Carlton led the Phillis, winning 24 games and striking out 286 batters. Offensive players who had the golden league mark were Pete Rose--42 doubles, and Mike Schmidt—48 homers, 342 TB, 121 RBIs and.624 SA. In team high marks, Schmidt scored 104 runs and walked 89 times. Bake McBride hit 10 triples, and had a .309 BA, while Pete Rose had 185 hits. Gary Maddox was their steals leader with 25.

Kansas City Royals, winning 97 games, copped the American League 1980 pennant while the Oakland Athletics drive petered out, leaving them 14 games behind. The Royals pitchers claimed two while the offense earned five high league highs. Closer Dan Quisenberry had 33 saves while position players Willie Wilson and George Brett claimed seven more: Wilson scored 132 runs, 15 triples, 79 stolen bases and had 230 hits while Brett had a .390 BA, .461 OBP and .664 SA. Brett was the only batter who was so close to the coveted .400 mark. Brett also hit 24 homers, 118 walks and 118 RBIs. Hal MacRae hit 29 doubles.

In the National League playoffs the Philadelphia Phillies (E) beat the Houston Astros (W) to win the pennant, 3-2. In American League playoffs, the Kansas City Royals (W) defeated the New York Yankees (E). The Philadelphia Phillies (NL) defeated the Kansas City Royals in the 1980 World Series. 4-2. It was the first time that the Phillies had won a World Series.

1981

The BBWAA elected Bob Gibson into the 1981 National Hall of Fame as the Veterans Committee chose Rube Foster and Johnny Mize.

The 1981 season was interrupted by a players strike. The season had been running smoothly from April 8 to June 12, when a disagreement between the owners and the baseball players union created a work stoppage. It involved with the owners demanding compensation for one of their players for a free agent being lost to another team. The strike lasted from June 12 to July 31 and play commenced on August 9 with the All-Star game. Play resumed the next day.

The 52nd Major League All-Star games was played in Cleveland Stadium on August 9 as the National League edge the American League in a 5-4 thriller.

A compromise was established as the owners would then receive a replacement player drawing from a pool of players unprotected by other clubs.

It was determined that when play had been resumed that the

season would be divided. The team in first half in the two leagues of both divisions would compete with the first place winner in the last half of the season on the same basis. The stats for the two teams finishing in the World Series are the Yankees and the Dodgers.

Rod Guidry, Dave Righetti and Goose Gossage led the pitching attack for the Yankees. Guidry had a 11-5 record, with a .688 WP and 104 strikeouts. Righetti earned a 2.05 ERA and Gossage saved 20 games.

Dave Winfield led the offense scattering 114 hits, including 25 doubles, 68 RBIs and 180 TB. Willie Randolph scored 59 runs while walking 57 times. Jerry Mumfrey had the best .307 BA. Graig Nettles and Reggie Jackson each had 15 round-trippers and Bobby Murcer was on top with a .470 SA.

Three pitchers paced the hill crew with Fernando Valenzuela, Jerry Reuss and Steve How leading the way, Rookie Valenzuela 13 wins, 2.48ERA, eight shutouts and 180 whiffs led the way as Reuss had ten wins, a .714 WP and a 2.30 ERA while Howe collected eight saves.

Ron Cey led the offense hitting 30 homers, a .372 OBP and a 474 SA. Steve Garvey scored 63 runs, hit 23 doubles and had 64 RBI. Dusty Baker rifled 128 hits, collected 178 TB and sported a .320 BA Davey Lopes spent a lot of time on the base, walking 40 times while stealing 20 bases.

In the American League, the Yankees defeated the Milwaukee Brewers 3-2 and Oakland Athletics beat the Kansas City Royals, 3-0. In the National League, the Los Angeles Dodgers won over the Houston Astros, 3-2 and Montreal Expos defeated the Philadelphia Phillies, 3-2.

In the American League championship round, the Yankees defeated the Athletics and the National League Dodgers beat the Espos, 3-2. The Dodgers defeated the Yankees in the 1981 World Series.

1982

The BBWAA elected Hank Aaron and Frank Robinson to the National Baseball Hall of Fame in 1982, while the Veterans Committee selected Travis Jackson and Happy Chandler (executive).

The National League topped the American League in the All Star game, 4-1 at Olympic Stadium in Montreal on July 13, 1982.

The St. Louis Cardinals was the National League champion winning 92 games, while the Philadelphia Phillies were three games behind. The St. Louis Cardinals Bob Forsch and Joaquin Andujar both won 15 games, and Closer Bruce Sutter saved 36 games. Lonnie Smith who scored a league high of 120 runs lead the offense with 182 hits including 35 doubles, 257 TB, sporting a .307 BA and stealing 68 bases. George Hendrick hit 19 homers, has a .404 OBP and a .450 SA. First baseman Keith Hernandez drew 100 bases-on-balls.

The American League titlist was the Milwaukee Brewers, winning 95 games and barely edged the Baltimore Orioles by one game. Pete Vuckovich won 18 games but earned a league high of .750 WP, while Rollie Fingers saved 29 games and pitched in the most games in the league. Robin Yount and Gorman Thomas collected five league summits. Thomas swatted 39 homers while Yount spread 210 hits, including 46 doubles, .331 BA, 387 TB and a .578 SA. Yount also had a .331 BA and a .379 OBP. Paul Molitor scored 136 runs and stole 41 bases. Yount, in previous years, played shortstop. In 1982 he was switched to the outfield.

In the National League playoffs, the St. Louis Cardinals (E) beat the Atlanta Braves (W) to win the pennant, 3-0. In the American League playoffs, the Milwaukee Brewers (E) defeated the California Angels (W), 3-2.

The St. Louis Cardinals (NL) defeated the Milwaukee Brewers (AL) in the 1982 World Series, 4-3.

1983

The BBWAA elected Juan Marichal and Brooks Robinson, to the National Baseball Hall of Fame in 1983, while the Veterans Committee selected George Kell and WalterAlston (manager).

The American League finally saw daylight, as they bombed the National League, in the All-Star game, 13-3 at Comiskey Park, in Chicago on July 6, 1983.

The Philadelphia Phillies in winning 90 games wrested the National League East Division championship from the Pittsburgh Pirates who stumbled behind by six games. Two Phillies pitchers grabbed the top league's spots in three categories. John Denny won 19 games and had a .760 WP, while Steve Carlton struck out 275 batters. Closer Al Holland saved 25 games. Mike Schmidt had two highs of his own, as he slammed 40 circuit clouts and was issued 128 walks. Schmidt did well in other categories too, as he scored 104 runs, sliced 136 hits, had 280 TB, 109 RBIs and .275 BA, a .399 OBP and a .524 SA. Second-baseman Joe Morgan swatted 20 doubles.

The Baltimore Orioles won 98 games to claim the American League East Division as the Detroit Tigers remained six games back. Mike Boddicker pitched a league high five shutouts. Scott McGregor had 18 wins, while Storm Davis stuck out 125 batters. Tippy Martinez saved 21 games. Cal Ripken, Jr. capture three high league categories: 121 runs, 211 hits and 47 doubles. Ripken also had 343 TB and a .318 BA. Eddie Murray socked 33 homers, 111 RBIs, a .398 OBP and a .538 SA. Ken Singleton was issued 99 walks.

In 1983, the Philadelphia Phillies (E) defeated the Los Angeles Dodgers (W) for the National League pennant, 3-1. The Baltimore Orioles (E) defeated the Chicago Whiter Sox (W) 3-1 for the American League championship.

The Baltimore Orioles (AL) defeated the Philadelphia Phillies (NL) for the 1983 World Series, 4-1.

1984

Peter Ueberroth, Sixth Baseball Commissioner

Peter Ueberroth was elected as the sixth baseball commissioner in 1984. He was active in suspending many players because of cocaine abuse. He negotiated a television contract with CBS and began an investigation into Pete Rose's betting habits. In 1985, he expanded the baseball championship series, from the best of five to seven games, At his urging, he convinced the Chicago Cubs, who only played daytime games, to install lights for night games.

The BBWAA elected Luis Aparicio, Don Drysdale and Harmon Killabrew to the National Baseball Hall of Fame in 1984, while the Veterans Committee selected Rick Ferrell and Pee Wee Reese.

The National League beat the American League 3-1, in the All-Star game, at Candlestick Park, in San Francisco on July 10, 1984.

The San Diego Padres were the National League West Division titlist in 1984, winning 92 games. Their closest competitor was the Houston Astros, that were 12 games behind. Mark Thurmond and Ed Whitson had identical 14-8 records. Tim Lollar struck out 131 batters and Goose Gossage saved 25 games. Tony Gwynn capture two league marks, spreading 213 hits and a .351 BA. He also hit 10 triples, a 269 TB and a .411 OBP. Tony Wiggins scored 106 runs and walked 76 times. Carmelo Martinez hit 28 doubles, Graig Nettles and Kevin McReynolds both hit 20 home runs, and Steve Garvey had 86 RBIs. McReynolds also had a .465 SA.

The 1984 American League East Division champion was the Detroit Tigers, which won 104 games. Runner-up Toronto Blue Jays were not in the running, finishing 15 games back. Jack Morris won 19 games for the Tigers, while Dan Petry had 18 and Milt Wilcox added 17 more. Willie Hernandez saved 32 games, but appeared in 80 games, a league high. Morris also struck out 148 batters. Kirk Gibson scored 92 runs, hit 10 triples and had a 274 TB. Alan Trammel spread 174 hits and equaled Chet Lemon with 34 doubles. Trammel also had a .314 BA and Lemon had a .495 SA. Lance Parish cracked 33 homers, while Darrell Evan received 77 walks.

In 1984, the San Diego Padres (W) defeated the Chicago Cubs (E) for the National League pennant, 3-2. The Detroit Tigers (E) defeated the Kansas City Royals (W) 3-0 for the American League championship.

The Detroit Tigers (AL) defeated the San Diego Padres (NL) in the 1984 World Series, 4-1.

1985

The BBWAA elect Lou Brock and Hoyt Wilhelm to the National Baseball Hall of Fame in 1985 while the Veterans Committee selected Enos Salughter and Arky Vaughn.

The 1985 All-Star game was played at the Hubert Humphrey Metrodome in Minneapolis, on July 16, 1985 when the National League defeated the American League, 6-1.

The St. Louis Cardinals won 101 games in their drive for the 1985 National League East Division. The New York Mets in the race for the championship were left behind as they finished three games-off-the pace. John Tudor won 21 games including 10 shutouts. He struck out 169 batters and finished with a 1.93 ERA. Joaquin Andujar matched Tudor in winning 21. Danny Cox added 18 wins Willie McGee and Vince Coleman collected four league summits. McGee had 216 hits, 18 triples and a .353 BA while Vince Coleman burned up the baselines in stealing 100 bases. McGee also scored 114 runs and had 308 TB. Tommy Herr sliced 38 doubles and had 110 RBIs while Jack Clark hit 22 fence-busters, had a .397 OBP and 83 bases-on-balls.

Kansas City Royals only needed 91 wins in winning the American League West Division championship just beating out the California

Angels by one game. Bret Saberhagen won 20 games and striking out 158 batters. Charlie Leibrandt won another 17 while closer Dab Quisenberry saved 37 league-topping games. George Brett led the Royals offensive attack scoring 108 runs, spaced 184 hits including 38 doubles, 322 TB, 112 RBIs, .335 BA and a .442 OBP. Brett and Willie Wilson were successful in gaining high league marks. Willie Wilson pounding 21 triples and Brett' had good hitting to get a .595 SA. Wilson also stole 43 bases and Steve Balboni swatted 26 homers.

In 1985 the league championships were decided in the best of seven. In previous years it was the best of five.

In 1985 the St. Louis Cardinals (E) defeated the Los Angels Dodgers for the National League pennant, 4-2. The the Kansas City Royals (W) defeated the Toronto Blue Jays (W) 4-3 for the American League championship.

During the series, Brett, who previously had hemorrhoid surgery, quipped that "All my troubles are behind me."

The Kansas City Royals (AL) defeated the St. Louis Cardinals (NL) in the 1985 World Series, 4-3.

1986

The BBWAA elect Willie McCovey to the National Baseball Hall of Fame in 1986 while the Veterans Committee selected Bobby Doerr and Ernie Lombardi.

The Atlanta Braves' Bob Horner was the 11th player in major league history to hit four home runs in a single game at Montreal on July 6, 1986.

The American League barely won in the All-Star game 3-2, defeating the National League at the Astrodome in Houston, on July 15, 1986.

The New York Mets, in their first "dance" since the 1969 season, copped the National League East Division with 108 wins. Their closest competitor, the Philadelphia Phillies, at 21.5 back were not even in the running. Bob Ojeda won 18 games, while Dwight Gooden had 17, Sid Martinez 16 and Ron Darling 15. Gooden and Martinez each struck out 200 batters. Keith Hernandez was the impetus for the Mets offensive attack as he scored 94 runs, scattered 171 hits including 34 doubles, 246 TB, .310 BA, .414 OBP and walking 94 times, the league high mark. Darryl Strawberry slugged 27 homers and had a .507 SA.

The Boston Red Sox, confident that they finally would win a World Series, won 95 games in the East Division while the New York Yankees fell behind by 5.5 games. Roger Clemens won 24 games, lassoed the .857 WP and a 2.48 ERA all of which were league highs. Bruce Hurst pitched four shut outs. Bob Stanley saved 16 games. Wade Boggs captured three league highs in a .357 BA, .455 OBP and 105 walks. Boggs also scored 107 runs, spaced 207 hits including 47 doubles and a .490 SA. Don Baylor smashed 31 homers while Jim Rice collected 110 RBIs.

In 1986 the New York Mets (E) defeated the Houston Astros for the National League pennant, 4-2. The Boston Red Sox (E) defeated the California Angels (W) 4-3 for the American League championship.

New York Mets (NL) defeated the Boston Red Sox (AL) in the 1986 World Series, 4-3.

A crucial play occurred during the 1986 World Series. On October 26, 1986, the Boston Red Sox were at the cutting edge of winning that World Series. They were winning, 5-3 in game six and were one out from winning the World Series. This is the reason why baseball is so exciting. In baseball, there is never a sure thing. This was supposed to be the first World Series win since the Red Sox won it in 1918. The Red Sox gave up hits to Gary Carter, Kevin Mitchell and Ray Knight. Bob Stanley threw a wild pitch to allow Mitchell to score. Then Mookie Wilson hit a soft bouncing grounder to Bill Buckner, and, as if by magic, it went through his legs, allowing Knight to score give the Mets an unimaginable 6-5 win. It was a simple error, but it led to the Mets winning the game. And in the following, seventh game, the Red Sox frittered away a three-run lead to lose the World Series. But Red Sox fans still blame Buckner for losing the series for the Red Sox. Some others blame it on "The Bambino's Curse." (Red Sox fans blame all of the team's problems through the years, because the Red Sox sold Babe Ruth's contract to the Yankees in 1919. It was dubbed "the Bambino's Curse.")

1987

The BBWAA elect Catfish Hunter and Billy Williams to the National Baseball Hall of Fame in 1987 while the Veterans Committee selected Ray Dandridge.
In a tightly fought All-Star game, the National League shutout the American League, 2-0 on July 14, 1987 at Oakland-Alameda Coliseum in Oakland.
The St. Louis Cardinals were 1987 National League East Division champions winning 95 games as the New York Mets failed to reach the top, only three games behind. The Cardinals pitching was a unique situation where Greg Mathews, Bob Forsch and Danny Cox each had 11 wins. Closer Todd Worrell saved 33 games. The offense was a conglomeration of efforts of five key players. Three of Jack Clark's performances netted him league highs as he had a .461 OBP, .597 SA and his ability to have a collection of 136 walks. Vince Coleman's penchant for stealing bases netted him 109 for another league high. Clark also hit 35 home runs and Coleman scored 121 runs. Acrobatic short stop Ozzie Smith sent 182 hits to different parts of the playing field, also smacking 40 doubles. Willie McGee hit 11 triples and had 269 TB.
During the season catcher Benito Santiago of the San Diego Padres put together a 34-game hitting streak.
The Minnesota Twins were the American League west division champion with only 85 wins as the Kansas City Royals, a constant competitor, ended the season two game out of first. Frank Viola won 17 games and Bert Blyleven won 15. The Twins closer Jeff Reardon saved

31 games.

Kirby Puckett led the Twins offense in scoring 96 runs, had 333 TB, a .332 BA , but also claimed a league high in scoring 207 hits while sharing that honor with Kevin Seitzer of the Kansa City Royals who also bunched 207 hits. Gary Guyette sliced 36 doubles and had 109 RBIs while Kent Hrbek rocketed 34 home runs, had a .389 OBP and received 84 walks. Tom Brunansky's hitting showed up on his .489 SA, while Dan Gladden pilfered 25 bases.

Paul Molitor of the Milwaukee Brewer kept hitting for a 39-game streak.

In 1987 the St. Louis Cardinals (E) defeated the San Francisco Giants (W) for the National League pennant, 4-3. The Minnesota Twins (W) defeated the Detroit Tigers (E) 4-1 for the American League championship.

The Minnesota Twins (AL) defeated the St. Louis Cardinals (NL) in the 1987 World Series, 4-3.

1988

The BBWAA elect Willie Stargell to the National Baseball Hall of Fame in 1988.

The American League beat the National League by a hair as they won 2-1 at the All-Star game on July 12, 1988 at Riverfront Stadium in Cincinnati.

The 1988 National League West Division champion was the Los Angeles Dodgers, who won 94 games, while second-place Cincinnati Reds was seven games back. Oriel Hershiser won 23 games, a league high, and had to share that with Danny Jackson of the Cincinnati Reds, who also had 23 wins. Hershiser had eight shutouts, while Tim Leary won 17 games, had six shutouts and struck out 180 batters. Jay Howell saved 21 games. Kirk Gibson led the Dodgers offense, when he scored 106 runs, hit 28 doubles,, smashed 28 homers, had 262 TB had a .290 BA, .377 OBP , .483 SA and received 77 walks. Steve Sax sprayed 175 hits, and stole 42 bases, while Mike Marshall had 82 RBIs.

The Oakland Athletics captured the American League West Division title, with 104 wins while the Minnesota Twins with 13 games behind, were not into the winning picture. Dave Stewart won 21 games, and struck out 192 batters. Bob Welch won 17 games, and Storm Davis won 16 games. Dennis Eckersley save 45 games for the Athletics. Jose Conseco scored 120 runs, had 187 hits, 347 TB, a .307 BA, .391 OBP, 78 bases-on-balls and 40 stolen bases. Conseco was cited for league-high performances when he slammed 42 home runs, 124 RBIs and .569 SA. Dave Henderson hit 38 doubles.

In 1988, the Los Angeles Dodgers (W) defeated the New York Mets (E) for the National League pennant, 4-3. The Oakland Athletics (W) defeated the Boston 4-0, for the American League championship.

The Los Angeles Dodgers (NL) defeated he Oakland Athletics (AL) in the 1988 World Series, 4-1.

1989

Bartlett Giamatti, Eighth Baseball Commissioner

A. Bartlett Giamatti was elect unanimously by the club owners on April 1, 1989. He had previously served as the president of the National League. He was responsible for reorganizing the roles and duties of the commissioner. He was the first commissioner to appoint a deputy commissioner when he appointed his friend Fay Vincent. Giamatti had a strong background in journalism, that helped him in dealing with the media. Soon after his election, Giamatti, in consulting with previous commissioner Peter Ueberroth, found that Cincinnati manager, and all-time hits leader, had been engages in betting on baseball, often betting on his team to win. Of course, Rose denied this. After intensive investigation, it was evident that Rose was guilty of having done those things, which circumvented the integrity of baseball. Rose agreed to the lifetime suspension from baseball imposed by Giamatti on August 23,

1989. A few short days later, on September 1, Giammati died of a heart attack.

Fay Vincent, Ninth Baseball Commissioner

Fay Vincent was elected by the club owners on September 7, 1989. He presided over the 1989 earthquake-delayed World Series, the owners lockout during Spring Training for 1990, and the expulsion of owner George Steinbrenner.

Vincent, in the 1989 World Series, was caught unawares with an earthquake, just before the beginning of a game being played in San Francisco. When the tremor started, Vincent decided that the game would be postponed and resumed 10 days later, but did not inform anyone of his decision to do that.

In February 1990, the owners announced that Spring Training would not start on schedule. That lockout, was the seventh work stoppage in baseball since 1972. The lockout was not resolved until 32 days later, wiping out Spring Training.

Vincent, in conjunction with owners and the players' union brokered a new Basic Agreement. Vincent's relationship with the owners was tenuous, at best. He resigned in 1992 after the owners gave him an 18-9 no confidence vote.

The BBWAA elected Johnny Bench and Carl Yastrzemski to the National Baseball Hall of Fame in 1989, while the Veterans Committee selected Red Schoendienst and Al Bartlick (umpire).

The American League won their second straight All-Star game, as they defeated the National League 5-3, at Anaheim Stadium, Anaheim, California on July 11, 1989.

The San Francisco Giants captured the National League West Division, winning 92 games. Second place San Diego Padres fell three games back. Rich Reuschel won 17 games and Scott Garrells had 14 wins and 119 strikeouts. Garrells was credited as having the lowest 2.28

ERA in the league. Craig Lefferts saved 20 games. Will Clark, Bobby Thompson and Kevin Mitchell were recipients of high league marks. Clark scored 104 runs, Thompson hit 11 triples and Mitchell had four marks—47 home runs, 345 TB, .635 SA and 125 RBIs. Clark also spread 196 hits, 38 doubles, a .333 BA, .413 OBP and 74 free passes, while Brett Butler stole 31 bases.

The Oakland Athletics took the American League West Division, winning 99 games, while second-place Kansas City Royals ended seven games back. Dave Stewart won 21 games, while Mike Moore and Storm Davis each won 19 gamess. Dennis Eckersley saved 33 games.

Mark McGwire hit 33 homers, league highs and had the highest home run total in the league. McGwire also had 17 doubles and a .336 BA. Dave Parker accumulated 97 RBIs and 239 TB as Rickey Henderson had a .425 OBP and pilfered 52 bases.

In 1989, the San Francisco Giants (W) defeated the Chicago Cubs (E) for the National League pennant, 4-1. The Oakland Athletics (W) defeated the Toronto Blue Jays (E) 4-1 for the American League championship.

The Oakland Athletics (AL) defeated the San Francisco Giants (NL) in the 1989 World Series, 4-0.

1990

The BBWAA elected Joe Morgan and Jim Palmer to the National Baseball Hall of Fame in 1990.

Nolan Ryan pitched a no hitter at the age 44, as the Texas Rangers whitewashed the Oakland Athletics, 5-0 at Oakland-Alemeda Coliseum, on June 11, 1990.

Wrigley Field in Chicago was the site of another All-Star win, for the American League, as they shutout the National League, 2-0 on July 10, 1990.

The Cincinnati Reds captured the Central Division of the National League, winning 91 games. The Los Angeles Dodgers was the second-place finisher at five games behind. Tom Browning won 15 games, while Jose Rijo won 14 and striking out 152 batters. Closer Randy Myers saved 31 games. Barry Larkin scored 95 runs, spread 185 hits, had a .301 BA and a .358 OBP. Chris Sabo sliced 38 doubles, slammed 25 home runs, had 270 TB and walked 61 times. Larkin and Billy Hatcher both stole 30 bases, while Mariano Duncan hit 11 triples.

The Oakland Athletics earned the National League West Division championship winning 103 games. The Chicago White Sox trailed them by nine games. Bob Welch was the best pitcher in the American League with 27 wins. Dave Stewart won 22, while Dennis Eckersley saved 48 games. On the offensive side, both Mark McGwire and Rickey Henderson were cited for league highs: McGwire for his 39 round-trippers and Rickey Henderson for his 65 base thefts. McGwire also had 108 RBIs and 110 free passes. Henderson had several more categories for league highs when he scored 119 runs, spread 159 hits, 33 doubles, a .325 BA, .577 SA and a .441 OBP.

In 1990, the Cincinnati Reds (W) defeated the Pittsburgh Pirates (W) for the National League pennant, 4-2. The Oakland Athletics (W) defeated the Boston Red Sox (E) 4-0 for the American League championship.

The Cincinnati Reds (NL) defeated the Oakland Athletics (AL) in the 1990 World Series, 4-0.

1991

The BBWAA elected Rod Carew, Ferguson Jenkins and Gaylord Perry into the National Baseball Hall of Fame in 1991, while the Veterans Committee selected Tony Lazzeri and Bill Veeck (executive).

Nolan Ryan pitched a no-hitter at the age 45, as the Texas Rangers whitewashed the Toronto Blue Jays, 3-0 at Arlington Stadium, on May 1, 1991. He was tied for the most no-hitters with Bob Feller of the Cleveland Indians at 12.

The American League made it three in a row, as they defeated the

National League 4-2, in the All-Star Classic, played on July 9, 1991, at the Skydome in Toronto.

Miami FL was awarded a National League expansion franchise and was called the Florida Marlins.

The Atlanta Braves conquered the National League West Division title, as second-placed Los Angeles Dodgers were left behind by only one game. The Braves Tom Glavine, and the Pittsburgh Pirates John Smiley, both won 20 games which was the league's summit. The Braves Steve Avery won 18 games, while Charlie Leibrandt won 15, and Tom Smoltz had 14. Glavine struck out 192 batters and Juan Berenquer saved 17 games. The Braves offense had some high league marks, as Terry Pendleton collected 187 hits, 303 TB and a .319 BA. Pendleton also had a .517 SA. Ron Gant scored 101 runs, had 105 RBIs and 71 walks. Lonnie Smith and David Justice had the same OBP at .377 as Otis Nixon swiped 72 bases.

The 1991 Minnesota Twins earned the West Division championship of the American League, winning 95 games, while the Chicago White Sox finished eight games behind. The Twins' Scott Erickson and Bill Gillickson of the Detroit Tigers, each had a league-highs with 20 wins. Erickson also had a league high with a ,714 WP. Teammate Jack Morris had 18 wins, but struck out 163 batters. Closer Rick Aguilera saved 42 games. Kirby Puckett scored 92 runs, scattered 195 hits, and had a .319 BA. Chili Davis hit 24 doubles, 29 home runs, 93 RBIs, 385 OBP and 95 bases-on-balls. Shane Mack had a .529 SA.

In 1991, the Atlanta Braves (W) defeated the Pittsburgh Pirates (E) for the National League pennant, 4-3. The Minnesota Twins (W) defeated the Toronto Blue Jays (E) 4-1 for the American League championship.

The Minnesota Twins (AL) defeated the Atlanta Braves (NL) in the 1991 World Series, 4-3.

1992

The BBWAA elected Tom Seaver and Rollie Fingers to the National Baseball Hall of Fame in 1992, while the Veterans Committee selected Hal Newhouser and Bill McGowan (umpire).

The American League defeated the National League, 13-6, at the All-Star game, played at Jack Murphy Stadium in San Diego, on July 14, 1992.

The Atlanta Braves were the National League's West Division champions winning 96 games, while the Cincinnati Reds were eight games behind. Two on the Braves pitching staff received high league marks. John Smoltz struck out 215 batters, and Tom Glavine won 20 games. Glavine shared his wins with Greg Maddux of the Chicago Cubs, who also won 20 games. Smoltz also won 15 games, as Alejandro Pena saved 15 games. Terry Pendleton and Dion Sanders had two league's best performances Pendleton sprayed 199 hits, and shared with Andy Slyke of the Pittsburgh Pirates, who also had 199 hits. Sanders sliced 14 triples while Pendleton also scored 98 runs, smashed 39 doubles had 303 TB, 105 RBIs, a .311 BA and a .473 SA. Pendleton and teammate David Justice both hit 21 home runs. Justice also walked 79 times, as Otis Nixon had 41 base thefts.

The Toronto Blue Jays captured the East Division of the American League, winning 96 games while the second-place Milwaukee Brewers were only four games behind. Jack Morris was the highest league winner with 21 games, which he shared with the Texas Rangers Kevin Brown, who also had 21 wins. Second baseman Roberto Alomar and center fielder Joe Carter, carried the Blue Jays offense, as Alomar scored 105 runs, had 177 hits, a .310 BA, .406 OBP, walked 87 times and stole 49 bases. Carter blasted 24 home runs, had 119 RBIs and 310 TB as David Winfield produced 33 doubles.

In 1992, the Atlanta Braves (W) defeated the Pittsburgh Pirates (E) for the National League pennant, 4-3. The Toronto Blue Jays (E) defeated the Oakland Athletics (W) 4-2 for the American League championship.

The Toronto Blue Jays (AL) defeated the Atlanta Braves (NL) in the 1992 World Series, 4-2.

1993

Bud Selig

Bud Selig was instrumental in the 1970 Milwaukee Brewers obtaining another franchise, when the Seattle Pilots went bankrupt, at the end of the 1969 season. The original Milwaukee franchise, the Milwaukee Braves, left in 1966, and transferred to Atlanta. Selig was the prime mover in his predecessor's Fay Vincent's no-confidence vote. Immediately after Vincent's resignation, Selig headed an owners group. Selig guided MLB, which was clearly a conflict-of-interest. In 1993 and 1998, Selig oversaw two expansions, the addition of two wild card playoff teams, the creation of inter-league playing, the World Baseball Classic and the introduction of instant replay as a tool for umpires. He resigned on January 24, 2015, and was voted into the Hall of Fame in 2017.

The BBWAA elected Reggie Jackson into the National Baseball Hall of Fame in 1993.

In 1993, Denver, Colorado was awarded a National league expansion franchise called the Colorado Rockies.

The Orioles Park at Camden Yards in Baltimore was the All-Star site, when the American League defeated the National League, 9-3 on July 13, 1993.

The St. Louis Cardinals' Mark Whiten was the 12th player in major league history to hit four home runs in a single game at Cincinnati, on September 7, 1993, driving in 12 runs.

The Philadelphia Phillies captured the East Division of the National

League, winning 97 games, while the Montreal Expos lagged behind by three games. Tommy Greene and Curt Schilling both won 16 games, as Schilling also struck out 186 batters, and Mitch Williams saved 43 games. Lenny Dykstra captured two league titles, scoring 143 runs and collecting 194 hits. Dykstra captured a team-high 129 walks and he also sliced 44 doubles, stole 37 bases and had 307 TB. Darren Daulton had 24 homers, 105 RBIs and both he and Dykstra had the same .482 SA.

The Toronto Blue Jays snatched the East Division of the American League, winning 95 games. Pat Hentegen won 19 games while Juan Guzman won 14 games, but posted a high .824 WP and struck out 194 batters. Paul Molitor and John Olerud won three league summit marks. Molitor had 211 hits while Olerud hit 54 doubles and sported a .363 BA. Olerud also had a 330 TB, walked 114 times, had a .473 OBP and a .599 SA. Joe Carter hit 33 four-baggers and was credited with 121 RBIs.

In 1993, the Philadelphia Phillies (W) defeated the Atlanta Braves (E) for the National League pennant, 4-2. The Toronto Blue Jays (E) defeated the Chicago White Sox (W), 4-2 for the American League championship.

The Toronto Blue Jays (AL) defeated the Philadelphia Phillies (NL) in the 1993 World Series, 4-2.

1994

The 1994 season was the first year in which each league had three divisions. In order for four teams to compete in the playoffs, another team selected to compete was called the wild card. The wild card was determined as being the one with the highest winning percentage, that was not in first in their division. The divisions were East, Central and West.

The division winners in the National League were (E) Montreal, (W) Los Angeles, (C) Cincinnati and (WC) Atlanta. In the American League division winners were New York (E), Texas(W), Chicago (C) and

Cleveland (WC).

The National League players held their breaths, as their team eked out a 8-7 victory over their American League rivals, 8-7, at Three Rivers Stadium, in Pittsburgh on July 12, 1994.

In the American League, the New York Yankees won 70 games for .619 WP only played 113 games. The achievements of both of the teams appear here despite the strike.

Montreal Expos probably would have played in the 1994 World Series, if it had been played.

Ken Hill was the best pitcher for the Expos, winning 16 games, and at that point, was the league's best pitcher. Pedro Martinez, who had won 11 games, struck out 142 batters. Moises Alou had 143 hits, 22 home runs, 250 TB, a .339 BA, .397 OBP and a ,.592 SA.

Marquis Grissom scored 96 runs, and stole 36 bases. Larry Walker had the league high in hitting 44 doubles, 86 RBIs and walked 47 times.

Jimmy Key's 17 Yankee wins, and closer Bob Wickman's who pitched in 53 games both had league highs, while Steve Howe saved 15 games. The offense was led by Paul O'Neill, who had a .359 BA, a league high, and collected 132 hits. O'Neill had a penchant for getting angry, if he didn't get a hit, especially in a key situation. He once was known to break the water cooler in the dugout, when that happened. He also smashed 21 homers, had 177 TB, 83 RBI, a .460 OBP, .603 SA and 72 walks. Center fielder Bernie Williams scored 80 times while slapping 29 doubles.

The division winners in the National League were Montreal (E), Los Angeles (W), Cincinnati (C) and Atlanta (WC). In the American League division winners were New York (E), Texas, (W) Chicago (C) and Cleveland (WC).

Since the players strike was held before the end of the 1994 season, there were no winners. Acting Commissioner, Alan "Bud" Selig canceled the season on September 14 after the players had been on strike for 34 days. There was no playoffs or a World Series in 1994 due to the strike.

1995

The strike continued into the beginning for the 1995 season.

Both the BBWAA and the Veterans Committee on the Hall of Fame continued to select the persons whom they voted for in 1995 even though the strike was still existent. The BBWAA elected Mike Schmidt, while the Veterans Committee selected Richie Ashburn, Leon Day, Vic Willis and William Hulbert (executive).

After 232 days of the 1994-1995 baseball season the players strike came to an end on April 25, 1995. Then, the major league teams began their 144-game-shortened season.

On April 2, 1995, it was established that it became legal to protest contested calls.

During a championship season game, All Star game or any post season game, a manager may request a "Replay Review" on a contested call, but it must be requested within a reasonable time.

In 1994, for the first time that there were three divisions in both the National and American Leagues, but because the players strike occurred then, their use in the playoffs were not implemented until the 1995 season.

The National league East division teams were the Atlanta Braves, Florida Marlins, Montreal Expos, New York Mets and the Philadelphia Phillies. In the Central division were the Cincinnati Reds, Chicago Cubs, Houston Astros, Pittsburgh Pirates, and the St. Louis Cardinals. In the West were: the Colorado Rockies, Los Angeles Dodgers, San Diego Padres and the San Francisco Giants.

The American League East division included The Baltimore Orioles, Boston Red Sox, Detroit Tigers, New York Yankees and the Toronto Blue Jays. The Central division was comprised of the Chicago White Sox, Cleveland Indians, Kansas City Royals, Milwaukee Brewers and the Minnesota Twins. Teams included in the West division were the California Angels, Oakland Athletics, Seattle Mariners and the Texas

Rangers.

On August 10, the Los Angeles Dodgers were forced to forfeit a game when inebriated fans threw baseball souvenirs onto the field.

The National League players were overjoyed as they had won a second game in a row, over the American League in the All-Star game, 3-2, at the Ballpark at Arlington in Arlington, Texas on July 11, 1995. They had won a previous All-Star game in 1994, breaking a string of American League annual wins. Jeff Conine of the Florida Marlins smashed a pinch-hit homer in the eighth, to win it for the senior league, as he accomplished this in his first All-Star at bat.

The Atlanta Braves captured the East division of the National League winning 90 games. Their closest competitor was the New York Mets, who were 21 games behind.

Greg Maddux claimed three high league pitching marks with 19 wins, 1.63 ERA and a .905 WP. John Smoltz struck out 193 batters, while Tom Glavine won 16 games. Mark Wohlers saved 25 games. Fred McGriff dominated the Braves offense as he scored 87 runs, drilled 144 hits, 27 doubles, 27 homers, 93 RBIs and a .258 OBP. A conglomerate of players served on the offense, including Chipper Jones scoring 87 runs and 73 walks, Ryan Klesko's .396 OBP, Javvy Lopez had a .315 BA and .498 SA, and Marquis Grissom stole 29 bases.

The Cleveland Indians won the American League East division, with an astonishing number of 100 wins, considering they accomplished this during a shortened season. The Kansas City Royals was the runner-up team, with a galaxy of 30 games being behind.

Charles Nagy and Orel Hirshiser both won 16 games, while Nagy struck out 139 batters. Closer Jose Mesa saved 46 games, a league high.

Albert Belle was recognized by the league, as one of two players who had identical 126 RBI scores. The other was Mo Vaughn of the Boston Red Sox. Belle excelled in other offensive categories, with 121 runs scored, drilling 52 doubles, 377 TB and a .690 SA. Belle was the best league home run hitter with 50 fence-busters, and Kenny Lofton was the league's best base-thief with 54 steals. He also hit 13 triples.

Eddie Murray had the highest batting average with .323, as Jim Thome had a .438 OBP and 99 walks.

On September 6th, Baltimore Orioles Cal Ripken Jr had played in 2,131 straight games. He broke Lou Gehrig's record of playing in 2,130 consecutive games. Ripkin continued to play in more games until he reached 2,632, before he took a day off.

With the change in all the team rosters in MLB, it was necessary to divide each league into three groups, east, west and central. In establishing a playoff series besides division champions of both leagues, an additional team would also compete in the playoffs designed as a "wide card." The wild card would be determined from the remaining teams, which would have the highest win-loss percentage.

In the playoffs, "wild card" games are given as the actual scores, but the difference in divisional league playoffs and World Series are given as the number of games won during that series.

The division games were the best of five, but the championship games would be the best of seven. In 1995, the Nationals League's playoff lineup was the Cincinnati Reds (C), the Los Angeles Dodgers (W), Atlanta Braves (E) and the Colorado Rockies (WC). The Reds beat the Dodgers, 3-0 and the Braves defeated the Rockies, 3-1. In the championship round, the Braves beat the Reds 4-0 for the National League title.

The American League playoff lineup was the Cleveland Indians (C), the Boston Red Sox (E), the Seattle Mariners (W) and the New York Yankees (WC).

In the division round, the Indians beat the Red Sox, 3-0, and the Mariners defeated the Yankees, 3-2.

In the American League championship round, the Indians beat the Mariners, 4-2.

In the 1995 World Series, the Atlanta Braves (NL) won 4-0, over the Cleveland Indians (AL).

1996

The Veterans Committee elected Jim Bunning, Bill Foster, Ned Hanlon (manager) and Earl Weaver (manager).

National League umpire, John McSherry collapsed during an Opening Day game in Cincinnati on April 1, 1996. He suffered a massive heart attack and was rushed to a nearby hospital, where he passed away.

The National League shutout the American League in an All-Star game, 6-0, played at Veterans Stadium in Philadelphia on July 9, 1996.

The Atlanta Braves captured the East division of the National League again, as they had been successful in 1995. The Braves won by 96 games and the Montreal Expos, trailing the Braves by eight games, did not qualify as a wild card for the playoffs.

John Smoltz received three league high citations, by winning 24 games, a .750 WP and striking out 276 batters. Greg Maddux and Tom Glavine each won 15 games. Maddux also earned a 2.72 ERA, while closer Mark Wohlers saved 39 games.

Chipper Jones led the Braves offense, as he scored 114 runs, collected 110 RBIs, .309 BA, .393 OBP and 87 walks. Fred McGriff hit 37 doubles, Marquis Grissom spread 207 hits, swiping 28 bases, and Ryan Kresko slugged 34 homers and a .530 SA.

New York Yankees won 92 games, as Baltimore Orioles were the runner-up in the East division of the American League, only four games behind, but they qualified for a wild card playoff spot.

Two American League high marks were achieved by rookie southpaw Andy Pettite, and closer John Wettland—Pettite for winning 21 games and Wettland for saving 43 games.

Bernie Williams led the scoring for the Yankees, scoring 108 runs, hitting 29 four-baggers, 295 TB and a .535 SA. Derek Jeter provided the team with 183 hits. Paul O'Neill hit 35 doubles and received 102 walks. Tino Martinez led the team in RBIs with 117.

In 1996, the Nationals League's playoff lineup was the St. Louis Cardinals (C), the San Diego Padres (W), Atlanta Braves (E) and Los Angeles Dodgers (WC). In the divisional playoff, the the Braves beat the Dodgers, 3-0, and the Cardinals defeated the Padres, 3-0. In the championship round, the Braves beat the Cardinals 4-0 for the National League title.

The American League playoff lineup was the Cleveland Indians (C), the New York Yankees (E), the Texas Rangers (W) and the Baltimore Orioles (WC). In the division round, the Yankees beat the Rangers 3-1, and the Orioles defeated the Indians 3-1. In the American League championship round, the Yankees beat the Orioles, 4-1.

In the 1996 World Series, the New York Yankees defeated the Atlanta Braves, 4-2.

1997

The BBAWW elected Phil Niekro while the Veteran Committee selected Nellie Fox, Willie Wells and Tommy Lasorta (manager) to the 1997 National Hall of Fame.

Acting Commissioner Bud Selig designated that all major and minor league teams would honor Jackie Robinson, by retiring his number 42. However, Mariano Rivera, an ace reliever for the New York Yankees since 1996, was allowed to keep his "42," until his retirement on September 26, 2013.

Mike DiMuro became the first American umpire to work a regular season game in the Japanese Leagues.

The American League began a new string of All-Star victories on July 8, 1997, as they defeated the National League, 3-1 in the All-Star game at Jacobs Field in Cleveland.

The Florida Marlins became the playoff wild card, winning 92 games in the East division of the National League. Even though they were the wild card entry, the team stats are included, because they were one of the two teams in the 1997 World Series.

Alex Fernandez won 17 games, while Kevin Brown struck out 205 batters, and the Marlins closer, Rob Nen saved 34 games. Edgar Renteria scored 90 runs while producing 171 hits. Bobby Bonilla was the best doubles hitter with 39, and Moises Alou hit 23 homers, 225 TB and 115 RBIs. Gary Sheffield accumulated a .424 OBP, a .446 SA and received 121 walks.

The Cleveland Indians became the champion of the American League Central Division, winning only 86 games, while the Chicago White Sox pursued them, finished six games back, but did not qualify as a wild card aspirant. Charles Nagy won 16 games and struck out 149 batters. Orel Hershiser won 14 games and closer Jose Mesa had 16 saves. Sandy Alomar scored 104 runs and had a 30-game hitting streak during the season. Manny Ramirez had 184 hits including 40 doubles and accumulated 302 TB. Dave Justice had a .329 BA, .323 OBP and a .596 SA. Jim Thome knocked out 40 homers and walked 120 times.

In 1997, the Nationals League's playoff lineup was the Atlanta Braves (E), Houston Astros (C) and San Francisco Grands (W) and the Florida Marlins (WC). The Braves beat the Astros, 3-0 and the Marlins defeated the Giants, 3-0. In the championship round, the Marlins beat the Braves 4-2, for the National League title.

The American League playoff lineup was the Cleveland Indians (C), the Baltimore Orioles (E), the New York Yankees (WC) and the Seattle Mariners (W). In the division round, the Indians beat the New York Yankees, 3-2 and the Orioles defeated the Mariners, 3-1. In the American League championship round, the Indians beat the Orioles, 4-2.

When the major leagues instituted the Wild Card in 1995, no one expected a Wild Card team to advance any further than the divisional round, but the Florida Marlins proved them all wrong. They not only won the divisional round beating the San Francisco Giants, 3-2 but the league championship round, defeating the Atlanta Braves, 4-2 and also they ultimately won the World Series too edging the Cleveland Indians in the 1997 World Series, 4-3.

1998

The BBWAA elected Don Sutton into the 1998 National Hall of Fame, while the Veterans Committee selected Larry Doby, Bullet Rogan, George Davis and Lee McPhail (executive).

The Milwaukee Brewers, in the American League since 1988, became a National League team in 1998 so that both the American League and National League would each have 16 teams.

Coors Field in Denver was the site of the All-Star game, when the American League won 13-8 over their National League rivals on July 7, 1998.

Mark McGwire and Sammy Sosa both passed Roger Maris' single-season home run record, with 70 and 66 respectively. It was later determined that both McGwire and Sosa had been using high performance drugs. The jury is still out about that.

Harry and Hunter Wendelstedt became the first father-son umpire combination to work a major league game together.

The San Diego Padres clinched the West Division of the National League, winning 98 games. The San Francisco Giants, finished in second place, 9.5 games out.

Kevin Brown won 18 games, struck out 257 batters and had a 2.38 ERA. Andy Ashley won 17 games, while Trevor Hoffman saved 53 games which was the league's best. Greg Vaughn scored 112 runs, as he rifled 156 hits, smashed 50 homers and had a .597 SA. Steve Finley hit 40 doubles, while Quilvio Veras had a .373 OBP, 24 stolen bases and received 84 walks. Tony Gwynn had a .321 BA.

The New York Yankees handily captured the East Division of the 1998 American League with 114 wins. Even though the Boston Red Sox were 22 games behind, they earned the Wild Card designation.

David Cone was the league's best pitcher sharing that mark with Rick Helling of the Texas Rangers, as they both won 20 games. David Wells pitched three shutouts and finished with a .818 WP. Mariano

Rivera was the league's best closer with 45 saves. Bernie Williams had the best league batting average with a .339. He also had a .422 OBP. Paul O'Neil finished with a .575 SA, hit 40 doubles and 207 TB. Derek Jeter scored 127 runs and had 203 hits. Chuck Knoblauch spent a lot of time on the bases walking 76 times while stealing 31 sacks.

David Wells pitched a perfect game on May 17, 1998 against the Minnesota Twins at Yankee Stadium, winning 4-0, before 49,820 fans.

In 1998, the Nationals League's playoff lineup was the San Diego Padres (W), the Houston Astros (C) and Atlanta Braves (E) and the Chicago Cubs (WC). The Padres beat the Astros, 3-1 and the Braves defeated the Cubs, 3-0. In the championship round, the Padres beat the Braves 4-2 for the National League title.

The American League playoff lineup was the New York Yankees (E), the Texas Rangers(W), the Cleveland Indians (C) and the Boston Red Sox (WC).

In the division round, the Indians beat the Red Sox 3-0, and the Yankees defeated the Rangers, 3-0. In the American League championship round, the Yankees beat the Indians, 4-2.

The New York Yankees defeated the San Diego Padres in the 1998 World Series, 4-0.

1999

The BBWAA elected George Brett, Robin Yount and Nolan Ryan into the 1999 National Baseball Hall of Fame, while the Veterans Committee selected Orlando Cepeda, Joe Williams, Frank Selee (manager) and Nestor Chylak (umpire).

The American League continued their winning ways in the All-Star game, as they defeated the National League, 4-1 at Fenway Park in Boston, on July 13, 1999.

The Atlanta Braves were the 1999 East division champions of the National League, winning 103 games. The New York Mets claimed second place in the division, they were behind by 6.5 games, but they were qualified as the Wild Card for the playoffs.

Greg Maddux won 19 games, while Kevin Millwood won 18 and struck out 205 batters. Closer John Rocker saved 38 games.

Chipper Jones scored 116 runs and peppered 181 hits. Bret Boone cracked 45 home runs, collected 359 TB, .441 OBP, .633 SA, 126 walks and swiped 25 bases.

In other action, in the National League, the Arizona Diamondbacks' Luis Gonzalez had a 30-game hitting streak in 1999.

The New York Yankees captured the 1999 East Division of the American League, winning 86 games. The runner-up for that division was the Boston Red Sox, and despite their falling 22 games behind the Yankees, they were eligible as the American League Wild Card team for the playoffs.

Orlando "El Duque" Hernandez won 17 games, and David Cone, won 12 games and struck out 177 batters. Mariano Rivera was the American league's best closer with 45 saves.

Derek Jeter led the offense, scoring 134 runs, collecting 219 hits, 346 TB, a .339 BA. .435 OBP and a .552 SA. Tino Martinez blasted 28 home runs, while Paul O'Neill slashed 39 doubles. Bernie Williams drove in 115 runs and received 100 bases-on-balls. Swifty Chuck Knoblauch stole 28 bases.

David Cone, of the New York Yankees, on July 18, 1999, pitched a perfect game against the Montreal Expos in Yankee Stadium, winning 6-0. That no-hit game was the first in Intra-league history.

In 1999, the Nationals League's playoff lineup was the Atlanta Braves (E), the Houston Astros (C) and Arizona Diamondbacks (W) and the New York Mets (WC). The Braves beat the Astros 3-1, and the Mets defeated the Diamondbacks, 3-1. In the championship round, the Braves beat the Mets 4-3, for the National League title.

The American League playoff lineup was the New York Yankees (E), the Texas Rangers (W), the Cleveland Indians (C) and the Boston Red Sox (WC).

In the division round, the Yankees beat the Rangers 3-0, and the Red Sox defeated the Indians, 3-2. In the American League championship round, the Yankees beat the Red Sox, 4-1.

The New York Yankees defeated the Atlanta Braves in the 1999 World Series, 4-0.

2000

The BBWAA elected Carlton Fisk and Tony Perez into the 2000 National Baseball Hall of Fame, while the Veterans Committee selected Bid McPhee, Turkey Stearnes and Sparky Anderson (manager).

The Chicago Cubs and New York Mets opened the season in Tokyo, Japan to help inspire the game globally.

On February 24, 2000, the World Umpires Association ("WUA") was certified as the exclusive collective bargaining agent for all regular full-time major league umpires. The umpires would no longer be designated National League or American League umpires; they umpired games in both leagues, and were from that point, called Major League umpires.

Some baseball fans don't realize that both the National League and American League, since the two have played in unison with one another, that they beat with a "different drummer." The umpires in the National League continued to wear outside chest protectors long after the American used inside protectors, National League umpires only worked National League games, now they all as the WUA work both leagues, under one combined group.

The American League continued to win in the All-Star games, and on July 11, 2000, defeated the National League, 6-3, at Turner Field in Atlanta.

The New York Mets finished as runner-up in the East division of the National League, one game behind the Atlanta Braves and was the wild card, winning the National League pennant.

The Mets Al Leiter won 16 games, and struck out 200 batters.

Mike Hampton won 15 games, while closer Armando Benitez saved 41 games.

Edgar Alfonso was the offensive dynamo for the Mets, scoring 109 runs, with 176 hits including, 40 doubles, an .425 OBP and 95 walks. Mike Piazza slammed 38 homers, had 296 TB, 113 RBIs and a .614 SA. Piazza and Alfonso both batted .314.

The New York Yankees were the East Division champions of the American League as they won 87 games. The Boston Red Sox, who were only behind by 2.5 games, did not earn the Playoffs Wild Card, which was won by the Seattle Mariners from the West division.

Andy Pettite won 19 games, while strikeout-leader Orlando "El Duque"Hernandez whiffed 140 batters. The Yankees perpetual closer, Mariano Rivera, saved 36 games that time.

Bernie Williams lassoed most of the offensive categories scoring 165 runs, blasting 30 four-baggers, 304 TB, 121 RBIs and a .566 SA. Derek Jeter got the most hits with 201, and 22 stolen bases. Jorge Posada led with a .417 OBP and was a recipient of 107 walks. Williams and Tino Martinez both hit 37 doubles.

In 2000, the Nationals League's playoff lineup was the St. Louis Cardinals (C), the Atlanta Braves (E) and San Francisco Giants (W) and the New York Mets (WC). The Cardinals beat the Braves, 3-1, while the Mets defeated the Giants, 3-1. In the championship round, the Mets beat the Cardinals 4-1 for the National League title.

The American League playoff lineup was the New York Yankees (E), the Oakland Athletics (W), the the Chicago White Sox (C) and the Seattle Mariners (WC).

In the division round, the Yankees beat Athletics,, 3-2, and the Mariners defeated the White Sox, 3-0. In the American League championship round, the Yankees beat the Mariners, 4-2.

The New York Yankees (AL) defeated the New York Mets (NL) in the 2000 subway World Series, 4-1. This subway series was the first since the New York Yankees played the Brooklyn Dodgers in 1956.

2001

The National Baseball Hall of Fame

As we begin the new millennium in 2001, the annual National Baseball Hall of Fame is constantly in the sight of the baseball fan. Those knowledgeable fans are aware of the first Hall of Fame selection in 1936, to honor recent baseball retirees who have contributed to the game itself.

In the election of these great players, it became necessary to establish a criteria for their selection. These are some of the rules. First, a player needed to play at least 10 years. Second, the election was done by members of the Baseball Writers Association, who were members in good standing for at least 10 years. At the election, only those who had received 75 percent or more of the votes, would be inducted into the Hall. Only those on the ballot who received a least five percent of the vote would be grandfathered in all future elections. All candidates with less than five percent of the votes would be deleted. Those who have been retired for longer than 15 years, would no longer be retained on the ballot. Former players who died between annual elections, were considered for election held at least six months after their deaths.

Another group was established in 1937 called the Era Group. This group would submit those players who were no longer on the BBWAA election list, together with managers, umpires and executives. In one group of the Eras contingent was devoted to other recognizable players of gone-by years. Players who have been on the Baseball Commissioner's ineligible list can never be considered for election.

The BBWAA, in 2001, elected Dave Winfield and Kirby Puckett into the National Baseball Hall of Fame, while the Veterans Committee selected Bill Mazeroski. The Negro League Committee chose Hilton Smith for the Hall.

The American League defeated the National League in the All-Star game, 4-1, played at the Safeco Field, in Seattle, on July 10, 2001.

The Arizona Diamondbacks won the West division of the National League in 2001. Their division runner-up was the San Francisco Giants, who fell two runs behind, but were not eligible for the Wild Card spot.

Both Curt Schilling and Randy Johnson had high league pitching marks. Johnson had a low 2.49 ERA and a high 372 strikeout count. Schilling had 22 wins, but needed to share it with St. Louis Cardinals' Matt Morris who also won 22 games. Diamondbacks closer Byung-Hyun Kim saved 14 games.

Luis Gonzalez was the team's offensive hero all season long, scoring 128 runs, drilled 198 hits including 36 doubles, and 57 home runs. Gonzalez also had 419 TB, .688 OBP, 142 RBIs, a .325 BA, 100 walks, a .429 OBP, and a .688 SA. Second-baseman Tony Womack stole 28 bases.

The New York Yankees captured the East division of the American League, winning 95 games while the Boston Red Sox, who were 13.5 games behind did not qualify for the Wild Card position.

Roger Clemens won 20 games, with a .870 WP, while Mike Mussina won 17 more, pitched two shutouts and struck out 214 batters.

Derek Jeter scored 110 runs, while scattering 191 hits and a 295 TB, which he shared with Tino Martinez who also had 295. Martinez also led the team with 34 homers and 113 RBIs. Bernie Williams swatted 38 doubles, had a .395 OBP, .522 SA and 78 walks. Fleet-footed Alfonso Soriano led the team with 43 thefts.

The National League playoffs scheduled for the 2001 season included Atlanta Braves (E) Arizona Diamondbacks (W), Houston Astros (C), San Francisco Giants (WC). The Braves beat the Astros, 3-0. The Diamondbacks defeated the Cardinals, 3-2. In the championship round, the Diamondbacks beat the Braves 4-1 for the National League title.

The American League playoff lineup was the Cleveland Indians (C),

New York Yankees (E) the Seattle Mariners (W) and the the Oakland Athletics (WC).

In the Division round, the Mariners beat the Indians, 3-2, the Yankees defeated the Athletics, 3-2. In the Championship round, the Yankees beat the Mariners, 4-1.

The Arizona Diamondbacks (N) defeated the New York Yankess (AL) in the 2001 World Series, 4-3.

The Home Run Mania

Home runs hit during a single season has always stimulated the fans, since Babe Ruth hit his maximum number of home runs of 60 in 1927. Due to his natural abilities, it was expected that no one would exceed that number.

In the early 1900s, Frank Baker would hit between 10 and 12 home runs during one season. However, Sam Crawford's single season total for 1901, when he played for the Cincinnati Reds, was 16. At that time, it was thought that that would be the most homers that any one could expect to be the maximum. Then, came Baker, but his total each year was less than that. But that was the era of the Dead Baseball, when balls were mainly constructed with materials like women might make from their clothes. Then, about 1910 to 1912, cork material was used for the center of the ball. It became easier to throw the ball faster and further. In 1911, Frank Schulte, while playing for the Chicago Cubs hit 21. That increased after the Chicago Black Sox Scandal, but the fans interest changed as 25-year old Babe Ruth hit 29 over the fences for the Boston Red Sox in 1919. What further stimulated fans interest, was that the Babe hit those while pitching—amazing! When the Red Sox owner sold Ruth to the New York Yankees, all the fans wanted to see was more home runs. During his first season with the Yankees in 1920, the Babe cleared the fences with a new record—54 home runs. The fans flocked to see the Babe hit more homers. He didn't disappoint them. He hit 59 in 1921. He slacked off a little, but his home run total reached 714 career homers by 1935. After the Babe retired, no one thought that that record would ever be broken—until 1961, a mere 26 years later. The fans wondered, "Did Roger Maris' 61 home runs count as the new record or not?" 1961 was the first year that the American League's season was 162 games long—Ruth's record was established when the length of the season in 1927 was 154 games. After much harangue about the problem, it was established that Maris had broken the record with his 61 zingers.

Another 37 years had elapsed, with no one coming close to breaking the Maris record. In 1998, Mark McGwire broke that record with 70 homers. Most people were happy to see the old record broken, but wait a minute. Many people noticed that during the year McGwire claimed the record, that the proportions of his body had increased tremendously. Enter the news of steroid use. Three years later, Barry Bonds had broken that record when the misuse of steroids had reached its peak. Bonds hit 73 home runs in 2001, under the specter of Bonds use of steroids. If he did indeed used the drug, that could invalidate his record. As of 2018, that has not been resolved.

2002

The BBWAA elected Ozzie Smith into the 2002 National Baseball Hall of Fame.

The Seattle Mariners' Mike Cameron was the 13th player in Major League history to hit four home runs in a single game, at Chicago White Sox's Comiskey Park on May 2, 2002. Later that month, Sean Green of the Los Angeles Dodgers became the 14th baseball player to hit four home runs in a game at Miller Park, Milwaukee on May 23, 2002.

The 2002 All-Star game resulted in a second tied game in All-Star history. The opening ceremonies were spectacular, with the greatest moments in baseball history being shown on an outside screen, and featured 30 of the greatest participants of the past classics. All thought that it might be the greatest All Star game ever played, but all were disappointed when at the end of 11 innings, it remained a 7-7 tie. Everybody wanted a winner! Both managers. Bob Brenly (NL) and Joe Torre (AL) asserted that they had both used a total of 19 pitchers. Both had tried to use them all, but there were none left to continue playing the game. The game was declared a tie. Later, Commissioner "Bud" Selig declared that the league winner of all future All Star games would be entitled to the home-field advantage in that year's World Series.

The Arizona Diamondbacks won their West Division of the National League with 98 wins. They possibly might repeat their performance of 2001, and win the World Series in 2002, The runner-up, San Francisco Giants, qualified for the Wild Card, with a .590 win-loss percentage.

It would appear that it wasn't the pitching that propelled the Giants. Kirk Rueter won 14 games, as did Russ Ortiz. Jason Schmidt struck out 196 batters, while winning 13 games. Their closer, Rob Nen might have been their answer, as he saved 43 games.

Barry Bonds scored 117 runs, while Jeff Kent garnered 195 hits, including 42 doubles. Kent also collected 352 TB. However, Bonds continued his barrage in other areas: 46 home runs, .370 BA, 110 RBIs, .582 OBP, .799 SA and 198 walks. Reggie Sanders led the Giants in stolen bases, with 18.

The Oakland Athletics won the West Division of the American League, with 103 wins, but the Anaheim Angels, who finished four games behind Oakland, may have assured that the 2002 World Series might be a first time Wild Card World Series.

The Angels won 99 games as they won the wild card designation in the American league. They had finished in second place in the West Division, four games behind the Oakland Athletics. Jarrod Washburn won 18 games, while Ramon Ortiz who won 15, struck out 162 batters. Troy Percival, the closer, saved 40 games. Shortstop Dave Eckstein, scored 107 Angels runs and also had a .312 BA, Tim Salmon had 178 hits. Garrett Anderson hit 56 doubles and collected 344 TB and 173

RBIs. Adam Kennedy sported .380 OBP, Brad Fulmer, a .531 SA, while Troy Gauls slammed 30 four-baggers and walked 88 times.

In 2002, the Nationals League's playoff lineup was the Atlanta Braves (E), St. Louis Cardinals (C), the Arizona Diamondbacks (W) and the San Francisco Giants (WC). The Cardinals beat the Diamondbacks, 3-0. The Giants defeated the Braves, 3-2. In the championship round, the Giants beat the Cardinals 4-1, for the National League title.

The American League playoff lineup was the Oakland Athletics (W), the Minnesota Twins (C), the New York Yankees (E) and the Anaheim Angels (WC). In the division round, the Twins beat the Athletics, 3-2, and the Angels defeated the Yankees, 3-1. In the American League championship round, the Angels beat the Twins, 4-1.

The Anaheim Angels (AL) defeated the San Francisco Giants (NL) in the 2002 World Series. 4-3. The Japanese player, Tsuyoshi Shinjo, was the first from his country to participate in a World Series, when he played for the San Francisco Giants in 2002.

2003

The BBWAA elected Gary Carter and Eddie Murray into the 2003 National Baseball Hall of Fame.

The All-Star game was played at the U.S. Cellular Field in Chicago on July 15, 2003, won by the American League 7-6, over the National League.

The Toronto Blue Jays' Carlos Delgado was the 15th player in major league history to hit four home runs in a single game, at Tampa Bay on September 25, 2003.

In 2003, the Florida Marlins qualified for the East division of the National League Wild Card position, in the playoffs, even though they were 10 games behind the first place Atlanta Braves. Dontrelle Willis and Mark Redman each won 14 games, while Willis posted a .700 WP. Josh Beckett struck out 152 batters. Closer Branden Looper saved 28 games. Juan Pierre captured a league high with stealing 65 bases, while he scored 100 runs and rifled 204 hits. Luis Castillo had a .314 BA and a .381 OBP. Mike Lowell cracked 32 home runs and had 105 RBIs, while Derek Lee had 224 TB and collected 88 walks.

The New York Yankees won the East division of the American League with 101 wins. The Boston Red Sox, the division runner-up, were six games behind, but qualified as the Wild Card in the playoffs.

The Yankees southpaw, Andy Pettite won 21 games, while Roger Clemens and Mike Mussina notched 17 games apiece. Mussina was the strikeout leader with 195 whiffs, while closer Mariano Rivera saved 40 games.

Second-baseman Alfonso Soriano was hot that year, as he scored 114 runs while contributing 198 hits, 358 TB and swiped 35 bases. Soriano also had a .527 SA which he shared with Jason Giambi, also at .527 SA. In addition, Giambi was the Yankees top home run hitter with 41 blasts. Other teammates contributed as well: Hidecki Matsui cracked 52 doubles, Nick Johnson had a .422 OBP and Derek Jeter's at .324 BA, are were the league's highest.

In 2003, the Nationals League's playoff lineup was the Chicago Cubs (C), the San Francisco Giants (W) and Atlanta Braves (E) and the Florida Marlins (WC). The Marlins beat the Giants, 3-1. the Cubs defeated the Braves, 3-2. In the league championship round, the Marlins beat the Cubs 4-3 for the National League title.

The American League lineup was the New York Yankees (E), the Minnesota Twins (C), The Oakland Athletics (W) and the Boston Red Sox (WC). In the division round, the Yankees beat theTwins, 3-1, and the Red Sox defeated the Athletics, 3-2. In the American League championship round, the Yankees beat the Red Sox, 4-3.

The Florida Marlins defeated the New York Yankees in the 2003 World Series, 4-2.

2004

The BBWAA elected Paul Molitor and Dennis Eckersley into the 2004 Baseball Hall of Fame.

The American League continued winning the All-Star game, defeating the National League, 9-4, on July 13, 2004, at Minute Maid Park.

The St. Louis Cardinals were the National League's Central Division champion in 2004, winning 105 games, 13 games ahead of the Houston Astros, who, despite their deficient showing, won the Wild Card designation.

Jason Marquis and Chris Carpenter both had 15 wins, as Carpenter struck out 152 batters. Closer Jason Isringhausen saved 47 games.

Albert Pujois scored 133 runs and drilled 196 hits including 51 doubles, 46 four-baggers, 389 TB, .331 BA and a .657 SA. Scott Rolens, Jim Edmonds and Tony Womack contributed some offense of their own: Rolens had 124 RBI, Edmonds had a .418 OBP and received 101 walks, while Womack stole 26 bases.

The Boston Red Sox was runner-up behind the New York Yankees, and at the end of the season had fallen three games behind the Yankees, but they won the Wild Card designation for the playoffs.

Curt Schilling won 21 games, and a .778 WP, as Pedro Martinez struck out 227 batters and Keith Foulke saved 32 games. Johnny Damon scored 173 runs and drilled 189 hits. Manny Ramirez provided the offense, with 43 home runs, a .308 BA, .397 OBP and a .613 SA. David Ortiz balanced the offense with 47 doubles, 351 TB, 139 RBI. Shortstop Mark Bellhorn was given 88 walks.

A once-in-a-lifetime event occurred in 2004 that had never occurred since 1918 for the Boston Red Sox—they won a World Series. They had participated in four others over that 84 year period always ending up losers. In 1946, they lost to the St. Louis Cardinals, 4-3; the

1967 series they lost to the same team, by an identical, 4-3 score; in 1975, they lost to the Cincinnati Reds, 4-3 again, and the last time, in 1986, they lost again 4-3 to the New York Mets.

In 2004, the Nationals League playoff lineup was the St. Louis Cardinals (C), the Los Angeles Dodgers (W) and Atlanta Braves (E) and the Houston Astros (WC). In the Division Series the Cardinals beat the Dodgers, 3-1. the Astros defeated the Braves, 3-2. In the championship round, the Cardinals beat the Astros 4-3 for the National League title.

The American League's playoff lineup was the New York Yankees (E), Minnesota Twins (C), the Los Angeles Angels (W) and the Boston Red Sox (WC). In the division round, the Yankees beat the Twins, 3-1, and the Red Sox defeated the Angels, 3-0. In the American League championship round, the Red Sox beat the Yankees, 4-3.

The Boston Red Sox, won their first World Series in 84 years, by defeating the St. Louis Cardinals, 4-0.

2005

The BBWAA elected Wade Boggs and Ryne Sandberg into the 2005 National Baseball Hall of Fame.

The All-Star game was played at Comerica Park in Detroit, when the American League defeated the National League, 7-5 on July 12, 2005. The Houston Astros were the runner-up team in the Central division of the National League, and were 11 games behind the division winner, St. Louis Cardinals, and still the Wild Card designate for the 2005 playoffs.

Roy Oswalt pitched 20 wins, and he had help from Roger Clemens and Andy Pettite. Pettite. had 17 wins and Clemens had 13, with his low 1.87 ERA. Closer Brad Lidge saved 42 games.

Craig Biggio scored 94 runs and hit 40 doubles. He received a balanced offense from teammates Willie Taveras, Lance Bergman and

Morgan Elsberg: Taveras peppered 172 hits and 34 steals; Berkman, had a .293 BA, .411 OBP and 91 walks; Elsberg clubbed 36 homers, 293 TB and 101 RBIs.

The Chicago White Sox captured the Central Division of the American League, winning 99 games. Their constant competitor, the Cleveland Indians, weren't able to keep up, and were the runner-up, six games behind. Jon Garland was the leader of the White Sox pitchers, winning 18 games. Mark Buehrle and Jose Contreras were not far behind; Buehrle had 16 and Contreras had 14 wins. Contreras also had a high winning percentage of .682, as he only lost seven games, and struck out 154 batters. Closer Dustin Hermanson saved 34 games.

Multi-year all-star, Paul Konerko dominated the offense all season, scoring 98 runs, scattering 163 hits, including 40 home runs, collecting 307 TB, 100 RBIs, .375 OBP., a .534 SA and 81 free passes. Konerko seemed to forget that there were teammates who wanted to contribute too, and he shared with Aaron Rowland who hit 30 doubles and Scot Posednik sported a .290 BA, and even stole 59 bases, a league high.

In 2005, the Nationals League playoff lineup was the St. Louis Cardinals (C), the San Diego Padres (W) and Atlanta Braves (E) and the Houston Astros (WC). In the division series, the St. Louis Cardinals beat the San Diego Padres, 3-0, and the Astros defeated the Braves, 3-1.

In the championship round, the Astros beat the Cardinals 4-2, for the National League title.

The American League playoff lineup was the the Los Angeles Angels (W), the New York Yankees (E), the Chicago White Sox (C), and the Boston Red Sox (WC). In the division round, the Angels beat the Yankees, 3-2, and the White Sox defeated the Red Sox, 3-0. In the American League championship round, the White Sox beat the Angels, 4-1.

The Chicago White Sox (AL) defeated the Houston Astros (NL) in the World Series, 4-0.

2006

The BBWAA elected Bruce Sutter into the 2006 National Baseball Hall of Fame, as the Negro Leagues Committee selected Ray Brown, Willard Brown, Andy Cooper, Frank Grant, Pete Hill, Biz Mackey, Effa Manley (executive), Jose Mendez, Alex Pompez, Cum Posey, Luis Santop, Mule Suttles, Ben Taylor, Cristobol Torriente, Sol White, J.L. Wilkerson and Jud Wilson.

John "Buck" O'Neil

Buck O'Neil's legacy continued to grow through the realization of his dream. John Jordan "Buck" O'Neil was born on November 13, 1911. Since he became 12, he was in love with baseball. He was denied entrance to the high school in Saratoga, but he eventually receive a high school diploma, went to college for two years, and then began playing for the Kansas City Monarchs. He played first base and became the first African-American manager in the Negro Leagues. He won the batting title twice in Negro American Baseball League. He became committed to the Negro Baseball Leagues, and was instrumental in forming a Negro Baseball Museum. He became the first African-American baseball coach working for the Chicago Cubs. He was one of the contributors for Ken Burns' video, Baseball.

In 2006, Buck was in line to be elected into the National baseball Hall of Fame, when the Negro Leagues Committee was formed to elect various members of the Negro leagues. But discrimination seemed to follow him there too, as he lacked one vote from being elected. There was no racial discrimination, however, because all of the 18 inductees were from the African-American Race. Buck had been the best ambassador for baseball. In retribution for that wrong, of his not being elected by that one vote, the Hall of Fame has a full sized statue of Buck to greet all visitors. Maybe someday Major League Baseball will come to realize that having that statue was picayune, compare to what baseball owes Buck, and that is to finally induct him into the Hall of Fame.

The American League won another close All-Star Game, as they defeated the National League, 3-2, at PNC Park in San Francisco on July 11, 2006.

The St. Louis Cardinals earned the Central division crown of the National League by winning 83 games, while runner-up Houston Astros played really close, but ultimately finished 1.5 games behind, and lost out in consideration for the Wild Card race.

Chris Carpenter won 15 games, striking out 184 batters, while Jason Isringhausen saved 33 games. Albert Pujois scored 119 runs, managed 117 hits, including 49 home runs, collected 359 TB, 137 RBIs, .331 BA, .431 OBP, .671 SA and 92 walks. Scott Rolens hit 48 doubles.

The Detroit Tigers were a participant in the 2006 World Series. They were runner-up behind the Minnesota Twins in the Central division of the American League. Even though the Tigers were one game behind in the final standings, they were eligible to compete as the American League as a Wild Card.

Kenny Rogers won 17 games for the Tigers, while Jeremy Bonderman won 14 and struck out 202 batters. Their closer, Todd Jones, saved 37 games.

In 2006, the Nationals League's playoff lineup was the St. Louis Cardinals (C), San Diego Padres (W) New York Mets (E) and the Los Angeles Dodgers (WC) The Cardinals beat the Padres, 3-1, and the Mets defeated the Dodgers, 3-0. In the championship round, the Cardinals beat the Mets 4-3 for the National League title.

The American League playoff lineup was the Minnesota Twins (C), the New York Yankees (E), the Oakland Athletics (W) and the Detroit Tigers (WC). In the division round, the Athletics beat the Twins, 3-0, and the Tigers defeated the Yankees, 3-1. In the American League championship round, the Tigers beat the Athletics, 4-0.

The St. Louis Cardinals (NL) defeat the Detroit Tigers (AL), in the 2006 World Series, 4-1.

2007

The BBWAA elected Tony Gwynn and Cal Ripkin, Jr. into the 2007 National Baseball Hall of Fame.

The American League had a close win, as they defeated the National League, 5-4 in the All-Star game at the AT&T Park in San Francisco, on July 10, 2007.

On August 4th, Barry Bonds broke Hank Aaron's home run record hitting his 756th four-bagger.

On December 13th, U.S. Sen. George Mitchell presented his infamous report regarding baseball players use of steroids.

The Colorado Rockies were the designated Wild Card team of the National League. They finished only one-half game behind the West division Arizona Diamondbacks. Jeff Francis won 17 games for the Rockies and, struck out 165 batters as Brian Fuentes saved 20 games.

Matt Holliday had 216 hits, 137 RBI and owned a .340 BA, all were the best league's marks. He also scored 120 runs, hit 50 doubles and 36 home runs, a .424 OBP and received 116 walks. Teammate Willie Taveras stole 33 bases.

The Boston Red Sox earned the East Division championship winning 96 games, but so did the New York Yankees, but the Yankees had two more losses, and qualified for the playoff wildcard.

Pitcher Josh Beckett was designated to be the best pitcher in the American League by winning 20 games. Tim Wakefield, the team's excellent knuckleball pitcher, won another 17 games. Daisuke Matsuzaka won 15 games, while striking out 201 batters. Closer Jonathan Papelbon saved 37 games.

David "Papi" Ortiz scored 116 runs, hit 52 doubles and 35 round-trippers, a .332 BA, .445 OBP, .621 SA and was walked 111 times. Mike

Lowell drilled 191 hits and had 121 RBIs while their elite base stealer, Julio Lugo stole 33 bases.

In 2007, the Nationals League playoff lineup was the Chicago Cubs (C), the Arizona Diamondbacks (W) and Philadelphia Phillies (E) and the Colorado Rockies (WC).

In the division series, the Rockies beat the Phillies, 3-0, and the Diamondbacks defeated the Cubs, 3-0.

In the championship round, the Rockies beat the Diamondbacks 4-0 for the National League title.

The American League playoff lineup was the Cleveland Indians (C), the Boston Red Sox (E), the Los Angeles Angels (W) and the New York Yankees (WC).

In the division round, the Indians beat the Yankees, 3-1 and the Red Sox defeated the Angels, 3-0. In the American League championship round, the Red Sox beat the Indians, 4-3.

The Boston Red Sox believed that they have finally dispelled the "Curse of the Bambino" as they defeated the Colorado Rockies in the 2007 World Series, 4-0.

The final game at the iconic Yankee Stadium was played on September 21, 2008.

The Tampa Bay Devil Rays team changed its name from the Tampa Bay Devil Rays to the Tampa Bay Rays on November 8, 2007.

2008

The BBWAA elected Rich "Goose" Gossage into the 2008 National Baseball Hall of Fame.

The American League edged passed the National League in the All-Star game, winning 4-3 at Yankee Stadium in New York, on July 15, 2008.

The Philadelphia Phillies earned the East division pennant of the National League, by winning 92 games. Runner-up New York Mets, three games behind the Phillies, became the designated National; League Wild Card.

The Phillies' Jamie Moyer won 16 games, while Cole Hamels won 14 and struck out 196 batters. Closer Brad Lidge saved 41 games. Chase Utley scored 113 runs, while collecting 177 hits, a .292 BA and a .380 OBP while Ryan Howard slammed 48 home runs, and had 146 RBIs, 47 stolen bases and had 331 TB and a .543 SA. Pat Burrell and Jimmy Rolens did their offensive work on the base paths. Burrell walked 102 times and and Rolens swiped 47 bases.

The Tampa Bay Rays won the East division of the American League, winning 97 games. Boston Red Sox finished in second place, two games behind. The Rays James Shields won 14 games as Scott Kazmir won 12, and struck out 166 batters. Their closer, Troy Percival saved 28 games. Akinori Iwamura scored 91 runs while producing 172 hits. Melvin Upton cracked 37 doubles, stole 44 bases, collected 97 bases-on-balls and sported a .383 OBP. Carl Crawford hit 10 triples, while Dioner Navarro finished with a .295 BA. Carlos Pena blasted 31 homers, collected 242 TB and 102 RBIs. Evan Longoria had the most multi-base hits giving him a .531 SA.

In 2008, the Nationals League's playoff lineup was the Chicago Cubs (C), the Los Angeles Dodgers (W) and Philadelphia Phillies (E) and the Milwaukee Brewers (WC).

In the division series The Dodgers beat the Cubs 3-0, the Phillies defeated the Brewers, 3-1. In the championship round, the Phillies beat the Dodgers 4-1, for the National League title.

The American League's playoff lineup was the Chicago White Sox (C), Tampa Bay Rays (E), Los Angeles Angels (W) and the Boston Red Sox (WC). In the division round, the Rays beat the White Sox, 3-0, and the Red Sox defeated the Angels, 3-1. In the American League championship round, the Rays beat the Red Sox, 4-3.

The Philadelphia Phillies (NL) defeated the Tampa Bay Rays (AL) in the 2008 World Series, 4-1. The 2008 World Series was the sixth time that a previous World Series winner failed to repeat the following year. In this case, it was the Boston Red Sox. This was the first time that the Tampa Bay Rays became a World Series participant.

2009

The BBWAA elected Rickey Henderson and Jim Rice into the 2009 National Baseball Hall of Fame, as the Veterans Committee selected Joe Gordon.

On January 15, 2009, the owners of the 30 Major League Baseball clubs approved two rule changes governing the playing of post season and one-game playoff game.

All post season games, and games added to the regular season, to determine qualifiers for the post season become suspended games, if they are called before nine innings are played.

Coin tosses will no longer be used to determine home-field advantage for one-game tiebreakers held to determine division champions or Wild Card teams. Instead, "performance-based criteria"—including head-to-head record between the tied clubs—will be used to determine home-field advantage.

The National League succumbed to the same identical score as they did last year in the All-Star game, as they lost to the American League 4-3, on July 15, 2009, at Busch Stadium in St. Louis.

The Philadelphia Phillies captured the East division of the National League, winning 93 games, while runner-up the Florida Marlins were six games behind.

Joe Blanton won 12 games and so did J.A. Happ and Cole Hamels. Hamels also struck out 168 batters, while closer Brad Lidge saved 31 games.

Chase Utley scored 112 runs, and a had a .397 OBP. Shane Victorino posted 181 hits, 39 doubles and 13 triples. Ryan Howard was cited for 141 RBI, and together with the same mark for Price Fielder of the Milwaukee Brewers, were league highs. Howard also hit 45 homes and collected 352 TB and a .571 SA. On the bases, Jimmy Rollins stole 31, while Jason Werth had 91 bases-on-balls.

The New York Yankees earned the 2009 crown for the East division of the American League, winning 103 games. Runner-up Boston Red Sox were eight games behind, but nailed down the American League Wild Card. CC Sabathia was the American League's co-winner for the most wins at 19, which he shared with Felix Hernandez of the Seattle Mariners. Andy Pettite won 14 games as Sabathia struck out 197 batters while Marino Rivera saved 44 games.

Mark Teixiera was honored by the league with having the most home runs at 37, and best 172 RBIs and he collected 344 TB and a .565 SA. Johnny Damon scored 107 runs, but Derek Jeter had most offensive marks with 212 hits. .334 BA, .406 OBP and he even stole 39 bases. Robinson Cano had 48 doubles and Nick Swisher had 97 walks.

In 2009, the Nationals League's playoff lineup was the St. Louis Cardinals (C), the Los Angeles Dodgers (W) and Philadelphia Phillies (E) and the Colorado Rockies (WC).

The Dodgers beat the Cardinals 3-0, the Phillies defeated the Rockies, 3-1. In the championship round, the Phillies beat the Dodgers 4-1, for the National League title.

The American League playoff lineup was the Minnesota Twins (C), the New York Yankees (E), the Los Angeles Angels (W) and the Boston Red Sox (WC). In the division round, the Angels beat the Red Sox, 3-0, and the Yankees defeated the Twins, 3-0. In the American League championship round, the Yankees beat Angels, 4-2.

The New York Yankees (AL) defeat the Philadelphia Phillies (NL) in the 2009 World Series, 4-2.

2010

The BBWAA elected Andre Dawson into the 2010 National Baseball Hall of Fame, while the Veterans Committee selected Doug Harvey (umpire) and Whitey Herzog (manager).

The National League players breathed a sigh of relief when they finally won a game from the American League, 4-3 on July 13, 2010, at Angel Stadium in Anaheim, California. It marked a win for the senior league after losing 13 straight All-Star games.

The San Francisco Giants won 92 games to secure the crown in the West division of the National League in 2010. The San Diego Padres were in second place by two games, but did not qualify for the Wild Card in the playoffs.

Tim Lincecum struck out 231 batters and Brian Wilson saved 48 games. Both marks were league highs. Aubrey Huff almost dominated the Giants offense as he scored 100 runs, spreading 165 hits including 35 doubles, 26 home runs, 288 TB, 86 RBIs, .385 OBP and 83 walks. Buster Posey batted .305 and Pat Burrell had .509 SA.

The Texas Rangers won 90 games to claim the American League West Division title. The Oakland Athletics were second and behind by nine games, but their win percentage was too low to be considered for the Wild Card spot in the playoffs.

C. J. Wilson won 15 games, while Colby Lewis struck out 196 batters, and closer Neftali Feliz saved 40 games. Michael Young scored 99 runs and had 186 hits, as teammate Josh Hamilton hit 40 doubles, 32 home runs, 328 TB, .411 OBP and a .623 SA and was recognized as having the league's best bating average at .359. Shortstop Elvis Andrus received 64 walks and stole 32 bases.

In 2010, the Nationals League's playoff lineup was the Cincinnati Reds (C), the San Francisco Giants (W) and Philadelphia Phillies (E) and the Atlanta Braves (WC). In the division series, the Phillies beat the Reds, 3-0, as the Giants defeated the Braves, 3-1. In the championship round, the Giants beat the Phillies 4-2, for the National League title. The American League's playoff lineup was the Minnesota Twins (C), the Tampa Bay Rays (E), the Texas Rangers (W) and the New York Yankees (WC). In the division round, the Rangers beat the Rays, 3-2 and the Yankees defeated the Twins, 3-0. In the American League championship round, the Rangers beat the Yankees, 4-2.

The San Francisco Giants (NL) defeat the Texas Rangers (AL) in the 2010 World Series, 4-1.

2011

The BBWAA elected Roberto Alomar and Bert Blyleven into the 2011 National Baseball Hall of Fame, while the Veterans Committee selected Pat Gillick (executive).

The Los Angeles Angels celebrated their 50th Anniversary in 2011. During that time they were knowns as the California Angels, the Los Angeles Angels, the Anaheim Angels and finally, the Los Angeles Angels At Anaheim.

This All-Star game marked a new beginning for the National League, as they won two consecutive years, with a win over the American League, 5-1, at Chase Field, in Phoenix on July 13, 2011.

The St. Louis Cardinals was the runner-up in the Central division of the National League, but their winning percentage of .556 was higher than the other division runners-up to qualify them for the Wild Card position in the playoffs.

The Cardinals Kyle Lohse won 14 games while 11-game winner Chris Carpenter struck out 180 batters, and closer Fernando Salas saved 24 games. Albert Pujois led the Cardinals offense by scoring 105 runs while spreading 173 hits, including 37 round-trippers, 313 TB and 99 RBIs. Matt Holliday knocked out 36 doubles while Yadier Molina sported a .365 BA. Lance Berkman received 92 walks and had a .412 OBP and a .547 SA.

The Texas Rangers earned 96 wins for the American League West Division title. The Los Angeles Angels were the runner-up team, but did not qualify for the Wild Card in the playoffs. The Rangers C. J. Wilson and Derek Holland each won 16 games, as Wilson struck out 266 batters. Closer Nefali Feliz saved 32 games. Ian Kinsler scored 121 runs and hit 32 homers while Michael Young had 123 hits which were equally shared with Boston Red Sox's Adrian Gonzalez. Young also hit

41 doubles, 299 TB, 106 RBIs, a .338 BA and a .380 OBP. Adrian Beltre had a .561 SA as teammate Elvis Andrus swiped 27 bases.

In 2011, the Nationals League playoff lineup was the Milwaukee Brewers (C), the Arizona Diamondbacks (W) and Philadelphia Phillies (E) and the St. Louis Cardinals (WC). In the divisional round, the Brewers beat the Diamondbacks, 3-2 and the Cardinals defeated the Phillies, 3-1. In the championship round, the Cardinals beat the Brewers 4-2, for the National League title.

The American League playoff lineup was the New York Yankees (E), the Detroit Tigers (C), the Texas Rangers (W) and the Tampa Bay Rays (WC). In the division round, the Tigers beat the Yankees, 3-2, and the Rangers defeated the Rays, 4-1. In the American League championship round, the Rangers beat the Tigers, 4-2.

The St. Louis Cardinals (NL) defeated the Texas Rangers (AL) in the 2011 World Series, 4-3.

2012

The BBWAA elected Barry Larkin into the 2012 National Baseball Hall of Fame, while the Veterans Committee selected Ron Santo.

The Florida Marlins, who began play in 1993, changed their name to the Miami Marlins for 2012.

The American League suffered their third consecutive loss in the All-Star game to the National League, in a smashing 8-0 loss, played at Kauffman Stadium on July 10, 2012.

The Texas Rangers' Josh Hamilton was the 16th player in major league history to hit four home runs in a single game at Baltimore on May 8, 2012.

The San Francisco Giants finished in first place in the West Division of the National League in 2012 by winning 94 games.

Matt Cain and Madison Baumgarner each won 16 games and they struck out 193 and 191 batters, respectively. Santiago Casilla saved 25 games.

The Giants' Angel Pagan scored 95 runs, hit 15 triples and hustled to steal 29 bases.

Buster Posey was a virtual batting ram with 205 hits, including 40 doubles, 44 homers, 39 RBIs, 291 total bases and driving in 103 runs. He also walked 67 times, had a .408 OBP, .549 SA. He is credited as posting a .336 BA for the league batting title. The records show that Melkey Cabrera had a higher .346 BA, but he was ineligible for the league title, because he was suspended for testing positive for testosterone.

The Detroit Tigers captured the 2012 Central Division, winning 88 games as the Chicago White Sox were close, only three games behind. Justin Verlander won 17 games, a 2.64 ERA and whiffed 239 batters. Jose Valaverde saved 35 games.

Miguel Cabrera led the Tigers offense, scoring 169 runs, peppering 205 hits including 40 doubles, 44 four-baggers, 139 RBIs, 377 TB. .330 BA and .606 SA. Prince fielder walked 85 times and had a .412 OBP.

In 2012, it wasl be the first year in which there would be two wild cards for each league. After the divisional winners have been decided in each league, the remaining two teams who have the highest winning percentage, will be designated as the league's two Wild Cards.

The two Wild Cards will oppose one another in a single-game playoff. The winner will then compete with one of the divisional winners, in the best of five-game playoff.

In the National League playoff lineup were the Washington Nationals (E), Cincinnati Reds (C), San Francisco Giants (W) Atlanta Braves (WC) and St. Louis Cardinals (WC). In the Wild Card game, the Cardinals beat the Braves, 6-3. The Cardinals defeated the Nationals, 3-2.; The Giants beat the Reds 3-2; The Giants defeated the Cardinals, 4-3.

In the American League lineup were the New York Yankees (E), Detroit Tigers (C), Oakland Athletics (W), Baltimore Orioles (WC) and Texas Rangers (WC). In the Wild Card game, the Orioles beat Rangers, 5-1; The Yankees defeated the Orioles 3-2; The Tigers edged the

Athletics, 3-2; The Tigers won the American League pennant over the Yankees, 4-0.

The San Francisco Giants won the 2012 World Series. defeating the Detroit Tigers, 4-0.

The Talent of Johan Santana

Johan Santana started pitching with the Minnesota Twins in 2000 when he was 21. He played with them, and in 2006 he was the highest American league pitcher in 2006 with 19 wins, and only 6 losses and another high 2.77 WP. In 2008 he was traded to the New York Mets. On June 21, 2012 he pitched the first no-hitter in the Mets history, The problem was that skipper Terry Collins left his in the game until he had pitched 134 pitches. Many considered his large pitch count to later back injuries. When he pitched in that game, he had only pitched in 11 games in 2012. He was out for back surgery in 2011. Then, pitchers were supposed to be relieved from the game when they had thrown 100 pitches.

Pitchers occasionally go over that limit by a few extra pitches, but his 134 pitches were consider exorbitant. The rest of the season he suffered additional back injuries. In 2013 he opted out of his contract for $3.3 million, entitling him to be a free agent. He signed with Baltimore and later with the Toronto Blue Jays on minor league contracts, but he never made it back to the majors.

2013

The Veterans Committee elected Deacon White, Hank O'Day (umpire), and Jacob Ruppert (executive) into the 2013 National Baseball Hall of Fame.

On December 11, 2013, the Playing Rules Committee voted overwhelmingly to outlaw home-plate collisions between runners and catchers. On February 24, 2014, the new rule was put into effect as Rule 7.13.

The 84th All-Star game was played at Citi Field in New York on July 16, 2013 with the American League shutting out the National League 3-0.

The St. Louis Cardinals were in first place at the end of the 2013 season in the National League's Central Division with 97 wins. Their closest opponent was the Cincinnati Reds who were seven games behind, but qualified as a wild card team in the playoffs.

Adam Wainwright won 19 games including two shutouts and striking out 219 batters. Edward Muiica saved 37 games. Matt Carpenter led the Cardinals attack scoring 126 runs, gathering 199 hits including 55 doubles, a .398 OBP and amassed 301 TB. Carlos Beltran blasted 24 homers with a .491 SA. Backstop Yadier Molina had the best .319 BA.

In the American League, the Boston Red Sox were successful in another East Division title with 97 wins, as runner-up Tampa Bay Rays lagged behind by 5.5 games, but nonetheless won a wild card spot. Jon Lester won 15 games for the Sox while striking out 177 batters. Koji Uehara save 21 games. Jacoby Ellsbury led the Red Sox, scoring 92 runs while driving the opposition crazy in stealing 52 bases. Jarrod Saltalamacchia sliced 40 doubles while Dustin Pedroia added 193 hits. David Ortiz smashed 30 four-baggers, had 103 RBIs, .395 OBP and .514 SA.

The National League playoff lineup was the Atlanta Braves (E), St. Louis Cardinals (C), Los Angeles Dodgers (W), Pittsburgh Pirates (WC) and Cincinnati Reds (WC). In the Wild Card game, the Pirates beat the Reds, 6-2. In the divisional round, The Cardinals edged the Pirates, 3-2; The Dodgers beat the Braves, 3-1. The Cardinals won the National League pennant over the Dodgers, 4-2.

The American League playoff lineup was the Boston Red Sox (E), Detroit Tigers (C), Oakland Athletics (W), Cleveland Indians (WC) and Tampa Bay Rays (WC). In the Wild Card game, the Rays beat the

Indians, 4-0. In the divisional round, the Red Sox topped the Rays, 3-1 and the Tigers defeated the Athletics, 3-2. The Red Sox captured the American league crown, over the Tigers, 4-2.

The Boston Red Sox (AL) defeated the St. Louis Cardinals (NL) in the 2013 World Series, 4-2.

2014

The BBWAA elected Tom Glavine, Greg Maddux and Frank Thomas into the 2014 National Baseball Hall of Fame while the Veterans Committee selected managers Bobby Cox, Tony LaRussa and Joe Torre into the Hall.

In the 2014 season managers were allowed to challenge questionable umpiring calls, but it must be made within 30 seconds of the call. The request for checking the replay would be made to a central location. Only two challenges can be made during a game.

The American League team made it two in a row, defeating the National League in the All-Star game, 5-3, at Target Field at Minneapolis on July 14, 2014.

In 2014, the Los Angeles Dodgers won the West Division of the National League winning 94 games, but the divisional runner-up San Francisco Giants, which finished six game games behind, claimed one wild card spot, and eventually represented the National League in the World Series.

Representing the Giants pitching staff, Madison Bumgarner won 18 games while Tim Lincecum won 12. Bumgarner also struck out 219 batters, and closer Sergio Romo saved 23 games. Hunter Pence led the Giants offensive drive by scoring 106 runs, scattered 180 hits and collected 289 TB, however, Buster Posey powered the Giants with 22 four-baggers, 89 RBI, a .311 BA, .364 OBP and .490 SA. Mike Morse was the doubles leader with 32, while Angel Pagan stole 16 bases as Brandon Crawford walked 59 times.

The Detroit Tigers in 2014, won the Central divisional crown, but by virtue of the playoffs, runner-up Kansas City Royals, which was one game behind in the standings eventually became an American League representative in the World Series.

The Royals James Shields won 14 games and struck out 180 batters, and Yordano Ventura notched another 14 wins and whiffed 159 swingers. Closer Greg Holland saved 46 games. Alex Gordon spearheaded the Royals attack in several areas, including scoring 87 runs, blasting 19 homers, a 243 TB, 74 RBIs, a .432 SA and crafted 65 walks. Alcides Escobar peppered 154 hits and stole 31 bases. Several others who made offensive contributions, were Eric Hosmer with 35 doubles, as Lorenzo Cain sported a .301 BA, and Norichika Aoki had a .349 OBP.

In 2014, the Nationals League's playoff lineup was the St. Louis Cardinals (C), the Los Angeles Dodgers (W), the Washington Nationals (E), the Pittsburgh Pirates (WC) and the San Francisco Giants (WC). In the National League wild-card game, the Giants beat the Pirates, 8-0. In the Divisional Series, the Cardinals beat the Dodgers, 3-1, and the Giants defeated the Nationals, 3-1. In the championship round, the Giants beat the Cardinals 4-1.

The American League's playoff lineup was the Detroit Tigers (C), the Baltimore Orioles (E), the Los Angeles Angels (W) and the Kansas City Royals (WC) and the Oakland Athletics (WC). In the American League wild-card game, the Royals beat the Athletics in 12 innings, 9-8. In the division round, the Royals beat the Angels, 3-0 and the Orioles defeated the Tigers, 3-0. In the American League championship round, the Royals beat the Orioles, 4-0. The San Francisco Giants (NL) defeated the Kansas City Royals (AL) in the 2014 World Series, 4-3.

2015

Rob Manfred, Tenth Baseball Commissioner

On January 25, 2015. Rob Manfred became the tenth person to be elected as the Baseball Commissioner. He replaced Allan "Bud" Selig who retired. Manfred was born in Rome, N.Y on September 28, 1958.

He previously served as Chief Operating Officer of MLB. In 1987, he began working with MLB during Collective Bargaining. During the 1994-1995 MLB strike, he served as outside counselor for the owners. In 1998, he joined MLB on a full-time basis as Executive Vice President of Economies and League Affairs. He negotiated MLB's first drug testing agreement with the Major League Baseball Players Association (MLBPA), and represented MLB in negotiations in 2002, 2006 and 2011. In 2013, he led the MLB investigation in the Biogenesis Scandal. He stated that his primary goals as commissioner were with youth outreach, embracing technologies, slowing the pace of the games, strengthen player relations and creating more unified business situations.

There were several rule changes in 2015. They were: (1) Any manager requesting a replay challenge will stay in the dugout; (2) Each batter must keep one foot in the batter's box between pitches. Foul balls, foul tips, wild pitches or an umpire's calling time, could not be used as an excuse to step out; (3) There will be no delays coming back from Television commercials; and there will be timed pitching changes —violations will incur fines.

The BBWAA elected Craig Biggio, Pedro Martinez, Randy Johnson and John Smoltz into the 2015 National Baseball Hall of Fame.

The Great American Ballpark in Cincinnati was the site of the 2015 All Star game, as the American League made it three in a row, defeating the National League, 6-3 on July 14, 2015.

The New York Mets captured the East division of the National League, winning 90 games. The Washington Nationals, the runner-up, was seven games behind, but was not eligible to play in the National League wild card game.

The Mets Forty-two year old Bartolo Colon won 14 games, as

Jacob deGrom also had 14 wins of his own, while striking out 205 batters. Closer Jeurys Familia saved 43 games.

Lead-off hitter, Curtis Granderson supplied the Mets with plenty of punch, as he scored 98 runs while collecting 150 hits, 265 TB, a .364 OBP and walked 91 times. Second-baseman Daniel Murphy slapped 38 doubles and had 73 RBIs, in which mark he shared with first-sacker Lucas Duda. Duda also clouted 27 homers and sported a .486 SA.

The Kansas City Royals were successful in defending the Central Division of the American League in winning 95 games. Their chief rival, the Minnesota Twins were 12 games behind—too far to be eligible as a Wild Card team in the playoffs.

Edinson Volquez and Yordano Ventura both won 13 games, as Ventura also struck out 156 batters. The Royals closer Greg Holland saved 32 games.

Many of the position players contributed to the offense, such as Lorenzo Cain, who scored 101 runs, batted .307 and stole 28 bases as Eric Hosmer spread 178 hits, had a .363 OBP and walked 61 times. Kendrys Morales, the team's DH, hit 51 doubles, had 276 TB, 106 RBI and a .481 SA. Morales also shared 22 home run honors with teammate Mike Moustakas.

In 2015, the Nationals League's playoff lineup was the St. Louis Cardinals (C), the Los Angeles Dodgers (W) the New York Mets (E), the Pittsburgh Pirates (WC) and the Chicago Cubs (WC).

In the National League wild-card game, the Cubs beat the Pirates, 4-0. In the National League divisional series, the Mets defeated the Dodgers, 3-2, and the Cubs beat the Cardinals, 3-1. In the championship round, the Mets beat the Cubs 4-0 for the National League title.

The American League's playoff lineup was the Kansas City Royals (C), the Toronto Blue Jays (E), the Texas Rangers (W) the New York Yankees (WC) and Houston Astros (WC). In the American League wild-card game, the Astros beat the Yankees, 3-0. In the division round, the Blue Jays beat the Rangers, 3-2, and the Royals defeated the Astros, 3-2. The Royals beat the Blue Jays, 4-2, in the American League championship round.

The Kansas City Royals (AL) defeated the New York Mets (NL) in the 2015 World Series, 4-1.

2016

The BBWAA elected Ken Griffey, Jr. and he had the highest percentage of surpassing all other National Baseball Hall of Fame winners in 2016 with a 99.32 mark. He surpassed Tom Seaver's 98.84 1992 mark. The great Babe Ruth was only able to tie Honus Wagner with a 95.13 vote in 1936.

The new rule for 2016 was that base coaches will remain in the coaches boxes before every pitch. The BBWAA elected Ken Griffy, Jr. and Mike Piazza into the 2016 National Baseball Hall of Fame.

In February 2016, Major League Baseball and the Major League Baseball Players Association agreed to two rule changes. Rule 6.01(j) delineates criteria for a legal slide, while trying to break up a double play, which is defined as making contact with the ground before reaching the base, being able to and attempting to reach the base with a hand or foot, being able to and attempting to remain on the base at the completion of the slide (except at home plate), and not changing his path for the purpose of initiating contact with a fielder. This is intended to protect infielders, while still allowing for aggressive base running.

The second rule change, limits managers and coaches visits to the mound to 30 seconds, and shortens between innings break times by 20 seconds, to match television commercial breaks.

The American League continued its winning ways, as they defeated the National League, 4-2, at Petco Park in San Diego on July 12, 2016.

The Chicago Cubs, who waited 108 years for a World Series Championship, as did their fans, they both thought that 2016 might be the end of their quest, even though the Cubs had won the World Series last in 1908. They later managed to get into seven World Series and lost them all. Their opponents then were the Philadelphia Athletics in 1910 and 1929, the Boston Red Sox in 1918, the New York Yankees in 1932 and 1938 and finally to the Detroit tigers in 1935 and 1945. Last year, they made it all the way to the league championship, but lost to the New York Mets. The Cubs hoped 2016 would be different, and it was!

In 2016, when Cubs were in the Central division of the National League, winning 103 games, they did it in style, leaving their closest challenger, the St. Louis Cardinals 17.5 games behind. Jon Lester lead the Cubs pitching staff with 19 wins and struck out 197 batters. Jake Arrieta won 18, striking out 190, and had a .692 WP. Kyle Hendricks won 16 games, and had a low 2.13 ERA. Chris Bryant led the Cubs attack scoring 121 runs, peppering 176 hits, hit 39 four-baggers, accumulated 334 TB and a .554 SA. First baseman Anthony Rizzo hit 43 doubles and 109 RBIs. Dexter Fowler claimed a .393 OBP and swiped 13 bases. Rizzo and Bryant had an identical .292 batting averages.

The Cleveland Indians, in search of their next World Series title since they last won one in 1948, had thoughts of another one in 2016 too! Their last trip at the 1954 World Series, they had a American League record of 111 wins and they unfortunately lost when they were swept in four games by the then-New York Giants.

Corey Kluber, the Indians' mainstay pitcher, won 18 games, striking out 227 batters. Closer Cody Allen helped the Indians by saving 32 games. Rajai Davis was the lone Indians player who led the league with 43 steals. In the attack for the division title, shortstop Francisco Lindor scored 99 runs as his teammates helped in other offensive areas: Jason Kipnis collected 168 hits; Jose Ramirez knocked out 46 doubles; Carlos Santana had 290 TB, walked 99 times and shared 34 home run highs marks with Mike Napoli. Napoli also drove in 101 runs. Tyler Naquin achieved a .372 OBP and a .514 SA.

In 2016, the Nationals League's playoff lineup was the Chicago Cubs (C), the Los Angeles Dodgers (W), Washington Nationals (E), the

New York Mets (WC) and the San Francisco Giants (WC). In the National League wild-card game, the Giants beat the Mets, 3-0. In the divisional series, the Dodgers beat the Nationals, 3-2 and the Cubs defeated the Giants, 3-1. In the championship round, the Cubs beat the Dodgers 4-2 for the National League title.

The American League's playoff lineup was the Cleveland Indians (C), the Boston Red Sox (E), the Texas Rangers (W), the Toronto Blue Jays (WC) and the Baltimore Orioles (WC). In the American League wild-card game, Blue Jays beat the Orioles in 11 innings, 5-2. In the divisional round, the Indians beat the Red Sox, 3-0 and the Blue Jays defeated the Rangers, 3-0. In the American League championship round, the Indians beat the Blue Jays, 4-1.

The Chicago Cubs (NL) won their first World Series since 1908, by defeating the Cleveland Indians (AL), 4-3.

2017

The BBWAA elected Jeff Bagwell, Tim Raines and Ivan Rodriguez into the 2017 National Baseball Hall of Fame, while the Veterans Committee selected John Schuerholz (executive) and Bud Selig (executive).

New rules in effect during the 2017 baseball season are: (1) To save time, when a batter is being intentionally walked, it can now be done without pitching any balls. The offensive manager shall signal to the plate umpire that the batter in the batters box is going to be walked, and the batter will proceed to first base; (2) A manager will have 30 seconds after a play, to call for a replay; a second challenge will allow managers to make challenges, up to the seventh inning. Additionally, when a manager has exhausted his challenges for the game, the crew chief may request a replay review for non-home run calls, beginning the eighth inning, instead of the seventh inning; (3) A conditional two minute guideline for Replay Officials to render a decision on replay review. There are various exceptions allowed; (4)

There will be no markings on the field for defensive positioning; (5) A new rule will prohibit a pitcher from lifting or shifting his pivot foot during a pitch. If there is a runner or runners on base when a violation occurs, it will be called a balk, and the runner or runners will advance a base without jeopardy of being put out. If there are no runners on base, it will be called an illegal pitch.

    In a joint meeting between the baseball commissioner and the major league players union, they determined that the 14-year rule, where the league winner of the All-Star Game would allow that league winner to have a home field advantage in that year's World Series, it would no longer be in effect. The new rule is that the team in the World Series with the highest win-loss percentage at the conclusion of the season, would receive the home-field advantage, starting in 2017. During the 2017 season, Aaron Judge, a New York Yankee rookie, hit 52 home runs, which won him the Rookie of the Year Award for the American League. It was the most home runs hit by a rookie since Mark McGuire hit his rookie year homer record of 49 when he played for the Oakland Athletics in 1987. Judge also set a negative major league mark for striking out 37 straight times. Judge's performance has been considered as nothing less than phenomenal. Even Joe DiMaggio in his 1936 rookie season only hit 29 homers, and even in his 1937 season he hit 47. DiMaggio's replacement, Mickey Mantle equaled the 52-home run mark, but it came in 1956, in Mickey's sixth season.

    Also occurring during the 2017 season, another long-distance home-run hitter, Giancarlo Stanton clubbed 58 for the Miami Marlins. During the off-season the new owners of the Marlins were looking to trade Stanton because of his 13-year $325,000,000 contract. Now Stanton whose contract was purchased by the New York Yankees, hoping that they will have two solid home-run hitters. One problem with a home-run hitter, is that they also tend to be large strikeout hitters too!. Only time will tell!

On June 6, 2017, Scooter Gennett became the 17th player in Major League history to hit four home runs in one baseball game. Gennett was also successful in driving in 10 runs in that game.

J.B Martinez with the 18th MLB player to hit four home runs on September 4, 2017 as his Arizona Diamondbacks defeated the Los Angeles Dodgers, 13-0.

The National League playoff lineup was Washington Nationals (E), Chicago Cubs (C), Los Angeles Dodgers (W), Arizona Diamondbacks (WC) and Colorado Rockies (WC). The Diamond-backs defeated the Rockies in a Wild Card Playoff, 11-8. The Dodgers defeated the Diamondbacks, 3-0 and the Chicago Cubs defeated the Nationals, 3-2. The Dodgers won the National League championship defeating the Chicago Cubs, 4-1.

The American League Playoff lineup was the Boston Red Sox (E), Cleveland Indians (C), Houston Astros (W), New York Yankees (WC) and the Minnesota Twins (WC). In the Wild Card Playoff, the Yankees defeated the Twins, 8-3. The Yankees beat the Indians, 3-2. The Astros defeated the Red Sox, 3-1. The Astros won the American League championship beating the Yankees, 4-3.

The Houston Astros defeated the Los Angeles Dodgers in the 2017 World Series, 4-3.

The 2017 MLB All Star game was played at the Marlins Field, Miami on July 11 with the American League edging the National League 2-1. Since the 2002 All-Star game, the league which won the All-Star since then was awarded the home-field advantage in that World Series. Beginning with the 2017 All-Star game, now the World Series team which has the highest win-loss percentage will be awarded with home field advantage.

As the history of Baseball is being uncovered, anyone who has grown to love baseball can look forward to many new developments in the variety of teams and players in the future, but also can look forward to many rules that develop to enrich the game. There have been 267 no-hitters pitched since 1876 in Major League Baseball, but many fans don't realize the turmoil which goes on in the dugout while the pitcher is struggling to get three outs every inning.

One of the most common superstitions in baseball is that when it is bad luck to mention a no-hitter while it is in progress after five innings, when the pitcher is starting to pitch one. At this point, it is an unwritten rule not to mention the possibility of one possibly occurring. After that fifth inning, one would think that the pitcher had an incurable disease as every other player stays away from him between innings. No one even mentions the possibility of a no-hitter.. In fact, no one communicates to the pitcher during this time at all. The pitcher during this time feels isolated and is treated as a pariah.

Some radio or television commentators at a game in question, adhere to that unwritten law, while others, who although they are not being heard by those players in the dugout, blatantly tell their audiences about the possibility of a no hitter occurring. The pitcher, in the middle of a no-hit game, definitely does not mention that it looks like a no-hittter might happen. In his mind, it'll be bad luck, if he does. However there are some pitchers, who either are not aware of that unwritten law of perpetual silence, or really don't care about it at all, blabbed like there's no tomorrow.

Don Larsen, the New York Yankee pitcher was one of these, who not only pitched a no-hitter in the fifth game of the 1956 World Series, but it was a perfect one. There were no walks issued by him, nor any errors committed by his teammates during the course of that game. His teammates were aghast as he rambled on that "he was pitching a no-hitter." Despite Larson's lack of adherence to the "unwritten law," at the end of the game, he didn't pitch a no-hitter--he pitched a perfect game, which has never been matched since at any World Series Classic.

There are other superstitions that players, managers and even some fans have, that might be noticed by other fans. Most players will not step on either foul line, when either going into the field or coming back at the end of the inning. Some of them, that might have forgotten to measure their gait, so not to step on the line, instead of walking over the line, realize that they are almost there, and everyone will see them hop over the line.

Many of the superstitions occur when a player in on a string of several hits, or that the team is trying to extend the winning streak, whether its the team's winning or the player's hitting steak that is on the line. In those cases, a player or several players will adopt some outrageous superstition, in hopes that that omen will continue the winning or hitting string. Some players will not changes their underwear while the string is continuing. When a player, for example, found that if he eats a certain type of food before a game, his string continues. He will eat the same food, like eating chicken, until the string is broken.

When a team is in the process of losing a game, players or fan fans, will wear their caps in an unorthodox kind of way (inside out or in a reversed direction). They will do that until the last out of the game, when all is lost.

2018

A new rule for the 2018 baseball season was that there would only be six allowed visits, either by a coach or player, to the pitcher's mound during game. In the event of an extra inning, only one additional visit will be allowed. Pitching change visits are not counting in these limits.

The BBWAA elected Vladimir Guerrero, Trevor Hoffman, Chipper Jones and Jim Thome to the 2018 National Baseball Hall of Fame while Veterans Committee selected Alan Trammel and Jack Morris.

The All Star game, played on July 17, 2018 at the Nationals Park, Washington DC, the American League defeated the National League, 8-6.

As of 2018, the American League has won 44 games, the National League, 43. There was a total of 89 games played. There were two tied games which were called: in 1961, a 1-1 tie called because of rain; in 2002, a 7-7 tied game called at the end of 11 innings because both teams had used all of their pitchers.

This book was published September 2018, just prior to the World Series. Enjoy the future competition and play ball!

Baseball Museums

At the end of a baseball season, many fans feel they did not get enough baseball. There is an outlet for them. They can go to a baseball museum that might be close to where they live, or they might trek to see more than one museum. There are many of them, but those ones that are most frequently visited by fans are: The Baseball Hall of Fame and Museum, the Baseball Wax Museum, the American Youth Hall of Fame Museum, all in Cooperstown, NY; Babe Ruth Museum, Baltimore; Ty Cobb Museum, Royston GA; Shoeless Joe Jackson Museum, Greensville SC; the Negro League Museum, Kansas City, MO; the Louisville Slugger Museum and Factory, Louisville; Yogi Berra Museum, Campus of Montclair State University, Little Falls, NJ; B's Baseball Museum (the National Ballpark Museum), Denver; Baseball Heritage Museum (adjacent to the old park), Cleveland; Little League Baseball Museum, South Williamsport, PA. The Bob Feller Museum was established in 1995 at Feller's home town in Van Meter, IA. As it was ready to close because of the lack of finances, Feller's museum was moved to Cleveland, and is located in the third floor of the Terrace Club Restaurant at Progressive Field.

As we have surveyed the history of baseball, we have learned a lot about all of our past heroes who have been instrumental in evolving what we see in baseball today. Each of them have been unique or we otherwise have shuttered them as one of many baseball has-beens. It has also been surprising how the rules which have been evolved over the years, makes us really aware how great the game has become. How many of us can realize that at one time a pitcher tossed the ball to the batter underhand, a mere forty feet away. Can we visualize how it was possible for an infielder to catch a line drive with his bare hand or that the original baseball was exceedingly soft that a player fielding the ball in the outfield was unable to throw the ball as far as one does today?

    The baseball fan of the present day and into the future will be exposed to an increasingly different way baseball is being played, so that they will be excited about watching a game. One thing that a fan now and in the future can expect to see is something new in every game will occur that he/she has never seen before. Such is the lifelong romance that we all have for baseball.

BIBLIOGRAPHY

BOOKS

DiMaggio, Joe. Baseball for Everyone. New York: Doubleday, 1948.

Graham, Frank. McGraw of the Giants. New York: C.P. Putnam Sons. 1944.

Lovello, Thom. The Encyclopedia of Negro League Baseball. New York: Facts on File, 2003.

Smith, Curt. Storied Stadiums: Baseball's History Through Its Ballparks., 2001.

Smith, H. Allen and Smith, Ira L. Three Men on Third. New York:The Country Life Press, 1963.

Thorn, John et al. Total Baseball. (7th edition) Kingston, N.Y.: Total Sports Publishing, 2001.

Vincent, Fay T. The Last Commissioner. (New York Simon and Shuster. 2002.

WEB SITES

Wikipedia

Baseball Almanac

DVD

Burns, Robert. Baseball

Made in the USA
Middletown, DE
15 February 2019